Teacher Education and the Struggle for Social Justice

"… Clear, articulate, and cogent…. [Zeichner] exhibits a commitment to a vision of social justice that rightly demands the very best both from society and from those of us who work in schools, communities, and teacher education institutions…. *Teacher Education and the Struggle for Social Justice* is a testament to the life and work of someone who deserves to be listened to by all of us who share his belief in an education that is worthy of its name."

–Michael W. Apple, From the Foreword

Kenneth M. Zeichner examines the relationships between various aspects of teacher education, teacher development, and their contributions to the achievement of greater justice in schooling and in the broader society in this selection of his work from 1991–2008. The focus is on issues of equity and social justice in teacher education and teacher professional development.

One major theme that comes up in different ways across the chapters is Zeichner's belief that the mission of teacher education programs is to prepare teachers in ways that enable them to successfully educate everyone's children. He cautions against uncritical acceptance of concepts and practices in teacher education, such as social justice, reflection, action research, and professional development schools, without closer examination of the purposes toward which they are directed in practice and the actual consequences associated with their use. A second theme is an argument for a view of democratic deliberation in schooling, teacher education, and educational research where members of various constituent groups have genuine input into the educational process.

Teacher Education and the Struggle for Social Justice is directed to teacher educators and to policy makers who see teacher education as a critical element in maintaining a strong public education system in a democratic society.

Kenneth M. Zeichner is Hoefs-Bascom Professor of Teacher Education and Associate Dean, School of Education, University of Wisconsin-Madison.

Teacher Education and the Struggle for Social Justice

Kenneth M. Zeichner
University of Wisconsin-Madison

Routledge
Taylor & Francis Group

NEW YORK AND LONDON

First published 2009
by Routledge
270 Madison Ave, New York, NY 10016

Simultaneously published in the UK
by Routledge
2 Park Square, Milton Park, Abingdon, Oxon OX14 4RN

Routledge is an imprint of the Taylor & Francis Group,
an informa business

Typeset in Sabon by Swales & Willis Ltd, Exeter, Devon
Printed and bound in the United States of America
on acid-free paper by Edwards Brothers, Inc.

Library of Congress Cataloging-in-Publication Data
Zeichner, Kenneth M.
Teacher education and the struggle for social justice/
Kenneth M. Zeichner.
p. cm.
1. Teachers—Training of. 2. Action research in education.
3. Social justice. I. Title.
LB1707.Z45 2009
370.71'1—dc22
2008045334

ISBN 10: 0–8058–5865–2 (hbk)
ISBN 10: 0–8058–5866–0 (pbk)
ISBN 10: 0–203–87876–0 (ebk)

ISBN 13: 978–0–8058–5865–5 (hbk)
ISBN 13: 978–0–8058–5866–2 (pbk)
ISBN 13: 978–0–203–87876–7 (ebk)

For my granddaughter, Elana Lee Zeichner

Contents

Foreword

Like Ken Zeichner, I began my teaching in the schools of the urban areas where I too had grown up. And like him as well, I was deeply distressed by the lack of resources, the conditions of the schools, the out-of-touch curriculum, and the ways teachers and community members were treated. But these are not the only things that bind us together. Zeichner is correct when he says that many of these things have not gotten better. Indeed, they may have gotten significantly worse. As he reminds us, we live in a society where growing inequalities have been exacerbated to such a degree that they can only be described as disgraceful. His honesty in confronting these conditions and in grounding his work as a teacher educator in movements to alter them is to be applauded.

The importance of Ken Zeichner's work and the commitments and perspectives that underpin it were made very clear to me recently. At this past year's meeting of the American Educational Research Association in New York, there was a seven-storey billboard near Times Square that advertised a contest to find the "ten worst union-protected teachers in America." The competition was supported by a conservative foundation that had given over $1,000,000 to the campaign for the billboard and for advertisements in major national newspapers. It asked children to nominate teachers for the contest. The teachers who "won" would be given $10,000 if they quit the profession.

Thus, the problems of schooling are not poverty, underfunding, disrespect, increasingly difficult working conditions, being asked to compensate for a society that is markedly disrespectful in terms of income distribution, health care, nutrition, etc. Economic policies that are racialized and racializing have nothing to do with it; nor does the redistribution upwards of the wealth of the nation and the world (Davis, 2005). Rather, the problems are largely the fault of teachers. Schools and children will be saved if we hold teachers' feet to the fire of competition, undercut their organizations, and make certain that they are teaching what we all supposedly know is "real knowledge" that is measured on standardized tests. It seems that attacking teachers is now something of a national sport. Teacher education institutions have been a consistent object of such criticism as well.

The fact that teachers and teacher education are currently being attacked so vociferously needs to seen as part of a larger ideological and political project that in *Educating the "Right" Way* (Apple, 2006) I call conservative modernization. We are told that "private" is necessarily good and "public" is necessarily bad. We are told to standardize the curriculum along lines that simply ignore the long and intense debates over what and whose knowledge should be counted as official (Buras, 2008). We are told that the best way to make certain that we get good achievement is through ensuring that teachers teach for the test, thus also guaranteeing that they only give their students what is on these tests. There is powerful empirical evidence that these policies do not necessarily do what their proponents say they do (e.g. Valenzuela, 2005; Lipman, 2004), and there is a good deal of public conflict over these policies. But this has not seemed to make the combination of neoliberals and neoconservatives pause in their almost religious fervor to remake schooling. All of this has had a predictable impact on teacher education, where the contradictory combination of deregulation, marketization, and further centralization and standardization have arisen as powerful forces as well.

The effects of these attacks on public schools and on teachers and teacher education are increasingly visible. For example, the rapid growth of home schooling speaks to the growing mistrust of teachers (Apple, 2006; Apple & Buras, 2006). Conservative think tanks have become factories for the production of reports that are scathing in their condemnations of teachers and teacher education institutions, often in the absence of robust empirical evidence to support their claims. The effects are also apparent when one speaks to both teachers who work so very hard in our often under-resourced schools and communities and to teacher educators who strive to build and defend programs that are responsive to the realities that these teachers face. For many of these committed educators, the situation they face can be best seen as "management by stress."

Ken Zeichner is not an apologist for all of the current teacher education practices. Far from it. While he supports some practices that are in place now, he wants to transform other policies and practices. But he wants them to change them in much more socially critical and democratic directions than those envisioned by the neoliberal and neoconservative critics who both seek to shift the blame from larger structures of inequality and change the very meaning of democracy from a collective sensibility to that of the possessive individual (Liston & Zeichner, 1991; Apple, 2006).

The problems with which we need to be concerned do not end there, however. No matter how smart or articulate they may be, many people who think about teacher education and educational policy in general in the United States have a bit of arrogance. As Zeichner argues, they do not think critically enough about the kinds of democratic relationships that can and must be built between schools and universities, and between researchers and teachers. The book you are about to read shows why we need to think more critically and democratically about both of these things.

But there is another kind of tacit arrogance that sometimes characterizes educators here in the United States. Too many people assume that the experiences of other nations have little to teach us about the limits and possibilities of educational reforms. This is not true in all cases, of course, since many of us may know of examples from other nations that have influenced us. The work of the great Brazilian educator Paulo Freire may be a case in point. Other examples of educational reforms could be noted as well.

There are, of course, very real problems with what has been called "policy borrowing." Reforms are taken out of their context of both the debates and the often serious conflicts over their meanings and differential results. Take No Child Left Behind Act as a prime instance. When I am lecturing internationally, I sometimes hear educational officials in nations with histories of strong state control say very positive things about it. They all too often mistake rhetoric for reality and have insufficient insight into how controversial these policies are, their hidden effects, their underlying ideological and political meanings, and who benefits the most from them (Valenzuela, 2005; Apple, 2006).

As someone who is truly an international educator, Ken Zeichner is clearly cognizant of the dilemmas associated with learning from other nations. He fully understands what is wrong with current policies here and elsewhere; and he just as fully understands that we have much to learn from programs of teacher education that are being built in places not only inside but also outside the borders of the United States. I have been fortunate enough to listen to him when he has spoken in these other nations about what is deeply problematic in educational policies and programs here, and I have also listened to him when he has discussed what we might learn from what is being built in other places. He is a model of doing this.

What sets Zeichner's work apart from so many others is not only his understanding of the strengths and weaknesses of what is happening in multiple nations (Zeichner & Dahlstrom, 1999) or his very evident and powerful grounding in issues of social justice, although I can think of few educators who take the issues of social justice as seriously. Something else characterizes his work: an equally compelling commitment to not leave these issues to the level of theory or mere talk. Speaking honestly, rather too much of critical educational literature remains rhetorical (Apple, Au, & Gandin, 2009). As this book demonstrates, Zeichner is not satisfied with that. He justifiably wants to take these commitments and put them into practice, both in teacher education and in the kinds of critically democratic research that connects the university with schools, teachers, and communities in powerful ways. As a colleague of his for three decades, I can attest that he is exemplary in this regard.

All too often, we are told that the only appropriate response to dominant policies in education and the larger society is a recognition of TINA—that is, "there is no alternative." Yet as Zeichner's articulate analyses and examples demonstrate, and as publications such as Rethinking Schools and the volume

Democratic Schools (Apple & Beane, 2007) so clearly show, there are workable alternatives if we but listen and learn. Zeichner is committed to creating teacher education programs that respond to these more critically democratic ways of educating.

I am not alone in having the highest respect for Ken Zeichner. As I noted earlier, his work has proven to be influential throughout Latin America and in China, Australia, many European nations, and elsewhere. The reasons for his influence will be more than a little visible in the chapters of this book. They are clear, articulate, and cogent. And like their author, they exhibit a commitment to a vision of social justice that rightly demands the very best from both society and those of us who work in schools, communities, and teacher education institutions. Taken as a whole, Teacher Education and the Struggle for Social Justice is a testament to the life and work of someone who deserves to be listened to by all of us who share his belief in an education that is worthy of its name.

Michael W. Apple
John Bascom Professor of Curriculum and Instruction and
Educational Policy Studies, University of Wisconsin-Madison

References

Apple, M. W. (2006). *Educating the "Right" Way: Markets, Standards, God, and Inequality*, 2nd edition. New York: Routledge.

Apple, M. W. & Buras, K. L. (Eds.) (2006). *The Subaltern Speak: Curriculum, Power, and Educational Struggles*. New York: Routledge.

Apple, M. W. & Beane, J. A. (Eds.) (2007). *Democratic Schools: Lessons in Powerful Education*. Portsmouth, NH: Heinemann.

Apple, M. W., Au, W., & Gandin, L. A. (Eds.) (2009). *Routledge International Handbook of Critical Education*. New York: Routledge.

Buras, K. L. (2008). *Rightist Multiculturalism*. New York: Routledge.

Davis, M. (2005). *Planet of Slums*. New York: Verso.

Liston, D. P. & Zeichner, K. M. (1991). *Teacher Education and the Social Conditions of Schooling*. New York: Routledge.

Valenzuela, A. (Ed.) (2005). *Leaving Children Behind*. Albany, NY: State University of New York Press.

Zeichner, K. M. & Dahlstrom, L. (Eds.) (1999). *Democratic Teacher Education Reform in Africa*. Boulder, CO: Westview.

Preface

It is a violation of the most basic principles of social justice that a country as wealthy as ours denies the opportunities that come with a high-quality education to a substantial portion of our young people (Bold Approach, 2008).

When I entered the Urban Teacher Preparation program at Syracuse University in 1969 to become an elementary school teacher I, and many others who entered teaching at that time, saw teaching as a way to broadly contribute to building a more just society in addition to the contributions that we hoped to make to our students through our classroom teaching. Then, and today, large numbers of young people in the U.S. are denied access to high quality public education.

My decision to become a teacher was an alternative form of service to my country instead of going to fight in what I and many others thought was an unnecessary and unjustified war in Vietnam. The 1960s and early 1970s were times of great unrest in the U.S. Many major cities were erupting in violence and progressive social leaders like Dr. Martin Luther King and Bobby Kennedy were assassinated. There was also great frustration about the failure of the society to provide all of its citizens with the economic and social supports that are needed to give everyone access to the opportunity to live a decent and productive life, such as access to decent housing, quality and affordable food, transportation, jobs that pay a living wage, health care, and quality education (including early childhood education). It was a time of great struggle for civil rights and against the war in Vietnam. There was much activity across the nation to eliminate poverty and racial inequality, and many of us who went into public school teaching during these times saw ourselves as part of a broad movement for social justice. While some progress has clearly been made in achieving the hopes that were widespread during these turbulent times, obviously much work remains to be done.

Poverty in the U.S. is more prevalent now than in the 1960s and early 1970s having escalated rapidly since 2000. For every 5 children who have fallen into poverty since 2000, more than 3 fell into extreme poverty (Children's Defense Fund, 2005, p.1).

In 2006, approximately 17.4 percent or 13 million children in the U.S. lived in families with incomes below the poverty level; over 9 million of these children did not have health insurance. Breaking this 13 million down by ethnicity and race, 35.3 percent of African-American children, 28 percent of Latino children, and 10.8 percent of white non-Latino children were living in poverty. This same disparity of ethnicity, race, and social class also exists for every other measure of wellbeing, such as access to health care, access to high quality and affordable transportation and food, freedom from violence, chance of being put in jail or prison, etc. (Annie E. Casey Foundation, 2008; Children's Defense Fund, 2007).

I began my career as a teacher educator in the federally-funded Teacher Corps.[1] I supervised Teacher Corps interns in an urban elementary school in Syracuse, New York that was attended primarily by African-American students who lived in poverty. This school, the same one in which I had taught, was a public community school where parents participated in decisions about teacher hiring and evaluation, the school curriculum, and the allocation of school resources. My own experiences of working in a school that shared governance with the community have influenced my views on the benefits of democratic deliberation in schools and teacher education institutions, which are articulated throughout this book. Throughout my teaching career and career as a teacher educator, I have focused my energy on the preparation of teachers for urban schools like the one in which I taught and those that I attended as a youth in Philadelphia. Over the years, I have become more familiar with the issues of poverty and educational inequality in rural areas and I have studied exemplary teacher education programs that focus on social justice issues in both urban and rural settings (e.g. Zeichner & Melnick, 1996; Zeichner, 2000).

The educational inequalities that existed when I went into teaching still exist and may even have gotten larger in the last 40 years. By almost every measure that exists, there continues to be a crisis of inequality in our public schools that denies many poor children and children of color a high quality education, despite the good work of many dedicated and talented teachers. A number of gaps in educational outcomes has persisted despite all of the reform efforts that have taken place in schools. These include inequalities in: achievement, as measured by standardized tests in reading and mathematics (Rothstein & Wilder, 2005); high school graduation rates (Heckman & LaFontaine, 2007); increased segregation of students according to their race, ethnicity, and social class backgrounds (Orfield & Lee, 2005); school funding (Carey, 2004); access to fully prepared and experienced teachers (Peske & Haycock, 2006); access to advanced mathematics courses that provide the gateway to scientific careers (U.S. Department of Education, 2003); and access to a broad and rich curriculum that educates students to think critically and develop their aesthetic and civic capabilities (Dillon, 2006; Kozol, 2005). There has also been documentation of the disproportionate assignment of children of color to special education classes (Artiles, Harry, Reschly, & Chinn, 2002).

Despite the picture often painted in the dominant corporate-funded media that the causes of these and other gaps lie primarily in bad schools and teacher education institutions (e.g. Dillon, 2006; Will, 2006), there is substantial evidence that the primary roots of school inequalities lie in the failure of our society to address the social and economic preconditions for student learning (Berliner, 2006; Rothstein, 2004). Further, efforts aimed at education-related social and economic disadvantages can, with continued school reform, improve school performance and student learning (Rothstein, 2004). Clearly, there is much to be done to improve both public schooling and teacher education, but these institutions need the resources and the support to do their work.

Critics of public schools and public universities, where the majority of U.S. teachers are still prepared, often neglect to discuss the persistent underfunding and forced budget cuts that P–12 school districts and public higher education institutions have faced for some years now. For example, according to recent data compiled by the National School Boards Association (2008), the cumulative shortfall in federal funding for Title I, which is the main source of federal funding for the Elementary and Secondary Education or No Child Left Behind Act (2002), between 2002 and 2007 was 43 billon dollars. Similarly, when Congress passed a law in 1975 to provide extra support for students who were classified as needing special education (Individuals with Disabilities Education Act or IDEA), it promised to pay an amount equal to 40 percent of the average per pupil expenditure rate. According to National School Boards Association (2008) compiled data, the current federal funding level is at about 18 percent, which is less than one half of the amount that Congress promised to fund.

One consequence of the lack of full federal funding of these mandates for public schools has been a continual reduction in the level of state support for public universities. This is because states need to make up the gaps between what the federal mandates require of schools and what federal money has been provided to meet these mandates (Lyall & Sell, 2006). When we discuss accountability as is the fashion today, in addition to the accountability of schools and teacher education institutions, we need to also address how accountable our government is in providing the resources that both public schools and public universities need to do their work well (Sirotnik, 2004).

A Brief Note on the Concept of Social Justice

Throughout this book, I continually examine the relationships between various aspects of teacher education and teacher development, and their contribution to the achievement of greater justice in schooling and the broader society. A substantial literature has evolved in philosophy and social theory that has analyzed the concept of justice, and a number of distinct positions on the meaning of justice have been identified (e.g. Gewirtz, 1998; Sturman, 1997; North, 2006, 2008). Recently, these discussions of the meaning of justice have begun to appear in the literature on social justice teacher education (e.g. McDonald, 2007), although most teacher education programs that claim to have a social justice orientation say very little about what they mean by the idea of social justice (McDonald & Zeichner, 2009). There are basically three broad categories of theories about the concept of justice: (a) distributive theories that focus on the distribution of material goods and services (e.g. Rawls, 2001); (b) recognition theories that focus on social relations among individuals and groups within the institutions in which they live and work (e.g. Young, 1990); and (c) theories that attempt to pay attention both to distributive and relational justice (e.g. Fraser, 1997). My own view of the concept of justice that has guided my work in teacher education comes the closest to those theories that seek to address both recognition (caring and respectful social relations where all individuals and groups are treated with dignity) and redistribution (where there is a fairer distribution of material resources).

About This Book

Throughout my 30-plus-year career at the University of Wisconsin-Madison, I have maintained close involvement with our teacher education programs, Wisconsin public schools, and the important job of preparing doctoral students to be teacher educators. This book includes a selection of my writing over these years that have focused on issues of equity and social justice in teacher education and teacher professional development. The work represented in this book ranges from papers that I wrote between 1991 and 2008. Although at times I refer to teacher education on an international scale, the bulk of the work represented in this book focuses on teacher education in the United States.

There are a number of themes that are present in this book and that come up in different ways in the various chapters. One theme is a belief that the mission of teacher education programs is to prepare teachers in ways that enable them to successfully educate everyone's children. Throughout the book, I caution against accepting concepts and practices in teacher education, including social justice, reflection, action research, and professional development schools, without closer examination of the purposes toward which they are directed in practice and the actual consequences associated with their use. I repeatedly argue that these practices and concepts are interpreted and used in various ways that do not necessarily contribute to building greater equity and justice in schooling.

A second theme present in this book is an argument for a view of democratic deliberation in schooling, teacher education, and educational research where members of various constituent groups have genuine input into the educational process. In schooling, this democratic deliberation would involve teachers, administrators, parents, community members, and, in some cases, students in negotiating school affairs (see Chapter 9). In teacher education, it would involve more closely connecting the preparation of teachers done by colleges and universities to both schools and communities (see Chapters 2 and 3). In educational research, it would involve a stronger interaction and exchange of knowledge produced in schools by education practitioners and knowledge produced by academics who are situated in colleges, universities, research centers, and think tanks (see Chapter 7).

In Chapter 1, I discuss and critique what I think represents the three major strands of contemporary teacher education reform: professionalization, deregulation, and social justice agendas.[2] When one examines the process of teacher education reform at individual teacher education institutions, aspects of all three of these perspectives can be found to be present. Although, different programs interpret the agendas in somewhat different ways and emphasize different elements. In this chapter, I point out that these reform agendas are not new, but they are an outgrowth of proposals for teacher education reform that have existed since the beginning of the twentieth century. I also argue that each of these agendas has strengths and weaknesses, and none is sufficient by itself for solving the problems of educational inequity that continue to plague our public schools.

In Chapter 2, Ryan Flessner and I examine the reform tradition of social justice teacher education in more depth. Although most teacher education institutions in the U.S. now claim to be preparing teachers to work for social justice, it is not always clear from the literature what these programs are like or what they are preparing teachers to do. Just as was the case with the concept of reflective practice in the 1990s (Zeichner & Liston, 1996), there is a danger that social justice teacher education will come to describe every reform initiative in teacher education and lose a specific meaning. Our analysis looks at the variety of perspectives and practices that have come to be associated with teacher education for social justice, including program admission and curriculum and instructional practices. We then illustrate these practices with brief portraits of three programs in the U.S., Canada, and Brazil. In the final part of this chapter, we elaborate on the critique of social justice teacher education in Chapter 1 and discuss ways in which we think the power of social justice-oriented work in teacher education can be strengthened with a particular focus on research universities.

In Chapter 3, I articulate my own sense of one of the key elements of the social justice agenda in teacher education: forming closer partnerships between schools and universities. In this chapter, I discuss how professional development schools offer the potential of both representing a clear break from traditional models of school and university relationships in teacher education and strengthening the preparation of teachers. I also share my concerns about what I have viewed as an uncritical glorification of partnerships in teacher education without sufficient attention to the core values that are associated with high quality partnerships.

Chapters 4 through 7 focus on different aspects of the practice of action research in social justice teacher education. In Chapter 4, I reflect upon the evolution of my use of action research with the education students in our elementary teacher education program at the University of Wisconsin-Madison. In this work, we have attempted to prepare teachers to develop habits and skills during their initial preparation for teaching that will help them continue to learn from and improve their teaching throughout their careers.

Chapters 5 and 6 are revised versions of keynote talks that I presented in 1992 and 2007 at the annual meetings of the Collaborative Action Research Network, an international network of individuals in education, health care, and social services that focuses on issues related to action research. In Chapter 5, I explore the tensions between action research as an enabler of individual teacher development, school change, and social change, and discuss ways in which action research can support social change within teachers' classrooms. In doing so, I criticize both an uncritical glorification of action research because of the alleged personal and social benefits that are often implied to be inevitably associated with it, and criticisms of teachers by academics for not directly seeking to change the structures of schooling.

In Chapter 6, I explore how action research in initial teacher education can serve to promote greater social justice in a climate in which there are efforts to privatize teacher education and impose harsh accountability requirements that I argue go beyond the bounds of reasonableness and divert teacher educators' energies away from the achievement of their goals. I examine how action research by both student teachers and teacher educators can serve to promote social justice even in the hostile environment in which teacher education exists.

In Chapter 7, I discuss the democratization of knowledge production in education—a quality of social relations that I think is consistent with the core values of social justice education and teacher education. Although there has been some progress in this direction since 1994 when I first made these remarks at a meeting of the Australian Association of Research in Education, the worlds of teacher research and academic research are still largely separate. There has been too little attention paid to utilizing the research that thousands of teachers all over the world are doing in their classrooms and schools in both teacher education programs and school reform and education policy making. In this chapter, I discuss ways in which academic and practitioner researchers can come together and take advantage of the strengths that each genre of research provides.

In Chapter 8, I discuss two issues that continue to undermine the authenticity and social value of efforts to promote teacher development. First, I argue that underlying the rhetoric of many efforts to "empower" teachers to take control of their own professional development is a reality in which teachers remain extremely limited in their power to influence the scope and conditions of their work. I also assert, using the concept of teachers as reflective practitioners as an example, that even when efforts to promote teacher development are not illusory, teacher development often becomes an end unto itself, unconnected to broader questions about education and equity in a democratic society. I conclude by arguing for efforts to promote forms of teacher development which are both genuine and connected to the promotion of equity and social justice.

In Chapter 9, I analyze several tensions and contradictions associated with efforts to restructure schools and give teachers more control over their work and professional development, including two potential pitfalls: (a) the potential to intensify teachers' work to a point where it begins to interfere with them accomplishing their goals with students and (b) the potential of deepening divisions between schools and communities. I then discuss ways in which I think teaching can be professionalized to a greater extent while avoiding these pitfalls. My argument is based on a belief in a broad view of school democracy that involves teachers, administrators, parents, community members, and, in some cases, students in deliberating school affairs. It is my view that this process of democratic deliberation is necessary for the achievement of greater equity in schooling processes and outcomes.

Chapter 10 includes a discussion of many of the issues raised in the preceeding chapters and represents a retrospective and prospective analysis based on my thirty-plus years as a teacher educator of college- and university-based teacher education in the U.S. In this chapter I make four recommendations for the future direction of college- and university-based teacher education that I think are needed to ensure that teacher education programs based in these institutions will make a contribution to preparing teachers who will contribute to weakening the link between social and economic disadvantage and student learning. These recommendations are: (a) to accept the need for multiple pathways into teaching and focus on the quality of a teacher education program rather than on who sponsors it; (b) to work to redefine policies related to the goals of schooling and teacher education beyond the raising of standardized test scores to include other important purposes of public schooling; (c) to connect teacher education programs more closely to schools and communities; and (d) to either take the education of teachers seriously or stop doing it.

This book is directed toward teacher educators who are associated with programs sponsored by colleges, universities, and other providers, and to policy makers who see teacher education as a critical element in maintaining a strong public education system in a democratic society.

Acknowledgments

In addition to my students and colleagues at the University of Wisconsin-Madison and local public schools who have helped push my thinking and improve my work over the 32 years that I have been in Madison, I would like to especially thank the following people who have provided me with helpful feedback or advice that informed the various essays in this book: Michael Apple, Marilyn Cochran-Smith, Hilary Conklin, Lars Dahlstrom, Ryan Flessner, Linda Darling-Hammond, Jennifer Gore, Carl Grant, Peter Grimmett, Pam Grossman, Gloria Ladson-Billings, David Imig, Morva McDonald, Sue Noffke, Connie North, Julio Pereira, Anna Richert, Ann Schulte. Lee Shulman, Bridget Somekh, Bob Tabachnick, Alan Tom, Linda Valli, Ana Maria Villegas, Lois Weiner, and my colleagues in the Global South Network.

I would also like to thank Yan Liu, Lois Opalewski, and Lois Triemstra for their expert assistance in the preparation of the manuscript. Finally, I would like to thank Naomi Silverman of Routledge with whom I have worked for close to 20 years. Naomi cares deeply about the creation of a more humane and just world, and her editorial advice has been enormously valuable to my work over the years.

The Adequacies and Inadequacies of Three Current Strategies to Recruit, Prepare, and Retain the Best Teachers for All Students[1]

In this chapter I discuss the research based on recruiting, preparing, and retaining good teachers for all of our children in relation to the different reform agendas that are currently being implemented in U.S. teacher education. Currently, there are three major agendas for the reform of teacher education being played out in teacher education programs across the country: (a) the well-publicized professionalization agenda, propelled by the National Commission on Teaching and America's Future (NCTAF) Report, National Council for Accreditation of Teacher Education (NCATE), Teacher Education Accreditation Council (TEAC), the National Board for Professional Teaching Standards, and other groups; (b) the deregulation agenda, supported by the work of the Fordham Foundation and other conservative think tanks and foundations like the Abell Foundation, the Pacific Research Institute, and the Progressive Policy Institute; and (c) the social justice agenda, implemented by individual teacher education practitioners in their teacher education classrooms and supported by groups like the National Association for Multicultural Education, policy centers like Tomas Rivéra Center and Center for the Future of Teaching and Learning, and grassroots organizations like Rethinking Schools in Milwaukee. There is a fourth agenda that Cochran-Smith (2001) has referred to as the overregulation agenda, which consists of efforts in some states to micromanage teacher education programs and the punitive Title II reporting requirements set by Congress. I am not going to discuss it here because this agenda is largely a reflection of aspects of both the professionalization and deregulation agendas.[2]

All three of the pathways to teacher education reform that I discuss acknowledge the gap between the rhetoric about providing all students with fully qualified and effective teachers and the reality of only some students having access to these teachers. Although advocates of these three reform agendas agree about certain things, such as the critical importance of teachers' subject matter knowledge and the importance of providing a high-quality education to all students in a society that professes to be democratic, they propose very different solutions for narrowing the educational quality and achievement gaps in U.S. public schools. My basic thesis is that none of these agendas for reform is adequate by itself for achieving the goal of providing every child with a high-quality education. All of them offer certain benefits but also have certain limitations and weaknesses. There are also important aspects of the reforms which are needed, but are not addressed by any of the agendas.

In this chapter, I discuss the adequacies and inadequacies of each of these reform agendas and point to the need to come together to find some common ground across these often warring camps. This cohesion is necessary to more effectively educate teachers to provide a high-quality education for everyone's children in our public schools and to establish the social preconditions that are needed for this quality of education to be realized.

I begin by briefly reviewing what has come to be referred to as the demographic imperative in teaching and teacher education and the gap that persists in the quality of education available to different groups. Following this, I sketch the central elements of each of the three reform agendas and discuss how each both contributes and fails to contribute to equalizing the quality of schooling for different groups. None of these three reform agendas is new. All of them are connected to long-standing traditions of reform in American teacher education that have been struggling with each other for the last one hundred years (Liston & Zeichner, 1991). In discussing each of the visions for teacher education reform, I identify its link to a long-standing reform tradition.

The Demographic Imperative

It has become quite familiar now to see discussions in literature and even in the popular press of the so-called demographic imperative in teaching and teacher education. Currently, about 47 million students attend public elementary and secondary schools in the United States. They are taught by about 3.3 million teachers and supported by thousands of paraprofessionals and administrative staff. Given a variety of factors, such as the aging of the teaching force, class size reduction initiatives, teacher attrition, and so on, it has been projected that at least two million new teachers will be needed by 2010 (U.S. Department of Education, 2001). Over the next four years, Illinois will need to hire about 55,000 teachers, more than one third of its current public school teaching force (Keller, 2002). This situation is similar in many other states. Noticeable aspects of this national situation are the large numbers of individuals who have not completed the minimum requirements for a teaching credential but who are teachers of record in a public school classroom and, among certified teachers, the large number of teachers who are teaching outside their fields of certification. This situation is more prevalent in certain fields, such as special education, ESL and bilingual education, science, and mathematics, as well as in certain geographical areas, such as urban and remote rural districts.

The situation in some states, such as California, is now reaching a point where the incentives for completing a teacher education program before assuming responsibility for a classroom are disappearing, and increasingly teacher education programs are serving students who are already full-time teachers of record. In a survey of California teachers with fewer than five years of experience conducted by the Center for the Future of Teaching and Learning in Santa Cruz, more than one half of those surveyed did some or all of their student teaching while working as the teacher of record in their own classrooms. At the time of this survey there were 42,000 classrooms in California headed by teachers who had not completed the minimum requirements for a teaching credential, which accounts for about 14 percent of the teaching force in the state. This represents an increase of 23 percent in under qualified teachers since 1997–1998 (Center for the Future of Teaching and Learning, 2001).

Nationally, the situation is more variable with some states, such as Wisconsin, exporting teachers in nonshortage subject areas to other parts of the country. Other importing states are in situations that are moving toward the situation in California. Even in the exporting states, however, large urban and remote rural districts often have the same types of shortages that are found on a more widespread basis in the states that import teachers. For example, in the exporting state of Wisconsin, 320 teachers and about 20 percent of new hires in the city of Milwaukee were teaching with emergency licenses last year (Milwaukee Public Schools, 2002).

Another critical aspect of the current demographic imperative in teaching and teacher education is the growing disparity between the students who attend public schools in the United States and their teachers. Currently, about 38 percent of public school pupils are from an ethnic/racial minority group, whereas close to 90 percent of their teachers are not (U.S. Department of Education, 2001). In large urban districts, the percentage of pupils of color is more than 70 percent; overall, one in five children under 18 lives in poverty; and more than one in seven children between ages five and 17 speak a language other than English at home (but more than one third of these are considered to be limited English proficient) (Villegas & Lucas, 2001).

This cultural divide between teachers and their students is further complicated by the lack of sustained attention to preparing teachers to teach across lines of ethnicity/race, language, and social class in most teacher education programs. The typical response of teacher education programs to the growing diversity of P–12 students has been to add a course or two on multicultural, bilingual/ESL, or urban education to the curriculum, leaving the rest of the curriculum largely intact (Ladson-Billings, 1999a; Villegas & Lucas, 2001; Zeichner & Hoeft, 1996). The white, monolingual, English-speaking teacher education professors and staff who are responsible for educating teachers for diversity often lack experience themselves in teaching in culturally diverse elementary and secondary schools. The lack of diversity among faculty, staff, and students in many teacher education programs undermines efforts to prepare interculturally competent teachers.

The Gap in Educational Quality

The most striking aspect of the current demographic situation in our public schools and teacher education institutions is that the effects of teacher short-ages and the provision of qualified teachers have been felt unequally by different groups. Kati Haycock (2000) of the Education Trust has argued, "Just under the surface is a system that, despite its stated goal of high achievement for all children, is rigged to produce high achievement in some kinds of children and to undermine it in others" (p. 1).

According to NCTAF reports (1996, 1997), the United States is producing enough teachers as a nation to fill all of the openings. The problem is that these graduates are not necessarily in the subject areas where they are needed, and they do not want to go to the schools where they are most needed.

What has been referred to as "leakage in the teacher education pipeline" or, more commonly, as teacher attrition, is partially responsible for the short-ages of fully qualified teachers in classrooms (Ingersoll, 2001). The NCTAF report describes a national attrition rate of about 75 percent from the beginning of an undergraduate teacher education program through about the third year of teaching (NCTAF, 1996). The Center for the Future of Teaching and Learning in California estimates that 40–60 percent of those who earn teaching credentials in the state do not seek employment as teachers (Gandara & Maxwell-Jolley, 2000). Also, as a result of teacher salaries and working conditions in much of the country and the general lack of public support for teaching as a profession, the percentage of teachers in urban schools who leave teaching within the first five years is generally about 30 percent, but can be as high as 50 percent (Gregorian, 2001). In 2001–2002, only 44 percent of teachers hired in New York City schools were certified (down from 53 percent the previous year), and only about one third of English language learners in California have a teacher who has earned a teaching credential of any kind (Gandara & Maxwell-Jolley, 2000). Only about one quarter of teachers who work with English language learners nationally have received any substantive preparation with regard to ESL teaching strategies and language acquisition theory. The preparation to teach English language learners consistently comes up as one of the lowest-rated items on follow-up studies of teacher education program graduates (e.g. Darling-Hammond, 2000b).

If one relied on a reading of the professional education literature alone, one might think that a lot has happened to alter this situation to provide the working conditions, mentoring, and professional development programs concerned with teaching diverse learners. One can pick up most education journals today and read about the professional development schools, teacher induction programs, and teacher-initiated professional development programs that are being implemented and producing wonderful results. These things are indeed happening, but unfortunately they are neither the norm, nor are they necessarily conducted in ways that contribute to the task of educating all teachers for diversity.

If one goes just a little further one can begin to see the stark reality that is currently confronting many states and local school districts. This reality threatens to undermine what progress has been made in recent years in providing more incentives to enter and remain in teaching and in enhancing teachers' abilities to be effective in promoting student learning. For example, in the spring of 2002, *Education Week* reported that many urban school districts across the country were pursuing cuts in teaching and support staff, professional development, bus services, supply purchases, and summer school programs, among other things, to meet mounting budget deficits. The Detroit school system, which is featured in the article (Blair, 2002), needed to cut 70 million dollars from its 1.2 billion dollar budget. Houston was dealing with 50 million dollar budget cuts and Miami-Dade was seeking to trim 81 million dollars. Even in my own state of Wisconsin, which is relatively better off on some indicators than others, the governor recently proposed phasing out the entire budget of one billion dollars per year of state aid to cities by 2004. The loss of this money, which is used to pay for basic city services such as fire and police protection, would threaten to devastate urban areas in Wisconsin, including the city of Milwaukee, whose public schools are already in a crisis situation.[3]

A comprehensive new teacher licensing bill with provisions for a career ladder for teachers, teacher induction programs, and teacher-directed professional development went into effect this same year. Currently, budget estimates are being finalized to finance this new bill, which includes new responsibilities for colleges and universities in the new performance-based licensing system. There is little chance in my view that the state will be able to pick up the tab for this new bill, which includes most elements of the NCTAF agenda. Once again, we may be left with only the pieces that are self-supporting, such as the state content examination for teachers. The pieces that require additional funding, such as mentoring for beginning teachers, may go unimplemented unless federal funds are obtained. Even if federal funds are obtained in the short run to pay for some of the new mandated features of the law, such as mentors for beginning teachers, this is not a permanent solution to the state's massive budget problems and its ability to support the professionalization agenda.

The effects of the shortages of fully qualified teachers are disproportionately borne by students who are in low-achieving schools, schools with high numbers of students of color, and schools with high numbers of students who qualify for free and reduced-price lunch. The Education Trust has clearly documented these inequities on a national level, and various groups, including Center for the Future of Teaching and Learning, have illuminated the gaps in the California schools. For example, Kati Haycock (2000) of the Education Trust has concluded the following:

> Large numbers of secondary teachers lack state certification to teach the subjects they are teaching. When certification data are disaggregated by

the economic composition of the school, clear patterns emerge. Students attending high poverty secondary schools (>75% poverty) are more than twice as likely as students in low poverty schools (<10% poverty) to be taught by teachers not certified in their fields. Youngsters attending predominately minority schools are also more likely to be taught by teachers uncertified in their subjects. In fact students attending schools in which African American and Latino students comprise 90% or more of the student population are more than twice as likely to be taught by teachers without certification to teach their subjects (p. 2).

An analysis of the 1999–2000 Schools and Staffing Survey data by the Education Trust (Jerald, 2002) confirmed their earlier analyses. This report concluded that "American secondary schools have unacceptably high rates of out-of-field teaching in core academic subjects, with classes in high-poverty and high-minority schools much more likely to be assigned an out-of-field teacher than classes in low-poverty and low-minority schools" (p. 4). In high-poverty schools, for example, classes are 77 percent more likely to be assigned an out-of-field teacher than classes in low-poverty schools. Also, classes in majority non-white schools are 40 percent more likely to be assigned an out-of-field teacher than those in mostly white schools.

It has been asserted by the Abell Foundation and others that teacher certification does not matter in determining a teacher's effectiveness, but it is unlikely that these critics of the idea of teacher certification send their own children to high-poverty or high-minority public schools filled with unlicensed teachers. The numbers cited by Kati Haycock (2000) with regard to the distribution of certified teachers are similar to those that emerged when she examined the distribution of teachers with academic majors in the fields they are teaching, teachers with high verbal and mathematics skills, and experienced teachers. In each instance, students who attend high-poverty schools, low-performing schools, or schools with high concentrations of African-American or Latino students have less-qualified teachers than students who do not attend these schools.

In California, as one would expect, the situation is the most pronounced and the problem of the misdistribution of under prepared teachers has gotten worse in the last few years. The Center for the Future of Teaching and Learning (2001) in Santa Cruz recently concluded in an analysis of the teaching force in the state in 2000–2001 that:

Students already exhibiting low academic performance, those most in need of investment and effective intervention, have a higher probability of being taught by an under prepared teacher …. On average, the lowest performing schools had 25% under prepared teachers. This is double the state average and five times the proportion of under prepared teachers at high achieving schools …. Schools with the highest percentages of students receiving free and reduced lunch … continue to have the highest percentage of under prepared teachers. A similar pattern emerges when examining schools by student minority level (pp. 23–24).

When we examine the data with regard to the achievement gap in P–12 public education, although there are some bright spots, such as the decline in the dropout rate for African-American students by 40 percent between 1972 and 1999 and a rise in college enrollment for African-American and white high school completers (U.S. Department of Education, 2001), disturbing gaps persist in the academic performance and educational participation among different ethnic/racial and socioeconomic groups. These gaps exist when children enter kindergarten and show few signs of closing throughout the grade levels (Lee, 2002; U.S. Department of Education, 2001).

One of the current major debates in the policy arena is whether teacher certification makes a difference in the effectiveness of teachers. Among others, Darling-Hammond and the Abell Foundation have issued detailed critiques and counter critiques of what the research that is often used in support of teacher certification means (e.g. Ballou & Podgursky, 2000; Darling-Hammond, 2000a, 2001; Darling-Hammond, Berry, & Thoreson, 2001; Finn & Kanstoroom, 2000; Goldhaber & Brewer, 2000; Madigan & Poliakoff, 2001; Walsh, 2001). Regardless of where one stands on this issue (in my view there are problems with both positions), it is hard to ignore the data on gaps in school achievement and the comments by teachers themselves about the variable quality of education that is available to different groups of students. The most recent MetLife Survey of American Teachers, for example, concludes the following:

> The premise that all children can learn is a concept that has been embraced by policy makers and the public alike. What is harder to ascertain is whether all students have access to the tools, knowledge, and guidance they need to succeed. In many areas addressed in this survey, from teacher quality, to school building conditions, to challenging curricula and high expectations, many low income students and ethnic minority students and their teachers and principals constantly give responses that indicate these students do not have the same opportunities to learn, when compared to responses of those in schools with largely high income populations or in schools with a low proportion of ethnic minority students (Markow, Fauth, & Gravitch, 2001, p. 6).

There is also the issue of the continued unequal spending on the education of students in different school districts. The Education Trust recently released a report that asserts that in 42 states, school districts with the greatest number of poor children have less money to spend per student than districts with the fewest poor children (Education Trust, 2001). The "savage inequalities" in educational provision so powerfully documented by Kozol (1991) are still with us. The facts are hard to ignore. The question is what to do about the situation. The professionalization, deregulation, and social justice agendas offer very different visions for how to remedy the current situation of inequality and injustice in public education. I now briefly examine each of these three visions for reform and identify what I think are their strengths and weaknesses. I also address the things I think none of the reform agendas addresses but are necessary if we are to see things change for the better.

The Professionalization Agenda

The first reform agenda, the professionalization agenda (or the regulatory agenda, as it is called by its critics), is propelled in its current incarnation by the NCTAF reports of 1996 and 1997, as well as a host of related developments stimulated by such groups as the Holmes Group and Partnership, the National Board for Professional Teaching Standards, Interstate New Teacher Assessment and Support Consortium (INTASC), and NCATE. However, this agenda did not originate in the 1990s. The current wave of reform to professionalize teacher education and teaching, which has resulted in the near-universal requirement for performance-based assessment in teacher education programs, represents the current incarnation of what has been referred to as the social efficiency tradition of reform in teacher education—the quest to establish a profession of teaching through the articulation of a knowledge base for teaching based on educational research and professional judgment (Liston & Zeichner, 1991). In the twentieth century, performance-based teacher education was clearly the dominant reform impulse in American teacher education. It resulted in several major attempts on a national scale to replace course completion as the basis for initial licensure with a system that assessed teachers' abilities to display certain knowledge, dispositions, and performances thought to be necessary for effective teaching (Gage & Winne, 1974; Zeichner, 2001).

Of course, what was going on throughout the 1970s and early 1980s was not exactly the same as what is happening now. In the current incarnation of performance-based teacher education, which some have referred to as performance standards-based teacher education (Valli & Rennert-Ariev, 2002) to distinguish it from its predecessors, there is no longer a focus on only behavioral competencies, as was the case in the 1970s. Contemporary statements of teacher standards are broader and attend to the cognitive and dispositional aspects of teaching in addition to the technical dimensions. The standards today are also fewer in number than the lists of hundreds of competencies that were common in the 1970s. Also, there is no longer a preoccupation with the empirical validity of the standards as there was in the 1970s. That is, there is no longer a preoccupation with whether educational research has established links between specific standards and student learning (Heath & Nielson, 1974). Instead, the validity of the standards is asserted based on the judgments of panels of experts, and careful attention is given to the process of standard development within committees of scholars and practitioners. We are closer today to the process of standard generation used in the infamous Commonwealth Teacher Training study of 1929, in which groups of experts came up with standards about what represents good teaching in particular domains (Charters & Waples, 1929), than we are to the quest for the key to teaching effectiveness through process–product research in the 1970s. This failure to establish clear links between teacher standards and pupil learning—even if they are broadly defined—has been pounced on by critics of the teacher education establishment. Critics use this failure as the basis for asserting that performance-based teacher education is of little consequence. In other respects, such as in the high cost of implementation and demands on the time and energy of faculty, what is going on today closely resembles the 1970s.

The main assertions made by advocates of the professionalization agenda have been translated into policy mandates that state education departments and NCATE have implemented in the program approval or accreditation process in most states. The main argument is that the inequities and injustices that exist in public education can be remedied by raising standards for both teaching and teacher education and investing more greatly in teaching and public schooling. The NCTAF and related reports have either proposed or actively supported a host of specific reforms toward the goal of raising the status of teaching as a profession. Such reforms include an end to issuing emergency teaching licenses and alternative routes that fail to provide adequate preparation for teaching, aggressive recruitment of teachers in high-need areas and a more ethnically diverse teaching force, implementation of higher standards for entry into and exit from teacher education programs, adoption of teacher standards linked to P–12 student standards, performance-based assessment of student teacher performance on these teacher standards, external examinations of teachers' content knowledge, extended programs of five years, professional development schools, establishment of professional standards boards in every state, mandatory national accreditation for teacher education programs, better teacher induction and mentoring programs, National Board certification as the benchmark for accomplished teaching, more support for high quality teacher professional development, and greater university-wide support and funding for teacher education programs.

A lot of positive results that have occurred from the implementation of pieces of the professionalization agenda in recent years have implications for dealing with the problems of inequality and injustice in public education. The first positive result is the way in which the advocates of this position have placed the problems of inequality and injustice in public education and the mistreatment of teacher education in higher education into center stage. More public discussion occurs today about these issues than ever before. There are also benefits that have clearly resulted from the increased dialogue and clearer articulation of the conceptual basis for teacher education programs and the knowledge, dispositions, and performances that teacher education students are expected to master.

Despite the many positive contributions that have been made so far by the professionalization agenda, there are a number of problems with the results of the implementation of this agenda that threaten to undermine the goal of equalizing educational outcomes. The first serious problem, in my view, is that teaching standards have often been defined in a way that enables programs to ignore what we know from research about what teachers need to know and do in order to likely be successful in teaching all students to high standards. In recent years, a substantial body of literature has converged on the identification of the attributes of teachers and instructional strategies associated with what has come to be called culturally responsive teaching (e.g. CREDE, 2002; Gay, 2000; Jordan-Irvine & Armento, 2001; Ladson-Billings, 1994; Villegas & Lucas, 2002a, b). The teaching standards that have come to be commonly used as the basis for performance assessment in teacher education programs, such as the INTASC standards, do not adequately incorporate what we know about culturally responsive teaching. For example, INTASC Standard 3 is the standard that most closely addresses the issue of student diversity, although others touch on it as well. This standard (INTASC, 1992) states, "The teacher understands how students differ in their approaches to learning and creates instructional opportunities that are adapted to diverse learners" (p. 18). Although the statements of knowledge, skills, and dispositions under this standard mention the need for teachers to understand how second languages are acquired, ESL teaching strategies, and the ways in which culture and community values in general influence learning, a whole lot is found in the literature on culturally responsive teaching that can easily be left out of the picture when the INTASC standards are implemented. I come back to this issue later when I discuss the social justice agenda for reform.

The second problem with the implementation of the professionalization agenda thus far has been the adverse effects raising standards has had on the diversity of the pool of teacher education students. There are at least two issues here. First, there is the issue of keeping people who are trying to come into the system from an uneven playing field out of teacher education programs. Rather than looking at a range of attributes and skills that applicants bring to teacher education—including academic performance and potential, the kinds of characteristics valued in Haberman and Post's urban teacher interview (Haberman, 1993, 1995)—programs continue to emphasize and, in some cases, exclusively use academic criteria such as GPA and test scores to determine who will be admitted.

Despite all of the rhetoric about the importance of bringing more students of color into teacher education programs and the existence of some very successful alternative programs that deliberately seek out applicants from underrepresented groups (e.g. Clewell & Villegas, 2001a, b), the picture of mainstream teacher education in the 1,300 or so institutions that offer programs is one of very little ethnic and racial diversity. While not denying the importance of academic performance and content knowledge, the practice of ignoring some of the additional strengths that diverse candidates bring to teacher education programs has worked against the goal of recruiting more diverse teacher education cohorts. This practice has also ignored the importance of some of the skills and experiences that are needed to be able to use content knowledge to promote pupil understanding and achievement (e.g. skills and experiences concerned with being able to relate well with pupils and parents in diverse settings).

Second, the performance assessments that have been used to evaluate teachers' work do not always value the attributes and skills of some effective teachers. The current debates about the disproportionate failure rates of teachers of color in the National Board Certification process are an example of this problem. Jackie Jordan-Irvine, Gloria Ladson-Billings, and others have raised some very important concerns about cultural bias in the performance assessment of teachers (Jordan-Irvine & Fraser, 1998; Ladson-Billings, 1999b).

The third problem with the implementation of the professionalization agenda has been the high cost of implementing the recommended practices in a time of declining budgets and economic recession. The teacher education literature throughout the 1970s was dominated by discussion of performance-based teacher education. In addition, the U.S. Department of Education funded the development of model performance-based programs and required performance-based assessment in all National Teacher Corps projects (Clarke, 1969; Houston & Howsam, 1972).The actual implementation of competency and performance-based programs, however, was very low: about 13 percent of teacher education institutions (Joyce, Yarger, & Howey, 1977). The problem was the lack of capacity to implement what had been designed on paper (Hite, 1973). Currently, the implementation of the new version of performance-based assessment in preservice teacher education is making many new demands on teacher education faculty and institutions while positions and budgets are being cut. There is also the question of whether state education departments, whose budgets are also being cut, will have the capacity to monitor the new performance-based programs. Furthermore, in research universities where there is already a tension between research and teaching and problems in finding faculty willing to work in teacher education programs (Goodlad, 1990; Zeichner, 1999a), the reemergence of performance-based teacher education has intensified the distaste of some faculty for being involved in teacher education. This is because the faculty is asked to write performance indicators and rubrics and to examine their courses to see if they are covering what will be covered on the state content examinations. The lack of the new financial and human resources needed to implement these more labor-intensive programs may once again lead to the demise of performance-based teacher education or to a superficial implementation. The implementation demands may just be too great, given the current economic situation and the continuing struggle by teacher education to gain respect in higher education.

It is assumed by many advocates of the professionalization agenda that establishing a performance-based assessment system in a teacher education program based on a set of teacher standards will necessarily lead to better teaching and learning for children. The efforts of thousands of teacher educators across the country are now necessarily focused at the micro level on how to implement the various state mandates for performance-based teacher education. The accreditation of their programs depends on it. There is a real danger here, however, of losing sight of the forest in the midst of the trees. That is, there is a danger of turning performance-based teacher education into a purely mechanical implementation activity that has lost sight of any moral purpose and the need to constantly step back from the daily grind of implementation to ask the hard questions about what is being accomplished and for whose benefit. In the end, we must be able to show that all of the effort now being expended on behalf of developing assessment systems, portfolios, and so on actually makes a difference in addressing the gaps in educational provision and outcomes.

The Deregulation Agenda

The second reform agenda for teacher education that has dominated the debates in the public policy arena is the deregulation agenda, or, as its advocates describe it, the reformist or commonsense agenda. This agenda, which has been moved forward by the Fordham Foundation and other conservative think tanks and foundations, has often been presented in direct opposition to the professionalization proposals and has clear links to the larger neoliberal and neoconservative agendas to privatize and deregulate P–12 schooling in the United States (Apple, 2001).[4] This agenda is an outgrowth of what Dan Liston and I have referred to as the academic tradition in teacher education reform (Liston & Zeichner, 1991), a reform tradition that began with Flexner's study of teacher education in 1930 and has produced a number of widely cited critiques of the teacher education establishment. Flexner (1930), whose study of medical education is ironically often cited by advocates of the professionalization agenda, raised a theme that has repeatedly appeared in the long list of attacks on the teacher education establishment. He concluded:

> Why should not an educated person, broadly and deeply versed in educational philosophy and experience, help himself from this point on? Why should his attention be diverted during these pregnant years to the trivialities and applications with which commonsense can deal adequately with when the time comes (pp. 99–100).

Since Flexner's (1930) critique, a number of highly visible, sharply pointed, and often emotionally charged assaults on teacher education have appeared, including Koerner's (1963) *Miseducation of American Teachers*, Bestor's (1953) *Educational Wastelands*, and Lynd's (1953) *Quackery in the Public*

Schools, as well as, more recently, Kramer's (2000) *Ed School Follies* and the Pacific Research Institute's *Teacher Quality and Teacher Training in California's Schools of Education* (Izumi & Coburn, 2001). The language in these critiques is often blunt and derogatory. For example, Koerner concluded his examination of teacher education in the United States with the following:

> Whatever they claim to do and be education courses deserve the ill repute that has always been accorded them by members of the academic faculty, by teachers themselves, and by the general public. Most education courses are vague, insipid, time wasting adumbrations of the obvious, and probably irrelevant to academic teaching (pp. 55–56).

Continuing with many of the same arguments made by Flexner and Koerner, and acknowledging the gap in the quality of education and educational outcomes for different groups, contemporary advocates of the deregulation agenda have sought to break what they see as the monopoly of colleges and universities on initial teacher education programs by encouraging alternative certification programs and the dismantling of state teacher certification. The argument is made that subject matter knowledge and teachers' verbal ability are the main determinants of teaching success, and it is asserted that much of what is offered in professional education methods and foundations courses can be learned on the job through an apprenticeship. Deregulation advocates assert that "there is no reliable link between pedagogical training and classroom success" (Fordham Foundation, 1999, p. 6). The knowledge base that is presented by advocates of professionalization and embedded in the teaching standards used to assess the performance of prospective teachers and teachers (e.g. INTASC and National Board standards) is described as vague and subjective and is thought to be without any basis in research. Hess (2001), whose recent report published by the Progressive Policy Institute offers one of the less emotional and more reasoned analyses of the situation from a deregulation perspective, asserts: "The simple truth is that professional educators have not constituted a cannon of essential knowledge or skills analogous to that which exists in law or medicine" (p. 27).

The recent reports of the Fordham and Abell Foundations and the Pacific and Progressive Policy Institutes (Izumi & Coburn, 2001; Kanstoroom & Finn, 1999; Walsh, 2001) call for both eliminating state certification and licensing teachers with bachelor's degrees who pass tests in the subjects they are to teach and criminal background checks. It is felt that the rest of what is offered in teacher education programs is either not necessary to be a good teacher or can be learned on the job through firsthand experience or professional development.

It is argued in these reports that the increasing requirements to get in and out of college- and university-based teacher education programs are discouraging many talented individuals, who could allegedly help reduce the gap in educational quality in the public schools, from going into teaching. The deregulators have encouraged opening the gates to teaching, and support is offered for three different kinds of alternative certification options: (a) "missionary" programs, such as Teach for America, where the goal is to find idealistic and smart young people to spend a couple of years working in high-poverty schools before they move on to the corporate boardrooms and other leadership positions in society; (b) private for-profit alternatives offered by Sylvan Learning, Edison, and so on; and (c) school-based alternative routes in which districts prepare their own teachers.

Another aspect of this reform agenda is the attack on what is described as a constructivist and multicultural bias in the teacher education curriculum in colleges and universities. Here, as can be seen in the Pacific Research Institute's recent critique of the curriculum and teaching methods used in several teacher education programs in the California State system (Izumi & Coburn, 2001), teacher educators are accused of indoctrinating students into student-centered teaching methods, being against high educational standards, and being overly concerned with political correctness. In oversimplified caricatures of what is referred to as student-centered instruction, teacher educators are accused of proposing that pupils should be able to construct their own knowledge without the teacher's intervention. Pointing to 25-year-old reviews of process–product research of the 1970s and 1980s, which allegedly lend support to teacher-centered and direct instruction, teacher educators are accused of ignoring the research evidence in their advocacy of student-centered methods. Selectively pulling quotes out of program materials, course syllabi, and text books, the authors of the Pacific Institute Report attack a range of identified evils in California State University teacher education programs. Such evils include constructivism, discovery learning, thematic and integrated curriculum, and cooperative learning, as well as the identified gurus of this poison propaganda, such as Dewey, Vygotsky, and Freire. One of the most disturbing aspects of this sophomoric diatribe, which has received a lot of public attention (e.g. "Too Many Teacher Colleges Major in Mediocrity," 2002), is the way in which multicultural education and concerns with preparing teachers to be advocates of social justice are positioned against support for high academic standards. Strangely, the remedies that are offered in this report for the California State University system and its public schools are mathematics instruction in Singapore and an after-school program in Japan. There are other aspects of the deregulation agenda that call for paying teachers who produce higher student learning scores more money and enabling principals to hire whomever they want as long as the basic conditions of a degree, subject matter test, and background check are met.

There are several major problems, in my view, with the deregulation agenda. Despite its contribution in drawing attention to both the problems with the subject matter preparation (and there are serious problems here) and the possibilities offered by alternative routes to certification, there are several flaws in its major arguments that are in conflict with the concern for academic standards that are expressed throughout these reports. First, the characterization of state certification as being obsessed with "course counting" that appears repeatedly in these reports may be an accurate description of what used to exist, but it no longer describes the near-universal performance-based approach to licensing that exists throughout the United States today. For example, in Hess's call for a radical overhaul of teacher certification, published in November, 2001 by the Progressive Policy Institute, he charges that "no state makes clear what teachers need to learn in teacher education courses or ensures that teachers have acquired essential knowledge or skills" (p. x). In Wisconsin, like many other states, we have been working for more than five years to phase in a performance-based assessment system in preservice teacher education programs that is linked to state teacher standards. All around the country, teacher educators, whether or not they are affiliated with NCATE, are spending much of their energy developing performance-based assessments linked to state standards. The characterization of state certification by some of the deregulation advocates is as outdated as their reliance on 25-year-old reviews of process–product research as evidence of the evils of learner-centered approaches to teaching.

Second, the assertion that subject matter knowledge alone is sufficient to be a successful teacher of that subject matter to diverse learners is a major problem. There is substantial research literature on the subject matter preparation of teachers that clearly documents the inadequacy of this simplistic view (Ball, 2000; Grossman, 1990; Hewson, Tabachnick, Zeichner, & Lemberger, 1999; McDiarmid, 1994; Wineberg, 2001). Majoring in a subject or passing a subject matter test, even if the bar is set high, is no guarantee that teachers understand the central concepts in their disciplines and have the pedagogical content knowledge needed to transform content to promote understanding by diverse learners. There is also no mention at all in the deregulation proposals of the need to develop teachers' intercultural sensitivities and competencies so that they can be effective with all students, including those who have cultural and linguistic backgrounds different from themselves. The attacks on multicultural education engaged in by some of the advocates of deregulation ignore the empirical evidence both about the importance of teachers' intercultural competence to being able to teach successfully our diverse schools (e.g. the research on culturally responsive teaching) and the research on teacher education experiences that enhance that competence (Zeichner, 2003a).

Third, the deregulation position's uncritical advocacy of alternative routes to certification without attention to the conditions that need to exist in these alternative programs for their educative potential to be realized is a weakness. Although deregulation advocates are correct in asserting that alternative programs have much to offer as legitimate pathways into teaching, there is no support in this literature for programs that put unqualified teachers into classrooms as teachers of record and provide them with little or no professional education and mentoring (Wilson, Floden, & Ferrini-Mundy, 2001; Zeichner & Schulte, 2001). Neither, by the way, does the literature support the assertion frequently heard from within the teacher education establishment that "the evidence against alternative certification seems to be definitive" (Scannell, 1999, p. 13).

The truth is that all forms of teacher education include a wide range of quality, from awful to excellent. Instead of continuing the debates over whether four- or five-year programs, undergraduate programs or graduate programs, or traditional programs or alternative programs is better, it would be more useful to focus on gaining a better understanding of the components of good teacher education regardless of the structural model of the program. Alternative certification programs of various kinds, including for-profit programs and those based on the use of distance technologies, are here to stay and are part of the solution to the tremendous inequities that exist in our public schools. We need to continue developing multiple pathways into teaching and focus on making sure that the components of high quality teacher education—something we are beginning to learn more about from recent in-depth case studies of teacher education programs (Darling-Hammond, 2000b; Howey & Zimpher, 1989)—are present in all of these various structural models. To assert, however, as is done by advocates of deregulation, that alternative certification of any kind is necessarily good, is not supported by any reasonable reading of peer-reviewed scholarly research on this issue.

The Social Justice Agenda

The third and final reform agenda I discuss is the social justice agenda. This agenda has been encouraged by the work that has been going on for many years within American Association of Colleges for Teacher Education (AACTE), Association of Teacher Educators (ATE), and other organizations, such as National Association of Multicultural Education (NAME), to place the preparation of teachers for cultural diversity at the center of attention. Often referring to the cultural gap between teachers and their pupils, advocates of the social justice agenda, which is an outgrowth of the social reconstructionist tradition of reform in American teacher education, see both schooling and teacher education as crucial elements in the making of a more just society (Liston & Zeichner, 1991). Despite the lack of infusion of multicultural and social reconstructionist perspectives throughout preservice teacher education programs, a great deal has been learned through research about both the teacher attributes and instructional strategies associated with successful teaching in culturally and linguistically diverse schools and teacher education strategies that are effective in preparing teachers to become these culturally responsive teachers.

Although much work remains to be done to clarify the elements of good teaching in a multicultural society, substantial literature has emerged in recent years on the attributes and strategies associated with culturally responsive teaching. Researchers such as Jackie Jordan-Irvine, Gloria Ladson-Billings, Geneva Gay, Ana Maria Villegas, Martin Haberman, Luis Moll, Michele Foster, Etta Hollins, Sonia Nieto, and Barbara Merino, among others, and research sponsored by research centers such as Center for Research on Education, Diversity and Excellence (CREDE) in Santa Cruz, California (e.g. CREDE, 2002; Foster, 1997; Gay, 2000; Jordan-Irvine, 1992; Jordan-Irvine & Armento, 2001; Ladson-Billings, 1994, 1995b; Merino, 1999; Moll & Vellez Ibanez, 1992; Murrell, 2001; Nieto, 2000; Nieto & Rolon, 1997; Villegas, 1991; Villegas & Lucas, 2001, 2002a), have identified remarkably consistent sets of knowledge, skills, and performances that are related to successful teaching in culturally diverse schools. Although the INTASC standards touch on these elements of this pedagogy, they do not capture the full force of what has been learned from this research.

Several years ago, I did work with colleagues in The Urban Network to Improve Teacher Education (UNITE, a network of 32 urban partnerships) to synthesize the various statements of the knowledge base for culturally responsive teaching and develop a set of knowledge, dispositions, and performances that can potentially be used to influence the definition of teaching standards so that the elements of culturally responsive teaching become more central.

When you look at this literature and the kinds of teacher attributes and instructional knowledge and skills that are associated with effective teaching for culturally and linguistically diverse students, many of the important pieces of this message are missing or are underemphasized in statements of the teaching standards that are used to assess prospective teachers for initial licensure. Currently, it is fairly easy to interpret the standards in ways that ignore or minimize the cultural and linguistic aspects of diversity that are so critical to effective teaching in today's schools. Here are three brief examples of knowledge, performances, and dispositions that I think would be easy to neglect with the use of the INTASC standards:[5]

- *Knowledge.* The teacher understands the ways in which life is organized in the communities in which his or her students live, as well as how students use and display knowledge, tell stories, and interact with peers and adults. The teacher knows something about the funds of knowledge that exist in these communities.
- *Performance.* The teacher is able to incorporate aspects of his or her students' abilities, experiences, cultures, participation styles, frames of references, and community resources into the class in ways that enhance student learning.
- *Disposition.* The teacher sees resources for learning in all students rather than viewing differences as problems to overcome. The teacher believes that he or she is responsible for making a difference in his or her students' learning.

These brief examples, which are part of an effort to transform some of the insights of a substantial body of research on effective teaching for culturally and linguistically diverse learners into the currency of standards, are aimed at making it more difficult for the knowledge base for culturally responsive teaching to be underemphasized in performance-based teacher education programs.

Research on teacher education has illuminated some of the factors in teacher education programs, including admission policies and instructional strategies used in courses and field experiences, that are effective in developing greater intercultural sensitivity and competence in prospective teachers. These include such things as: admissions criteria that screen applicants on the basis of their commitment to teach all students; carefully monitored and analyzed field experiences in culturally diverse schools and communities, including cultural immersion experiences in which prospective teachers live in culturally different communities and are forced to reexamine their worldviews; the use of uncertified adults in communities as teacher educators teaching prospective teachers cultural and linguistic knowledge; and teaching prospective teachers how to use various teaching and assessment strategies that are sensitive to cultural and linguistic variations and how to adapt classroom instruction to accommodate the cultural resources that their students bring to school (Grant & Secada, 1990; Ladson-Billings, 1995a, 1999a; Villegas & Lucas, 2001; Zeichner, 1996a, 2003; Zeichner & Hoeft, 1996).

Some of the advocates of social justice teacher education operate within the parameters of traditional undergraduate college- and university-based programs. Others, like Martin Haberman and Linda Post in Milwaukee and teacher educators in a number of places, including those that extend their programs outside of colleges and universities, have implemented high-quality alternative certification programs that provide legitimate professional preparation for teaching. Examples of these high-quality alternative programs are the Dewitt Wallace-Reader's Digest Fund's Pathways to Teaching Careers program, which includes such programs as the University of Southern California's Latino Teacher Project, and the Milwaukee Teacher Education Center (MTEC) program in Milwaukee, Wisconsin (Genzuk & Baca, 1998; Haberman, 1999; Villegas & Clewell, 1998).

Another aspect of the social justice agenda has been to make deliberate efforts to recruit, prepare, and retain more teachers of color. Here, we have learned a lot from evaluating successful programs, such as the Pathways to Teaching programs (e.g. Clewell & Villegas, 2001a, b; Villegas & Clewell, 1998), that could be used to improve the diversity of our teaching force.

Despite the important contribution made by advocates of the social justice agenda to the national discourse on teacher education, there are several problems with this reform agenda that have weakened its impact. The first major limitation of the social justice agenda is that much of what has been done by advocates of this agenda has been done at the level of the teacher education classroom as teacher educators have introduced activities and experiences into their programs that are aimed at preparing more culturally responsive teachers. Both the professionalization and deregulation agendas address the structures of the teaching profession and teacher education. Although one may not agree with some of the specific proposals their advocates make, it is clear that any solution to the problems of inequality and injustice in public education will need to address the larger contexts in which teaching and teacher education exist.

When my colleagues and I began a study of several exemplary teacher education programs for diversity about 10 years ago for the National Center for Research on Teacher Learning at Michigan State, we began with a very narrow focus on the instructional practices that teacher educators used in campus classes and field experiences. It very quickly became clear that we needed to broaden our focus to address both the ways in which students were selected into teacher education and the larger programmatic and institutional contexts in which the programs were embedded. Our reports of this research ended up paying a lot of attention to both the institutional conditions that are critical to the effectiveness of the work of teacher educators in their classrooms and the ways in which students are selected into teacher education programs (e.g. Melnick & Zeichner, 1997). The focus must be even broader than this and needs to consider, from a social justice perspective, the kinds of structures of the profession of teaching and of teacher education that are addressed by the other two reform agendas: program approval and accreditation, requirements for initial licensure, the induction of new teachers, the structure of teaching careers, and so on. Keeping the focus of proposals for social justice-oriented teacher education at the level of the teacher education classroom will not significantly impact the larger societal problem of inequality in education provision and outcomes.

The second major limitation of the social justice agenda is the lack of capacity in the teacher education group to do the job that we know needs to be done. Here, just as there has been a continuing low level of ethnic diversity among teacher education students, there has also been a problem with developing a more ethnically diverse group of teacher educators. Currently, about 14 percent of the faculty in higher education overall and about 15 percent of the faculty in education units are of color. This represents an improvement from where we were in the 1980s, but it is still pathetic. A diverse learning community in teacher education programs is critical to our ability to prepare teachers for diverse schools.

Also, although, contrary to public perceptions, many teacher educators have P–12 teaching experience, not many have had experience as successful teachers in the kinds of culturally diverse and high-poverty schools for which we need to prepare teachers today. Martin Haberman made the claim in the late 1980s that less than five percent of teacher education faculty had taught for even one year in an urban school district. His statement probably still holds true today. Even if we know a lot about the attributes and instructional strategies that teachers need to be successful in the public schools of today (which I think we do), we need to either have culturally responsive teacher educators who are able to develop these capacities in prospective teachers or figure out how to compensate for the limitations of the faculty.

Despite what we know from research about the value of closely connecting teacher education programs to diverse communities and employing community members as teacher educators (e.g. Mahan, 1982, 1993; Mahan, Fortney, & Garcia, 1983; Zeichner & Melnick, 1996), most teacher education programs continue to operate on the belief that developing interculturally competent teachers is primarily a matter of reading texts and discussing them on campus or placing student teachers in culturally different schools for field experiences. Integrally embedding teacher education programs and teacher education students into diverse communities, as has been done by some programs over the last 30 years with much success (e.g. Grinberg & Paz-Goldfarb, 1998; Noordhoff & Kleinfeld, 1993; Sconzert, Iazzetto, & Purkey, 2000; Stachowski & Mahan, 1998), is not that common in practice today. My experience as a teacher educator in the National Teacher Corps and my research on teacher education programs has convinced me that it is important to make diverse communities central aspects of teacher education for diversity and openly acknowledge the limitations of what can be accomplished when the center of gravity of teacher education is on a college or university campus.

The third major limitation of the social justice agenda is that it has almost exclusively focused on the transformation of white, monolingual English teachers, who are the majority of teacher education students, to teach students of color living in poverty. Sorely neglected in this work is the preparation of all teachers to teach all students. A literature has emerged in recent years documenting the failure of teacher education programs to adequately address the needs of student teachers of color who attend primarily white institutions (Delpit, 1995; Hood & Parker, 1994; Montecinos, 1995). This literature argues that although growing up as a person of color or as someone whose first language is not English in the United States results in a particular quality of life experience different from that of those who are white and English-speaking, one cannot necessarily equate being a person of color with being an effective teacher, even of students of a similar background. The task of teacher education for diversity needs to be reframed to one of preparing all teachers to teach all students, and the particular needs of prospective teachers of color need to be better addressed in teacher education programs, including many of those that have already incorporated multicultural education.

Also, as I alluded to earlier, much of the work that has occurred in multicultural teacher education has focused on issues of race, gender, and social class, ignoring the preparation of teachers to teach the increasing number of English language learners in our public schools. Despite the existence of Crosscultural, Language, and Academic Development (CLAD) Certificate in California, which includes a linguistic component (Walton & Carlson, 1997), and several other similar efforts around the country, such as the

English for Speakers of Other Languages (ESOL) endorsement in Florida, most teacher education programs do not give prospective teachers the background and training in applied linguistics that is necessary to work in today's public schools. According to research, elements of this preparation should include educating all prospective teachers about such things as the components of language, the process of language acquisition, and ESL teaching strategies (National Research Council, 1997; Reagan, 1997).

Another limitation of the social justice agenda that has undermined its legitimacy is that some of the published literature that presents a social justice perspective on teacher education is written by faculty who themselves have left the work of teacher education for a more comfortable and high-status existence within higher education. Although there has been some presence of social justice perspectives at the main teacher education gatherings at the national and state levels (e.g. AACTE and ATE), for the most part the most visible of these advocates do not attend the meetings of teacher educators to engage practicing teacher educators in a discussion of their ideas. The lowly status of teacher education within higher education and the persistence of promotion and tenure criteria which do not sufficiently value good work in the practice of teacher education continue to draw talented people away from the work of teacher education (Labaree, 1997).

Conclusion

In conclusion, although each of the three major reform agendas in teacher education today makes some positive contributions toward ameliorating the inequalities and injustices in education with which we are faced, each of these platforms has certain weaknesses. The professionalization agenda seeks to raise the status and working conditions of teachers in the country through a variety of integrated mechanisms that address the structures that govern teaching and teacher education. However, its definition of teaching standards does not always give enough explicit attention to what research says teachers need to know and be able to do to successfully teach the culturally and linguistically diverse students who are in our public schools. Likewise, it does not give enough explicit attention to teacher education strategies, such as community field experiences, that research has shown are effective in developing intercultural teaching competence. It has also failed to establish clear links between the efforts now being focused on the development of (even broadly defined) standards, assessments, portfolios, and pupil learning. Additionally, some of the mechanisms that have been put into place have worked against efforts to diversify the learning communities in teacher education programs, and the additional requirements for teacher education programs that have resulted from these new mechanisms have not always been followed with the resources to implement them.

The deregulation agenda, although drawing attention to the importance of teachers' subject matter knowledge, fails to recognize the importance of the pedagogical content knowledge that teachers also need to be able to translate content to promote student understanding. Advocates of this agenda often uncritically endorse alternative certification programs and denigrate the value of professional education courses by relying on process–product research from more than 20 years ago, ignoring much of the research on teaching and learning that has been done since then (e.g. Bransford, Brown, & Cocking, 2000). There is little or no attention paid by deregulation advocates to the cultural divide between teachers and their pupils and the need to develop teachers' abilities to be interculturally competent.

The social justice agenda brings the issue of preparing teachers to work in culturally and linguistically diverse schools into focus and draws attention to the things that research has identified we need to be able to do well in educating teachers if they are going to be able to be successful in promoting learning in the public schools that we have today. However, many advocates of this agenda have too narrowly defined the task as transforming white, monolingual teachers to teach students of color (instead of one of preparing all teachers to teach all students). Such advocates have mostly focused their efforts at the level of the teacher education classroom, often ignoring the contexts in which both teacher education programs and teachers operate. There are also serious questions about the capacity of teacher education faculties to be able to do what is required given the composition of teacher educators, the reward systems in higher education and in the public schools that devalue teacher education, and the limited resource base for teacher education programs. Finally, social justice teacher education has not given much attention to issues of linguistic diversity and the teaching of English language learners, even within programs that incorporate aspects of multicultural education.

There is also a sense in which none of these reform agendas has given attention to some of the most important issues that must be dealt with by all of us if the social preconditions for the equality of educational provision and outcomes are to be achieved. The discourse on teacher education is largely silent about the need to aggressively advocate for the societal conditions that need to be present if equality in the educational arena is to be achieved. Such conditions include access to quality food, housing, affordable health care, and jobs that pay a living wage. Currently, there are 11.5 million children under the age of 18 in the United States who live in poverty, and almost 11 million children under the age of 19 who do not have health insurance (Children's Defense Fund, 2001). Unless we are able to address these broader social conditions that affect students in our public school classrooms and their families, the slogan now attached to our new education act, No Child Left Behind, will be empty and meaningless. It will not help us move toward a world where what we all want for our children and grandchildren is also available to everyone's children. This is the only kind of world with which we should be satisfied.

Advocates of the three reform agendas who are currently vying for control of the education of teachers in the United States must look past their partisan interests and put together a plan for the future of our children, taking advantage of what each version has to offer while minimizing the negative aspects of each perspective. It is not a question of which view is the correct one. So far none of us has gotten it right.

In the end, the achievement gap in U.S. public schooling is largely a reflection of the other gaps that exist in the larger society. Although schooling and teacher education can play a role in lessening these inequalities, they must be viewed as only one aspect of a more comprehensive plan for the equalization of outcomes in society. Without the broader political work that needs to occur at many levels to change the ways in which our society's resources are allocated (e.g. for prisons, weapons, and sports stadiums, and not for educators and schools), the reform agendas in teacher education will be of little consequence in the long run.

Chapter 2

Educating Teachers for Social Justice[1]

Kenneth M. Zeichner and Ryan Flessner

> The duty of the teachers' colleges is thus clear. They must furnish over a
> period of years a staff of workers for the public schools who thoroughly
> understand the social, economic, and political problems with which this
> country is faced, who are zealous in the improvement of present conditions
> and who are capable of educating citizens disposed to study social prob-
> lems earnestly, think critically about them, and act in accord with their
> noblest impulses (Brown, 1938, p. 328).

In this chapter, we discuss the goals and practices that have been commonly
associated with preservice teacher education programs that emphasize the
preparation of teachers who are critical of the current inequities in public
schooling and the social, economic, and political structures of the society and
will work in and outside their classrooms for greater educational, economic,
and social justice. Following this discussion, we illustrate the ways in which
social justice-oriented preservice teacher education programs have been
implemented by presenting brief descriptions of the goals and practices in
three teacher education programs in Canada, the U.S., and Brazil. Finally, we
examine several aspects of current practice that we think need more attention
from teacher educators who identify with a social justice agenda.

Since the early part of the twentieth century, there have been a number of
efforts by teacher educators in a number of countries to prepare teachers as
agents of social change who will work with their colleagues and local communities to ameliorate problems of inequity and injustice in schooling and the
broader society.[2] Liston & Zeichner (1991) describe a number of examples of
these social reconstructionist teacher education initiatives in the U.S., including New College, an experimental teacher education program at Teachers
College Columbia University from 1932–1939 (Limbert, 1934), the introduction of an integrated social foundations component into the teacher education curriculum in the 1930s (Rugg, 1952), and the National Teacher
Corps program (Rogers, 2002). Rodgers (2006) describes a similar attempt
to link teacher preparation with broader movements for social justice at the
Putney Graduate School of Teacher Education in the 1950s and 1960s. Also,

Ladson-Billings (1995b) and Cochran-Smith, Davis, and Fries (2003) analyze specific elements of the multicultural education movement in teacher education in the U.S. that have focused on preparing teachers to work for greater equity and justice in schooling and society.[3]

Today, the term social justice teacher education (SJTE) has come to be used to describe these social reconstructionist-oriented teacher preparation programs. SJTE, like reflection in the 1980s and 1990s, has become a new slogan in teacher education among those teacher educators who identify themselves with a progressive agenda. It has come to the point where it is very difficult to find a teacher education program anywhere that does not claim that it has a social justice agenda and that it prepares teachers to work against inequities in schooling and society. One danger of the sloganizing that has emerged around the concept of social justice in teacher education is that the term will lose any specific meaning: It will come to justify and frame teacher education efforts that represent a variety of ideological and political commitments, including some that are not critical of the current social order or representing a change from the status quo. This has been the fate of other slogans in teacher education such as reflection and professional development schools (e.g. Zeichner, 2007; Zeichner & Liston, 1996).

One example of the proliferation of rhetoric about social justice in current discourse is the explosion of books that have flooded the market in recent years, such as *Walking the Road: Race Diversity and Social Justice in Teacher Education* (Cochran-Smith, 2004), *Learning to Teach for Social Justice* (Darling-Hammond, French & Garcia-Lopez, 2002), *Parallel Practices: Social Justice-focused Teacher Education and the Elementary Classroom* (Regenspan, 2002), *Urban Teacher Education and Teaching: Innovative Practices for Diversity and Social Justice* (Solomon & Sekayi, 2007), and *Teacher Education for Democracy and Social Justice* (Michelli & Keiser, 2005).

Many other recent books do not use the term social justice in their titles but essentially express the same commitments. They include *Revealing the Invisible: Confronting Passive Racism in Teacher Education* (Marx, 2006), *Partnering to Prepare Urban Teachers* (Peterman, 2008), *Teacher Education with an Attitude: Preparing Teachers to Educate Working-class Students in their Collective Self-interest* (Finn & Finn, 2007).

Despite the frequency with which the term teacher education for social justice has come to be used by teacher educators, most of the scholars who have produced this literature have not articulated or elaborated specific conceptions of social justice toward which teacher preparation is directed in particular programs (McDonald & Zeichner, 2009).[4] There are very different notions about the concept of social justice that exist in philosophical and social science literature (e.g. See Gewirtz, 1998; North, 2006; Sturman, 1997). There is also a number of other theoretical perspectives, such as critical race theory and critical multiculturalism (Wiedman, 2002), that have been used as conceptual anchors for social justice work in teacher education.

These various conceptions of justice and oppression have different implications for how one would organize a teacher education program and what one would expect teachers to be able to know and learn how to do. For example, a commitment to a distributive conception of social justice (Rawls, 1999) would be mainly concerned with the equitable allocation of material goods and educational resources (e.g. the teacher's time and attention, the quality of questions asked, etc.) among students as individuals. It would not necessarily be as concerned as other conceptions of justice (e.g. Fraser, 1997; Young, 1990) with combating forms of oppression experienced by individuals as members of various ethnic/racial, language, social class, and other groups that are rooted in particular institutional and societal structures (McDonald & Zeichner, 2009).

The Focus of Social Justice Teacher Education

Despite the vagueness in the literature about what is meant by working for social justice, it is possible to identify a set of goals and practices that repeatedly appear in the literature about teacher preparation programs in which teacher educators explicitly affiliate with the general goal of preparing teachers to work for social justice. First, with regard to the issue of goals, teacher educators who claim to prepare teachers to work for social justice usually express a vision of the kind of teaching that they hope to promote among their graduates. These conceptions of the knowledge, skills, and dispositions that teachers need to enact are usually expressed in terms of some version of culturally responsive teaching and provide a focus for a teacher preparation program (e.g. Cochran-Smith, 1999; Gay, 2000; Ladson-Billings, 1995a; Irvine, 2003; Villegas & Lucas, 2002b). One example of a vision of the knowledge, skills, and dispositions that teachers need to teach in culturally responsive ways in order to teach for social justice is the one proposed by Villegas & Lucas (2002) of Montclair State University in New Jersey. They argue that one element of preparing teachers to work for social justice is the development of teachers who

- are socioculturally conscious and recognize that there are multiple ways of perceiving reality that are influenced by one's location in the social order;
- have an affirming view of students from diverse backgrounds and see resources for learning in all students rather than view differences as problems to overcome;
- see themselves as both responsible for and capable of bringing about educational change that will make schools responsive to all students;
- understand how learners construct knowledge and are capable of promoting learners' knowledge construction;
- know about the lives of their students, including the funds of knowledge in their communities;
- use their knowledge about the lives of their students to design instruction that builds on what they already know while stretching them beyond the familiar.

(Abstracted from Villegas & Lucas, 2002).

These visions of the culturally responsive teacher go beyond a celebration of diversity. In their elaborated forms, they explicitly address issues of oppression and injustice that are linked to social class, race, gender, and other markers of difference that are embedded in the institutions and structures in a society, as well as in the minds of individuals. They also include an activist component that encourages teachers as agents of change to act within and outside of schooling to combat these injustices.

Second, teaching for social justice goes beyond a rhetorical commitment to social justice. It must include strong preparation in academic content knowledge and the instructional, assessment, relational, and management skills needed to translate that knowledge to students in a way that promotes understanding (Darling-Hammond & Bransford, 2005). As important as the kind of personal qualities noted earlier, the ability to teach all students for understanding in today's underfunded public schools is complex. It is important that social justice teacher education programs help give prospective teachers the practical tools that they need to transform their good intentions into effective actions.

Practices in Social Justice-Oriented Teacher Education

Two types of strategies have been reported in the literature on teacher education programs that claim to be driven by social justice goals. First, are the efforts by teacher educators to recruit more students and faculty of color. Second, are strategies concerned with the social relations, instructional strategies, and curriculum within teacher education programs.

Recruiting Faculty and Students of Color

The goal of recruiting more faculty and students of color into teacher education programs has been defended because (a) a more diverse teaching force is needed to provide all students within an increasingly diverse public school population with a high quality education (Villegas & Davis, 2008) and (b) diverse cohorts of teacher education students and diverse faculty are needed to create the learning conditions needed to educate teachers to be successful in today's public schools (Sleeter, 2007).

A number of approaches have been used to attempt to recruit more students of color into teacher education programs. One strategy has been to change admissions requirements for college and university-sponsored preservice programs away from a system that relies exclusively on academic criteria, such as grade point averages and test scores, to one that maintains high academic standards but is also more holistic, taking into account a variety of personal factors and life experiences. A second strategy has been to create various types of alternative teacher education programs that would be attractive to prospective teachers of color and focus on teaching in high-need urban and rural schools, where it has been hard to attract qualified teachers (e.g. Clewell & Villegas, 2001a, b). A third strategy for recruiting more students of color into teacher education programs is to establish articulation agreements with two-year community and technical colleges, which traditionally have enrolled more than one half of all ethnic/racial minority students who are in higher education (Villegas, & Lucas, 2004). These agreements have been designed to ease the transition of students from the two-year colleges into teacher education in colleges and universities. A fourth strategy that has been used in institutions that have post baccalaureate programs is to expand advertising outreach efforts to sources of students of color such as historically black colleges and universities (HBCUs) and other campuses serving large numbers of students of color. A fifth strategy is to increase financial aid and target it to students of color. A final strategy is to define a program as focused on teaching for social justice, follow through with changes in its curriculum, social relations, instructional practices, and teaching placements, and strengthen faculty commitment and competence with regard to issues of diversity through recruitment and professional development in order to attract and retain students of color in teacher education programs (e.g. Darling Hammond, et al. 2002). Despite these efforts and successes at some individual institutions, the teaching force in the U.S. remains predominately white and monolingual English speaking (Zumwalt & Craig, 2005).

In addition to recruiting more students of color into teacher education programs, more needs to be done than to ensure that students are supported and complete their programs successfully. The track record of predominately white colleges and universities for retaining students of color is very poor (Villegas & Davis, 2008). Also, there is a lot of evidence that the focus on diversity in teacher education programs in predominately white institutions has been aimed at preparing white students to teach students of color (Sleeter, 2001). There has been a neglect of the needs of candidates of color to learn how to teach in culturally responsive ways (e.g. Montecinos, 2004).

Many institutions across the U.S. have instituted policies that attempt to support the recruitment and retention of more faculty of color in colleges and universities. Education schools have utilized these policies to attempt to bring more faculty of color into their teacher education programs. These faculty recruitment efforts have been complemented at many campuses by efforts to improve the institutional climate and structures with regard to issues of equity and diversity (Melnick & Zeichner, 1997). It has been argued that the success of social justice teacher education requires an institutional context that is supportive of this work and that teacher education programs alone, without this larger contextual support, will not have much of an impact on prospective teachers (Zeichner, et al. 1998).

Social relations, Instructional Strategies, and Curriculum Within Programs

In addition to recruitment and admissions strategies that are designed to cre-ate more ethnically/racially diverse learning communities of faculty and stu-dents in colleges and universities within which to carry out the work of social justice teacher education and to build a more positive institutional climate for dealing with issues like racism within teacher education institutions, there are a number of common strategies that have been used within programs to sup-port social justice goals. These include the requirement of courses or parts of courses in programs that go beyond a celebration of diversity and focus explicitly on social justice issues and the development of teaching practices that promote equitable educational outcomes.[5]

There is some evidence that the study of multicultural and social justice-oriented concepts and practices is more effective when it is integrated throughout a coherent teacher education program than when it is restricted to specific courses or seen as the responsibility of only some faculty (e.g. Darling-Hammond, 2006; Moule, 2005). There is also evidence that preser-vice teachers learn more from the study of these issues when their teacher edu-cators exemplify and model the concepts and practices that they advocate to prospective teachers (Sleeter, 2008).

Within this coursework, various instructional strategies are used to develop the intercultural competence and teaching abilities of prospective teachers with regard to social justice ends. These include such practices as involving candidates in both the discussion of racism and white privilege and a reexamination of who they are and their attitudes and beliefs about others (e.g. Marx, 2006; McIntyre, 2002). This inclusion can be achieved through: reading, writing, and discussing autobiographies, including personal autobi-ographies; reading and discussing other literature (e.g. Abbate-Vaughn, 2008; Florio-Ruane, 2001; Vavrus, 2006); reviewing case studies (e.g. Noordhoff & Kleinfeld, 1993), film (e.g. Trier, 2003), and dialogue journals (e.g. Garmon, 1998); and engaging in action research (e.g. McIntyre, 2003).[6] It is important to note that these and other instructional practices can be used to support the development of a variety of visions of teaching and learning; they are not in and of themselves evidence that a program is seeking to prepare teachers to work for social justice.

In the empirical literature on social justice teacher education (e.g. Hollins & Guzman, 2005), teacher educators have often described student teachers resisting efforts to help them become more culturally sensitive and competent teachers. A lot of self-study research by teacher educators currently exists in which teacher educators have attempted to deal with what they define as stu-dent resistance (e.g. Schulte, 2004). In these studies, prospective teachers are sometimes portrayed in very negative ways. Given the important role that emotions play in learning (e.g. hooks, 2003) and the substantial amount of learning and personal transformation that sometimes needs to occur for prospective teachers to be successful teachers of all students (Hamerness, et al., 2005), some have argued that as a central element of social justice pedagogy in teacher education, teacher educators need to model the same kind of caring and compassionate relationships with their teacher education students that they want their students to create with their pupils in elementary and secondary schools (see Conklin, 2008 for a discussion of this literature).[7] This would lead to the same kind of culturally responsive teaching that builds on student teachers' strengths in teacher education classrooms as teacher educators hope to foster in P–12 classrooms. Grossman and McDonald (2008) have argued that any framework of teaching needs to give strong attention to the relational aspects of teaching, including teaching in teacher education programs.

Another important part of preparing teachers for social justice is the field experiences that are required for prospective teachers in schools and communities. There is substantial empirical evidence that traditional models of field-based teacher education that are disconnected from course-based content and pedagogy preparation are ineffective in supporting the enactment of teaching strategies advocated by teacher educators (Darling-Hammond & Bransford, 2005; Feiman-Nemser, 2001). There is also evidence that merely placing teaching candidates in "high need" urban or rural schools is not necessarily beneficial. Doing this may support or obstruct teacher educators' efforts to prepare interculturally competent teachers who can successfully engage in equity pedagogy depending upon the specific nature of these experiences and the quality of support provided to candidates (Hollins & Guzman, 2005). In fact, in some cases it has been shown that field experiences that were designed to develop intercultural sensitivity and competence actually strengthen and reinforce candidates' negative stereotypes (Haberman & Post, 2008).

There is substantial literature from several countries that documents the enduring problems associated with traditional models of field experiences (e.g. Vick, 2006; Zeichner, 1996b). Many teacher education programs are now moving away from traditional models and experimenting with various forms of partnerships with schools in which there is: (a) more careful attention to the curriculum of field experiences for prospective teachers and regular opportunities for student teachers to analyze their work in schools: (b) placements that are selected with greater consideration to the degree to which they can offer student teachers opportunities to observe and practice the teaching and assessment strategies they are learning about in their programs; (c) more attention given to the selection, preparation, and continuing support for the P–12 teachers who are expected to mentor student teachers; and (d) expertise embedded in the thinking of master P–12 teachers that becomes more accessible to preservice students (e.g. Boyle-Baise & McIntyre, 2008; Darling-Hammond, et al. 2005; Feiman-Nemser & Beasley, 2007; Zeichner, 2005a).

In addition to providing prospective teachers with school placements where they can gain experience teaching pupils from a variety of racial, ethnic, and socioeconomic backgrounds and observe and use culturally responsive teaching and assessment practices that build in positive ways on the cultural resources that exist in students' families and communities (Banks et al., 2005), it has become increasingly common for teacher educators oriented toward social justice to extend field experiences for prospective teachers into communities. Some of this work has focused on community field experiences as service learning (Boyle-Baise, 2002) as a way to develop the cultural teaching competence of prospective teachers. Many recent examples of community-based learning in teacher education have positioned prospective teachers as learners and have focused on helping them learn about the funds of knowledge and social networks in students' families and communities and how to utilize that knowledge in their teaching (e.g. Boyle-Baise & McIntyre, 2008; Buck & Sylvester, 2005; Sleeter, 2008). In some cases, teacher education programs have employed people from local communities to teach prospective teachers about their communities (Zeichner & Melnick, 1996).

Another way that programs have sought to enact social justice practices in the current climate of accountability and close surveillance of college- and university-based teacher education programs is by sharpening the often very general standards that are used to assess teacher candidates to better reflect social justice goals. Most states mandate that teacher education programs use some version of the INTASC standards[8] which, as Peterman (2008) points out, are very general and can be interpreted in many different ways. Some teacher education programs that have articulated a social justice mission have developed standards or assessment rubrics for general standards (like the ones proposed by INTASC) that explicitly focus on social justice goals. Vavrus (2002) and his colleagues at Evergreen State University have developed a set of assessment rubrics that clearly reflect their program's social justice mission.

For example, one of the standards for student teachers at Evergreen State University is concerned with assessing knowledge of multicultural, antibias curriculum planning. Different levels of development of this standard are identified, ranging from curriculum plans which do not incorporate multicultural perspectives and advance antibias goals to those which transform the conventional curriculum with multicultural and antibias goals (Vavrus, 2002, p.47). This explicit incorporation of social justice elements into the assessments that are used in the program reinforces the message that these are areas of importance for prospective teachers.

Programs That Exemplify Social Justice Teacher Education

Because the term social justice means many things to many people, it is important that we identify programs that genuinely address issues of equality, difference, and social action in the preparation of teachers for classroom practice. The following sections introduce three teacher education programs that exemplify the type of teacher education highlighted in this chapter. The programs that we highlight are the Urban Diversity Teacher Education Initiative at York University in Canada, the Center X Teacher Education Program at the University of California, Los Angeles in the United States, and the Landless Workers' Movement's *Pedagogia da Terra* in Brazil. Each of these examples provides an overview of the ways in which social justice teacher education has been actualized in practice. Each example illustrates aspects of social justice teacher education that we think are particularly important, but often neglected, in programs that are described as oriented toward social justice. Although there have been very few systematic examinations by outsiders of programs that focus on preparing teachers to teach for social justice (e.g. McDonald, 2005; 2007), there are many self-report accounts in the literature describing the social justice-oriented work of teacher educators in individual courses and field experiences (e.g. Seidl & Friend, 2002; McIntyre, 2003; Young, 2007).

York University's Urban Diversity Teacher Education Initiative, Canada

In 1994, the Ontario Ministry of Education issued a challenge to its teacher education programs. Noting an increasingly diverse population, the Ministry charged teacher preparation programs to become more "relevant and responsive to the province's growing racial and ethnocultural diversity" (Solomon, 2007, p. 2). In answering this call, York University, which is located in the Toronto metropolitan area, developed its Urban Diversity (UD) Teacher Education Initiative. This initiative attempts to incorporate teaching and learning opportunities that address issues of equity, diversity, and social justice across the program.

Rather than designing a program that addressed the Ministry's concerns in name only, the York faculty set for themselves an ambitious agenda that attends to the inequities in schooling and society. For example, as a requirement of the UD Initiative, at least half of the students admitted into each cohort are from culturally or racially diverse backgrounds. These students include "namely, People of Colour, Aboriginal/First Nations Peoples, people of refugee and immigrant backgrounds, and persons with disabilities" (Solomon, 2007, p. 2). This attention to the inclusion of marginalized populations that have typically been excluded from teacher education programs highlights the education faculty's acknowledgement of its role in instigating change.

Similarly, the design of the program shows a dedication to a socially just orientation to teacher education. Components of the UD Initiative include an inclusive curriculum and pedagogy, intergroup dyad partnerships, community development (service learning), ethno-racial identity development and teaching, and creating a community of learners (Solomon, 2007). Each of these components is discussed in the following sections.

Inclusive Curriculum and Pedagogy

In preparing educators to enter classrooms ready to teach all students, the faculty supports teachers-to-be in examining the ideological and political influences that shape schooling practices. The program asks students to examine how those ideas have played a role in the construction of curricular materials and schooling practices. Opportunities to engage in this type of reflection take many forms, including written and oral assignments, individual and group activities, in-class discussions, online conferencing, and seminar presentations. Future teachers are expected to examine formal and informal curricula in an attempt to uncover hidden messages that may be reinforced through the implementation of such materials. From the program's perspective, the objective in presenting future teachers with the opportunity to reflect, share ideas, and engage in a dialogue of important social issues is to share practical information, resources, and guidance, while bringing marginalized knowledge and resources into the mainstream curriculum (Solomon, 2007).

As Solomon, Manoukian, and Clark (2007) note:

> This pedagogical model is designed to promote in [teacher candidates] a desire to recognize borderlands within which they can begin to interrogate their own racial formation, but also to critique and challenge the power relations, institutional structures, and organizing forces that come together within the borders of schools (p. 73).

Inter-Group Dyad Partnerships

For all practica and community projects, teacher candidates are placed in cross-racial/cross-cultural dyads. The purpose of the dyad partnership is to promote the development of professional, collaborative, and interdependent relationships through the sharing of experiences, perspectives, and ideas. It is hoped that such experiences will create spaces in which future teachers can engage in a dialogue that examines their roles as educators in a diverse society. Solomon (2007) states,

> This provision is a response to the need to break down racial/ethnic barriers, own-group cleavages, and create instead a space for teachers of different backgrounds to engage collegially in long-lasting, prejudice-free appreciation for each other's perspectives, norms, values and traditions (p. 4).

Community Development (Service Learning)

Each student that enrolls in the Urban Diversity Teacher Education Initiative is required to engage in a community-based service learning project. A minimum of six hours of service per month is required of each teacher candidate. The purpose of the service learning project is to connect education and schooling with civic responsibility and social action, moving from altruism to social reconstruction in communities. In addition, the education faculty believes that such experiences will lead to teachers' use of culturally relevant pedagogies and a further examination of one's beliefs, perspectives, and assumptions about others. In discussing the service learning project, Solomon, Manoukian, and Clark (2007) observe:

> [O]ne of the challenges [teacher candidates] must confront is overcoming the tendency to see their placement as an add-on to their already heavy workload or in terms of charity orientation. ... Indeed, negotiation of this type of borderland is constitutive to their education as transformative individuals (p. 74).

Service learning projects have included a range of academic, health and safety, sociocultural, recreational, and political activities, such as collaborating in nutritional breakfast/snack programs, acting as support staff in ESL initiatives, providing academic programs at women's shelters and drop-in centers for youth at risk, and empowering parents by actively recruiting underrepresented parents for school councils.

Ethno-Racial Identity Development and Teaching

Students in the program are also asked to reflect on their own identities and how their experiences, beliefs, and worldviews shape them as individuals. Furthermore, the future teachers enrolled in the program are asked to examine the ways in which one's personal and professional identities intertwine and influence one another. Several protocols are employed in assisting students in identifying teacher candidates' "initial identity status" (Solomon, 2007, p. 4). These protocols include the Racial and Ethnic Identity Development Model developed by Helms (1995), Carlson Learning Company's (1996) *Discovering Diversity Profile,* and the *Multicultural & Antiracism Education Survey* (Solomon, 1994). These tools provide the teachers-to-be with information necessary to create and implement growth plans that will assist them in working effectively within diverse schools and communities (Solomon, 2007).

Community of Learners

In an effort to promote an environment of reciprocity and collegiality, the Urban Diversity Teacher Education Initiative creates a community of learners, involving teacher candidates, veteran practitioners, and teacher educators. All of the participants are positioned as valuable contributors of information, knowledge, and resources. For example, action research projects conducted by future teachers in their classrooms and the surrounding communities showcase the knowledge of these teacher candidates and are supported by the mentor teachers and the university faculty. In sum, the Urban Diversity Teacher Education Initiative at York University seeks to model the type of community involvement and partnership it hopes its graduates will develop and sustain as educational professionals.

Center X at the University of California, Los Angeles, United States

Following the uprising that resulted from the 1992 Rodney King verdict in Los Angeles, the education faculty of the University of California, Los Angeles took the initiative to create an urban teacher education program within the Graduate School of Education and Information Studies. In order to "highlight experimentation and the intersection of theory and practice" (Olsen, Lane, Metcalfe, Priselac, Suzuki, & Williams, 2005, p. 34), the program was named Center X and enrolled its first cohort during the 1994–1995 academic year. With an explicit commitment to social justice, Center X aims to examine social inequality and the results these injustices inflict upon public schools. The Center X Community of Educators (under review) note:

> One of the most compelling reasons to become a teacher is to help make the world a better place ... Yet figuring out how to translate this idealism into a long and meaningful career in education is an extraordinary challenge ... [A] group of UCLA educators took on this challenge and created a center ... [that] recruits, prepares, inducts and professionally supports hundreds of urban educators in Los Angeles' hardest to staff public schools (p. 1).

In the following section, Center X's teacher education program is examined. A brief description of the Center's support for its graduates who enter the field follows this introduction to the program.

The Teacher Education Program

Because of a teacher shortage typical of most urban centers, Center X offers a two-year program that leads to state certification as well as a master's degree for its graduates. During the first year, participants complete coursework and a student teaching placement. In their second year, participants are placed in full-time teaching roles in a high-poverty urban partner school. This format builds on the former program's one-year M.Ed. program in order to provide a scaffolded resident year of teaching with continued support from the program (Center X Community of Educators, under review; Olsen, et al., 2005).

The structure of the program focuses explicitly on the tenets of social justice teacher education. In the words of Olsen and his colleagues (2005):

> The Center X curriculum stresses views of inequity as structural, activism as necessary, multiculturalism as central, and the critical study of race

and culture as crucial to preparing teachers to teach successfully for social justice in urban schools (pp. 35–36).

Reading lists for courses include topics ranging from critical pedagogy and culturally responsive teaching to community organizing and second language acquisition. To build on this informational base, a community project asks those enrolled in the teacher education program to examine the resources, history, demographics, and community assets that surround the schools in which they are placed. These projects and the resulting portfolios created by teacher candidates are shared publicly with the program and with the community. To build on these practical experiences, faculty members engage students in conversations about complex issues such as oppression and privilege, the inequitable distribution of resources, and institutional structures that inhibit teaching and learning within schools today. Yet, these are not simply philosophical exchanges. The tying of theory to practice frames the discourse of the program and culminates in a master's inquiry project required of each graduate.

The evaluation of teacher candidates mirrors the type of assessment the program expects to see in the classrooms of its graduates. In-class tasks and discussions, the completion of inquiry-based projects throughout their coursework, a professional portfolio, and observations of classroom practice by university supervisors are just a few of the evaluative measures used in the program. Tied to these assessments, constant critique, feedback, and support from faculty members and peers provides rich opportunities for teacher candidates to deliberately reflect on their understandings of teaching, learning, and learners.

In addition to fostering an environment that utilizes authentic forms of assessment to foster teachers' continued development, Center X prioritizes supporting educators in their teaching practice. This support is typified by the requirement that teacher candidates accept positions in pairs as they enter urban schools. This built-in support mechanism fosters collegial relationships between members of the program while addressing the need for new teachers to have colleagues who can understand and appreciate the complex task of beginning to teach. Yet, the support does not cease upon graduation. The following section details the support networks put into place for graduates of the Center X Teacher Education Program.

Supporting Graduates of the Program

The faculty of Center X have put into place ways in which graduates of the program can continue to receive professional development and support. The Urban Educator Network was created as a way to continue the work of the teacher education program once teacher candidates graduate and enter the field as licensed professionals. Offerings of the Network include inquiry groups, seminars, and opportunities to write and exchange ideas through an online journal, *Teaching to Change LA* (Center X Community of Educators, under review).

The purpose of the Urban Educator Network is to "establish additional sites of collaborative practice for teachers within the school-university partnerships" (Olsen, et al., 2005, p. 45). UCLA inquiry groups are one example of such work. Graduates of the Center X program are invited to engage in inquiry-based discussion groups in order to examine issues surrounding educating for social justice. These groups are then used to build graduates' capacities to lead school-based inquiry groups in order to effect change within their school sites.

This continued effort to remain active in the professional lives of its graduates makes Center X a good illustration of social justice teacher education. This commitment exemplifies the type of work necessary to increase the odds that the capabilities developed during preservice training will be enacted once candidates complete their program.

Pedagogia da Terra, Brazil

The Landless Workers' Movement (*Movimento dos Trabalhadores Rurais Sem Terra* or MST) in Brazil has a strong history of grassroots activism. Originally, the movement's focus was to pressure the Brazilian government to adhere to constitutional regulations dealing with the distribution of idle farmland. This pressure was—and still is—realized through land occupations, street marches, hunger strikes, and other non-violent forms of protest (McCowan, 2003).

In the 1980s, the MST began to attend to the training of teachers.[9] Because the struggle for land and economic justice is closely tied to education (McDonald & Zeichner, 2009), the movement saw great potential in playing an active role in the educational arena. Through conversations with communities of landless families, education became a major piece of their movement to transform Brazilian society. According to Diniz-Pereira (2005):

> One of the principal lessons that the MST has learned from its history in Brazil is that it is not enough to struggle only for land .... Due to the high rates of illiteracy and low rates of schooling in the *acampamentos* (encampments) and *assentamentos* (settlements), the landless families consider formal education and schooling crucial (p. 2).

Building on the ideals of democratic participation, the MST has created two different teacher preparation programs. Completed at the high school level, the *Magistério* is one pathway to teacher certification. In addition, *Pedagogia da Terra* is a preservice teacher education program at the college level. The *Pedagogia da Terra* program is the focus of this vignette because of its positioning within a higher education setting.[10]

The *Pedagogia da Terra* program consists of two major strands: *Tempo Escola* (school time) and *Tempo Comunidade* (community time). During

Tempo Escola, preservice teachers take courses, enter into political dialogues, and familiarize themselves with curricular materials designed by the MST. Common features of *Tempo Comunidade* include practical experiences in schools, reflective reading and writing assignments, and an action research project (Diniz-Pereira, 2005).

Three main principles guide the education of preservice teachers within the *Pedagogia da Terra*: technical and professional preparation, political preparation, and cultural preparation (Diniz-Pereira, 2005). The technical and professional preparation of teachers entails the mastery of knowledge sets, behaviors, and ethics surrounding education. A heightened awareness of agrarian reform and social justice are stressed within this principle. In preparing teachers politically, instructors within the program stress consciousness of history and class. This awareness assists future teachers in linking their professional purposes to those of the broader political and social movements of the MST. Finally, cultural preparation stresses the ideals of cooperation and solidarity within the Landless Workers' Movement.

Acceptance into the program is based on more than traditional criteria. In addition to academic criteria, the MST program looks for candidates with diverse life experiences and a willingness to examine how those experiences shape them as individuals and educators. The program is designed to validate candidates from disenfranchised backgrounds because it is assumed that these candidates tend to readily identify injustices within society (Diniz-Pereira, 2005). While students from more privileged backgrounds are accepted into the program, intense self-examination is expected. Regardless of a students' background, the teacher education program stresses the importance of an attitude towards social transformation above all else.

Selected for their commitment to political action, the participants in the *Pedagogia da Terra* program are expected to become community activists in addition to their roles as teachers. This work outside of formal schooling is considered essential to the success of the movement. The notion of political involvement fosters a sense of belonging to a larger movement—a movement toward change—in teachers. Centralization of power is seen as counterproductive. By participating in local, state, and national politics, teachers model the participatory nature of representational democracy (McCowan, 2003). In fact, Diniz-Pereira (2005) contends that teacher education programs must encourage their teacher candidates to involve themselves with political movements in order to effect change within schools and the broader local, national, and global societies. In this way, "... the movement creates the schools in its image, but the schools in turn create the movement of the future" (McCowan, 2003, p. 11).

Each of the programs described above has begun the difficult task of rethinking the role that social justice teacher education plays in the preparation of classroom practitioners. While the descriptions of each of the programs are based on the self-reports of faculty members from the various institutions, all of the programs have gained international attention for the work that they have begun and the role that this work has played in contributing to the larger dialogue surrounding social justice teacher education. We are aware that there is often a gap between the ways in which teacher educators describe their programs and what is truly discovered to be happening by researchers from outside the programs.[11] Systematic studies by those outside of the programs are needed to more fully illuminate the complex realities of these and other similar programs.

As a group, these three programs illustrate a number of things that are often missing from preservice programs that espouse a social justice mission, such as close links with schools and communities and connections to broader movements for social change. We now examine some of the characteristics of current efforts at social justice teacher education as reported in literature and based on our own observations that we think need to be addressed if social justice teacher education is to realize its potential.

Strengthening the Impact of Social Justice Teacher Education

In 1969, the National Institute for the Study of Disadvantaged Youth published a book called *Teachers for the Real World* (Smith, 1969) in which it clearly and forcefully identified the failure of U.S. teacher education programs to prepare teachers to teach pupils living in poverty.

> Racial, class and ethnic bias can be found in every aspect of current teacher education programs. The selection processes militate against the poor and the minority. The program content reflects current prejudices; the methods of instruction coincide with learning styles of the dominant group. Subtle inequalities are reinforced in the institutions of higher learning. Unless there is scrupulous self-appraisal, unless every aspect of teacher training is carefully reviewed, the changes initiated in teacher preparation as a result of the current crises will be like so many changes which have gone before, merely differences which make no difference (pp. 2–3).

The report identified three major problems: (a) teachers were unfamiliar with the backgrounds of poor students and the communities where they live; (b) teacher education programs have done little to sensitize teachers to their own prejudices and values; and (c) teachers lack preparation in the skills needed to perform effectively in the classroom.

Since 1969, we have come a long way in giving teacher preparation in the U.S. more of a social justice focus, despite the widespread negative influence of neoliberal and neoconservative policies in undermining social justice goals in P–12 public education (Apple, 2006) and teacher education (Sleeter, 2007; Weiner, 2007). Many teacher education students in the U.S., for example, are now reading the works of scholars like Sonia Nieto, Gloria Ladson-Billings, and Lisa Delpit and realizing their own social location and biases. We are clearly doing a better job than before in sensitizing prospective teachers to their own values and prejudices and to how one's world view and life chances are influenced by one's social location.

As Smith (1969) pointed out though, this process of greater self-knowledge and knowledge about others different from oneself is not enough to prepare teachers who can succeed in and remain at the schools where they are most needed. There are several issues that we think need to be addressed by teacher educators who claim to be working for social justice if this work is to make a significant contribution to the realization of greater social justice within and beyond schooling. These issues include: (a) taking teacher education and the preparation, induction, and the continuing professional development of teacher educators more seriously in the research universities that prepare college and university teacher educators; (b) creating a teacher educator community that includes college and university faculty and staff, P–12 teachers, administrators, and people from local communities as full partners in the education of teachers; (c) focusing preservice teacher education on issues of practice in schools in addition to the conceptual focus on social justice thus far; (d) including issues of language diversity and the preparation of teachers to teach English learners within the scope of social justice teacher education; and (e) modeling the sorts of social justice-oriented practices in the preparation of teachers that are advocated for teacher candidates to use in schools.

In U.S. research universities that prepare most college and university teacher educators during their doctoral education, the low status of teacher education and the lack of engagement of many full-time tenure-track faculty in the work of teacher preparation in an intensive and sustained way has undermined the quality of the preparation of both teachers in these institutions (e.g. helping to make programs more fragmented) and the next generation of teacher educators (Labaree, 2008; Zeichner, 2006).[12] Although there are some cases where tenure-track faculty in research universities have devoted a lot of energy into creating innovative programs, applied their scholarly habits and skills to the renewal of their teacher education programs, and carefully mentored new teacher educators (e.g. Carroll et al. 2007; Darling-Hammond, 2006),[13] creating the best possible programs of teacher education and preparing new teacher educators to engage in cutting edge practice and research on teacher education have not been priorities in education schools in research universities. Instead, teacher education programs have often been underfunded, marginalized, and colonized on many of these campuses, sometimes serving as nothing more than financial aid for the doctoral students who staff them and "cash cows" to support other more highly rewarded types of activities and programs (Liston, 1995; Tom, 1997; Zeichner, 2006). There is also some evidence of a two-tiered system among faculty in these education schools; faculty who engage in the work of teacher education have lower status, receive less pay, and have fewer other benefits than faculty who limit their activities to those that are more highly valued within academe (Schneider, 1987).

> A good teacher education program would be an entire community, like a school and its parts—the sequence of courses and experiences—would fit together to make a whole. Its leaders would be able to make decisions shaping the program: it would not be a poor colony run from afar by faculty or administrators (Carroll, et al. 2007, p. 214).

The involvement of doctoral students in teaching and supervising in an institution's teacher education programs is a necessary and important part of the preparation of new teacher educators as it brings many talented educators with recent classroom experience in contact with prospective teachers. However, in our experience novice teacher educators' mentorship, support, and knowledge of the literature in teacher education of these varies considerably. In some cases, this variance leads to graduate students being sent out on their own with little support to work with prospective teachers.

Other problems in teacher education that is conducted in these universities are both the frequent disconnect between campus-based instruction and the complexities of the schools in which candidates teach and the failure to include P–12 staff and community representatives as full and equal partners in the teacher education team. For example, in her study of two social justice-focused preservice programs in California, McDonald (2005) concluded that there was a focus on conceptual tools related to social justice and multiculturalism and a lack of attention to practical tools and strategies needed to enact equity pedagogy. In our experience and reading of the literature, this finding represents a very common situation in teacher education programs in research universities. As argued earlier, we believe that good social justice teacher education ensures that student teachers have the knowledge and skills they need to begin teaching in addition to the attitudes, beliefs, and dispositions that complement them.

Also, despite the existence of school (and sometimes school and community) advisory committees in many teacher education institutions and the often token involvement of P–12 teachers in decisions about teacher education programs, it is less common to see P–12 staff and community representatives participating as full and equal partners in all aspects of program planning and renewal. Maintaining a hierarchical relationship with those outside of the academy and ceding to university academics the preferential right of interpretation about program planning and renewal are especially troublesome when university teacher educators are claiming to offer social justice-oriented programs. While it is not necessarily the case that socially just decisions will result from more inclusive and democratic social relations in teacher education programs (e.g. Zeichner, 1991a), we believe that it is not possible to have a genuine social justice-oriented program without such relationships.

One hopeful sign that can be observed in some education schools is the efforts of teacher educators to better connect their campus-based instruction to specific and often the most challenging school contexts by moving part or all of the instruction into the schools and working alongside P–12 teachers in educating pupils and new teachers. One of us, in his role as an external evaluator of the Teachers for a New Era project at the University of Washington, has observed the benefits to pupils in high needs urban schools and prospective teachers of this kind of situated instruction of novice teachers (Campbell, 2008). Lampert & Ball (1998) have been doing this kind of work for many years and it is now becoming more common for teacher educators to break out of the traditional model of distanced methods instruction that is not situated in relation to any specific school contexts. Some of this work, at universities including our own, is taking place within the context of some type of professional development school partnership.[14]

Moving a university course to a school or having a professional development school-type partnership, however, is no guarantee in and of itself that things will be any different from traditional and ineffective models of practice. The important element in these efforts to address a longstanding problem in teacher education is the careful mediation of the campus-based teaching in relation to the complexities of schools. This mediation can also be achieved through the strategic documentation of practice, using videotaped teaching and various artifacts of practice, such as teachers' plans, students' work, teachers' research studies, and curriculum materials (Ball & Cohen, 1999).

A related development in some programs has been the integration of experienced P–12 teachers into campus-based instruction (e.g. Benyon et al., 2004; Post et al., 2006). In such campus-based instruction the P–12 teachers often work alongside university faculty, staff, and graduate students in new boundary-spanning roles. They provide instruction and clinical supervision and enact ongoing program renewal as part of an inclusive teacher education community.

Another weakness in current efforts of many programs to prepare teachers for social justice is the lack of attention to issues of language diversity and the preparation of teachers to teach English learners. Although there has been much attention to issues of ethnicity and race, gender, and social class in the coursework that has become part of many teacher education programs, there has been a noticeable lack of attention within these courses and in programs as a whole to the teaching of English learners (Brisk, 2008; Lucas & Grinberg, 2008). Given the changing demographics with regard to English learners,[15] it is no longer sufficient to prepare specialist ESL and bilingual teachers. Preparation to teach English learners has consistently been one of the lowest rated items on follow-up studies of teacher education graduates, even in programs that are deemed to be exemplary (e.g. Darling-Hammond, 2006). An applied linguistics component and ESL teaching strategies need to be infused into all teacher education programs for general teachers as well.

Additionally, one of the most important ways to strengthen the impact of social justice teacher education is for teacher educators to exemplify and model the dispositions and practices that they hope their students will take up during their education for teaching. For example, prospective teachers need to work with politically committed college and university teacher educators who are willing to engage in respectful ways and on an ongoing basis with teachers and administrators working in P–12 schools for social justice. In addition, it is essential that teachers have contact with people in communities that are working to address the vast array of injustices that now exist beyond schooling, including access to housing, food, safety, health care and so on. This would join teacher education for social justice in colleges and universities with education for social justice in P–12 schools and movements for social justice in the broader society. This kind of alliance would ideally benefit the struggles in all three spheres, including efforts to stop the longstanding decline in state support for public higher education, which has also had a negative effect on teacher education (Lyall & Sell, 2006).

While reading and discussing ideas on a university campus are an important part of teacher education for social justice, this work cannot be limited to such activities. Teacher education for social justice must be situated more than is currently the case within schools and communities. College and university faculty who say that they are committed to working for social justice must learn how to put aside the individualistic and entrepreneurial aspects of their work culture in order to be able to build the kind of genuinely collaborative relationships that are consistent with the ideals expressed by social justice educators. All of this work needs to take place within schools, colleges, and Departments of Education that place teacher education as a central part of their missions (Ball, 2007). Good teacher education, including good social justice teacher education, requires this kind of faculty and institutional commitment.

Finally, probably the most important thing that can be done to strengthen the work of social justice teacher education is for teacher educators to adopt the same self-critical inquiry stance on their work in teacher education that they expect their students to take on in elementary and secondary schools. Although there are many fine examples in the literature of social justice-oriented teacher educators who critically analyze their own individual teaching in light of social justice goals (e.g. Schulte, 2004), there also needs to be more efforts from communities of teacher educators to critically analyze and renew their teacher education programs on an ongoing basis. This requires the creation of structures and a culture within teacher education programs that support the ongoing learning of everyone who works with prospective teachers. This critical stance on ongoing and collaborative inquiry and a serious commitment to offer exemplary teacher education programs are fundamental to the success of all kinds of teacher education programs, including those which purport to work for social justice.

Chapter 3

Professional Development Schools in a Culture of Evidence and Accountability[1]

In this chapter I reflect on the future of professional development schools (PDSs) in this time of high-stakes accountability for schools and education schools under the No Child Left Behind (NCLB) Act and the higher education act, and the pressures on educators and teacher educators to prove that what we do results in gains in student learning (Fallon, 2006). I share my understanding of: why PDSs were created as alternatives to traditional models of preservice teacher education, teacher professional development, and educational reform (which are my understanding of the core values in PDS work); where I see these institutions standing currently in relation to the larger picture of educational reform and teacher preparation in the U.S.; and some of my concerns about the future of PDSs. I will also comment on the nature of recent research on the effects of PDSs on various aspects of teacher quality and student learning.

Although I will address the different aspects of PDSs associated with professional development, inquiry, and institutional reform, because most of what I do on a daily basis is concerned with educating prospective teachers, I will focus on the role of PDSs in providing an alternative to traditional models of preservice teacher education. I will first briefly discuss traditional models of teacher education.

The Traditional Model of School and University Relations in Initial and Continuing Teacher Education

As long as there have been formal teacher education programs, teacher education institutions have had some relationship with schools so that student teachers could have places to practice their teaching skills. For many years, prospective teachers completed a student teaching experience for a few weeks either in a campus laboratory school that was run by a teacher education institution or in a public or private school (Stallings & Kowalski, 1990). This student teaching experience would often come at the very end of the preservice program and would usually be the first and only time that a prospective teacher would get a chance to practice his or her teaching skills with students.

Over the years, structured field experiences in mostly public schools have played a greater and greater role in the teacher education curriculum and almost all of the campus laboratory schools of the past are gone. In most college- and university-based programs today, student teachers usually complete a series of field experiences during their preparation, most often beginning at the onset of their preparation.

In the traditional relationship between teacher education institutions and schools there are assumptions that expertise lies only among the faculty within colleges and universities and that the job of schools is to provide places for student teachers to practice their craft and to apply theories learned in the university. It is also the function of schools to provide settings for the passive consumption of professional development activities provided for school staff by university or other outside experts.

Generally in this model there is a large disconnect between the curriculum of the teacher education program on the university campus and student teachers' work in schools. The mentor teachers who supervise the work of student teachers in their classrooms typically know very little about what takes place in university classes, and the university instructors typically know very little about what goes on in the student teachers' classrooms (Guyton & McIntyre, 1990; Zeichner, 1996).

The mentor teachers who work with student teachers typically have little voice in running the overall teacher education program, and university teacher educators make most of the decisions even about the field-based portions of the preparation that take place in schools. Research clearly shows that this disconnect between schools and universities in traditional practicum, student teaching, and internship experiences, together with the uneven quality of student teacher mentoring and inadequate funding that often supports these experiences, undermines the quality of teacher learning (e.g. Feiman-Nemser & Buchmann, 1985; Zeichner, 1996). In the traditional model (which I think is still the dominant model today), the placement of teacher candidates is in individual classrooms rather than schools, and placements which are often made at a distance by a centralized placement office are not necessarily made on the basis of what is best for the learning of student teachers.

University supervision of student teachers in a traditionally organized field experience is conducted either by permanent or adjunct faculty members or in research universities by faculty, staff, or doctoral students who travel to a number of different schools to supervise students. In the traditional programs at my university, for example, graduate student supervisors travel to up to 11 schools per semester and can only make a limited number of visits to each student teacher because of all of the time they spend traveling from school to school. These supervisors, who are mostly doctoral students, are often unfamiliar with the mentor teachers and their classrooms and sometimes work with a different group of mentor teachers each semester. The result, in my view, is a lower quality of student teacher supervision than is potentially possible in a PDS model in which university supervisors are more integrally connected to the schools where student teachers teach (Guyton & McIntyre, 1990; Zeichner, 1992a; Zeichner & Miller, 1997).

With regard to teacher professional development, the traditional model of university-sponsored professional development asks teachers to (sometimes physically, but often metaphorically) come to the university to participate in courses that the university has organized, often without regard to the participants and their contexts. In recent years, this model has been overtaken in many places by professional development provided to schools by nonuniversity outside experts, independent entrepreneurs of professional development, who are also unconnected to the schools in which the activities are to be provided. Research has shown that teachers often do not value these dominant forms of professional development that are disconnected from their professional workplaces because they often do not address their specific needs and concerns or build upon the knowledge that teachers bring to these experiences (Randi & Zeichner, 2004).

The PDS model rejects this top-down view of transferring knowledge from universities and independent outside experts to schools. The PDS model integrates teacher professional development opportunities with student teacher learning opportunities into the life of schools (Darling-Hammond, 1994; Whitford & Metcalf-Turner, 1999). While there is an appreciation of the value that can be gained from university expertise, there is also a recognition of university teacher educators as learners, and there is an attempt to take advantage of the knowledge and expertise that exists in both schools and universities. The expertise of university, school, and community members is respected and utilized as responsibility is shared for a number of tasks that are usually addressed in an isolated fashion.

The Movement to Professional Development Schools

Since the mid-1980s, teacher education institutions in the U.S. and a number of other countries have organized relationships with school districts for the initial and continuing education of teachers and the reform of teacher education and schooling. These partnerships have been called professional development schools, partner schools, clinical schools, or professional practice schools. Currently, there are over 1,000 of these schools in the U.S. and they are mostly public schools. It was recently estimated that over one third of NCATE-accredited institutions are involved in these partnerships. In the literature, at least, PDSs are now viewed as a central component of the professionalization of teaching. In practice, PDSs, for a variety of reasons, are still on the margins and are not the dominant vehicles for teacher education and teacher professional development.

PDSs in the U.S. focus on several goals while seeking to connect teacher education reform with school reform: the improvement of preservice teacher education; the improvement of professional development for existing staff, including university staff; and the establishment of closer connections between research and practice by fostering the development of an inquiry culture in schools and teacher education programs (Holmes Group, 1990). It is felt that all of these things will contribute toward improving the quality of education for P–12 students.

Different PDSs emphasize these goals in different ways and there is great variability across the country in what actually goes on in institutions that are called professional development schools. For example, in some PDSs, the focus is on improving the preservice preparation of teachers by more closely connecting the preparation of new teachers with real school contexts and attempting to take advantage of the expert knowledge that exists in schools in addition to knowledge from universities. In other PDSs, there is less of a focus on preservice teacher education and more focus on the induction of new teachers' continuing professional development, or collaborative inquiry.

Within our partnership in Madison, Wisconsin, for example,[2] there is a great deal of variation among the eight PDSs. There is variance in terms of which goals are emphasized beyond the concern of all of them with improving student learning for everyone's children. Some of the schools work with many student teachers while others do not. Some schools initiate many PDS-sponsored professional development activities for staff (and sometimes parents), while other schools initiate fewer activities. In some of the schools there is more of a focus on collaborative inquiry through action research or study groups and in other schools there is less of this activity.

One characteristic feature of PDSs is that they seek to take advantage of the expertise of school staff in educating student teachers and teachers in a way that is not typical in traditional preservice programs. For example, preservice teacher education seminars and courses typically held on the university campus are often moved to PDSs where school staff members participate in the teaching.

In a video that I recently showed to my graduate seminar in the study of teacher education, a mentor teacher in an elementary PDS in Michigan worked for a week with a group of interns placed at her school (in addition to the work that she did in mentoring the intern in her classroom) on the teaching of mathematics. The interns watched this teacher teach math everyday for a week—a practice similar to grand rounds in medical schools—and met with her before and after the lessons to discuss her thoughts on her teaching and her pupils' accomplishments (see Feiman-Nemser & Beasley, 2007).

Another aspect of taking advantage of the expertise of school staff in the education of new teachers is that experienced teachers are given a voice in the running of the entire teacher education program and participate in staff meetings with their university partners as respected colleagues. In our partnership in Madison for example, the PDS coordinators in our secondary teacher education program attend the monthly program meetings on campus and actively participate in discussions and decisions about admissions policies, curriculum, program structure, and so on. Their presence adds an important perspective to the discussions that is often not present in traditionally organized programs.[3]

Similarly, university staff members are sometimes given a voice that is typically not present in school improvement efforts. For example, I recently participated as a friendly observer of two of our PDSs. I spent time as part of a team that assisted each school in an audit of their self-studies, which were part of the district school improvement process. One of my colleagues, Hardin Coleman, who is the university liaison to one of our PDS middle schools, sits on the governance council of this school. Including university faculty and staff in school improvement in this way is common in PDS work and is consistent with the sharing of responsibilities that is fundamental to the idea of PDSs.

In many PDSs, including some of the ones in Madison, university classes and seminars are moved from the campus to the schools. P–12 teachers have opportunities to demonstrate particular teaching practices, to analyze their teaching in public with groups of preservice students and colleagues, and, in some cases, to assume responsibility for planning and teaching university classes. Often in PDSs, the university supervisors are based within the schools. The supervisors work with the interns in one school rather than traveling to and from different schools. Situating preservice teacher education in the context of real schools and communities is fundamental to the idea of PDSs.

Also, instead of placing student teachers and interns exclusively in individual classrooms with a single mentor teacher, prospective teachers are often placed in schools. In addition to their work with a mentor teacher or team of teachers, they typically engage in a variety of activities that are designed to help them take advantage of different areas of expertise both within and outside of the school. Any single mentor teacher, no matter how good she or he is as a teacher, only has a limited amount of expertise (Stones, 1984).

In our partnership in Madison, our teacher education students meet with a variety of staff within the schools and community members. For example, a number of our PDS students work in the African American Ethnic Academy, which is an Afrocentric program that is held on Saturday mornings and has been developed by a reading specialist and community liaison in one of the schools.[4] I have been involved in research that examines the e-portfolios of elementary education students in Madison. I have clearly seen the impact that these beyond-the-classroom activities have on students' development of intercultural teaching competence (Zeichner, Hutchinson, & Chagolla, 2007). This research is consistent with a growing body of research on the importance of community-based learning in teacher preparation (Boyle-Baise & McIntyre, 2008; Sleeter, 2008).

One characteristic feature of many PDSs is the ways in which the university supervision of teaching candidates has changed. I have already mentioned the traditional model in which staff, faculty, or graduate students travel from school to school, supervising student teachers in situations where they are outsiders. PDS work, in one way or the other, tries to embed university supervision of student teachers into the schools so that supervisors can get to know the classrooms and teachers and more intensively supervise student teachers. There are different models for accomplishing this, of course. In my partnership, we use both school staff and graduate students as university supervisors in the PDSs. These school-based university supervisors often hold weekly seminars in the schools. (In my partnership, the seminars are often co-led by university faculty liaisons and the school-based supervisors.) These school-based seminars, and sometimes classes which are also moved to the schools, involve many staff in the PDSs in instructional roles with novice teachers.

Generally, as I alluded to earlier, PDS partnerships entail the increased involvement of university faculty in the schools. We have several senior and tenured faculty members in Madison who serve as liaisons to particular schools. They work with preservice students and help generate professional development and inquiry opportunities for both prospective teachers and school staff. Recently, I have been focusing on building stronger connections between faculty in the arts and sciences and the professional development schools. I have also been focusing on bringing more community voices into the teacher education and school reform process.

It is not easy to achieve the shift in university faculty—school staff relationships that is necessary for a PDS to function well. Professors and students need to work together as equal colleagues. In my experience, this shift takes a lot of time to achieve but it is absolutely necessary for a PDS model to succeed. In the U.S., teachers are often socialized to either defer to or ignore the expertise of university professors, and professors are often socialized to believe that their only role is to disseminate knowledge to teachers. In my view, one of the key elements of PDS work is to achieve a situation in which the expertise of both teachers and professors is acknowledged, and both parties see themselves as learners and teachers of each other.

The literature on PDSs discusses the different cultures of schools and universities, as well as the difficulties that teacher education institutions have sometimes faced in getting professors to work in schools (especially in research-intensive universities like mine) (Stoddart, 1993). I have worked for many years to get this work counted as part of faculty members' teaching loads. I believe that unless this work is valued in this way in the reward systems in the academy, many faculty members will avoid it (Labaree, 2004). With recent cuts to public higher education, it has become more difficult for university departments with PDSs that run on hard money (like my own, instead of grants) to be able to afford to count PDS liaison work as part of teaching loads. Similarly, with all of the cuts in public education and pressures on schools, districts sometimes do not reward their staff for work in these partnerships and it is becoming increasingly harder for them to afford the extra costs associated with PDS work. In many ways, PDSs remain marginalized within schools and universities, despite their tremendous potential.

PDSs also provide a new kind of professional development to school staff. Instead of staff leaving their schools mentally and/or physically to participate in professional development activities, the PDS often integrates professional development into the life of schools. The goal is to embed a culture of inquiry into the school. These professional development activities are specifically designed for the staff involved. They often involve school staff in teaching and leading the activities, usually recognizing and building upon the knowledge that staff bring to the experiences. Of course, it is possible to inject what I have called "snake oil" staff development (Zeichner, 1993a) into PDSs. In the literature, I have, however, seen more discussion in PDS stories of the kind of empowering and transformational professional development that is often advocated in the literature but is so infrequently available to teachers in practice. These are just a few of the core values that I see connected to the work of PDSs.

There are lots of important issues being discussed across the country today about professional development schools, including how to: move them from the margins to the mainstream; sustain them in times of severe cuts in education, other social services, and so on; and do this important work in a climate in which there is a focus on narrow forms of accountability. In the remainder of this chapter I briefly discuss one of these key issues: a recent trend to use research about PDSs to attempt to document the value of them in a climate of evidence and accountability.

Research on the Effects of Professional Development Schools

Lee Teitel (2001b) has talked about the leap of faith associated with the benefits of PDSs and complained about the lack of careful documentation of their impact. He warned that without good documentation of the impact of PDSs on preservice and experienced educators and P–12 students, "the professional development schools that have grown so fast in the last decade will wither away" (Teitel, 2001b, p. 68).

In recent years, there has been an increase in research conducted on the effects of PDSs on aspects of teacher quality, student learning, and institutional change. This research has taken our understanding beyond the largely descriptive work that was prevalent in the early years of PDS development (e.g. Abdal-Haqq, 1998; Book, 1996; Clift & Brady, 2005; Teitel, 1997, 2001a, 2001b, 2004). This research has sought to illuminate the consequences for student teachers, teachers, schools, and pupils participating in these partnerships. In some cases, this research compares the experiences of those who have participated in a PDS with those who have not.

This research has begun to show some positive effects of PDS involvement for all role groups and schools in its comparison to non-PDS models. Such positive PDS effects include higher ratings of teaching effectiveness, stronger confidence and efficacy levels, enhanced ability to collaborate with colleagues for PDS student teachers, higher test scores for pupils in PDSs, and more enabling and empowering professional development. However, the research has not illuminated which particular aspects of PDSs are responsible for these effects, under what specific conditions they occur, or for how long they persist. Some of the effects attributed by researchers to PDSs could be the result of factors other than PDSs. Such factors could include longer time spent in schools for field experiences and more intense supervision of the teaching of student teachers.

As is the case in other aspects of teacher education, research has been of limited value in providing useful information for practitioners or policymakers or for theory development about the process of learning to teach. Because of the wide variation in what PDSs mean in different locations, it is important for research to identify the particular characteristics of these partnerships that are connected to desired outcomes. Another flaw in much of the existing research is the failure to design studies that would enable us to distinguish selection effects from those of the programs. In some cases, many of the differences attributed to PDSs could just as easily be attributed to the characteristics of the individuals who often self-select into these schools.

It has been suggested by some that the NCATE PDS standards (NCATE, 2001) provide a framework to enable researchers and those of us who work in PDSs to clearly describe the contexts under which these partnerships operate in particular settings. A few studies have emerged in the last few years that do this and self-describe a partnership according to some subset of the NCATE PDS standards. Generally—though even in studies that have gone through a peer review process—there is wide variation in how PDSs are defined. It is very difficult to know clearly what aspect of the PDS was responsible for the impact(s) on student teachers, teachers, or schools. It is not uncommon for researchers to assert that their studies show that (and I quote from a recent published study) "teachers prepared in PDS based preservice teacher education programs are indeed more effective than teachers prepared at a traditional campus-based program" (Ridely, et al. 2005, p. 54).

As a career-long supporter of the values and practices associated with PDSs, I am both heartened and troubled by these kinds of claims. On the one hand, I know through my long experience in working with schools and in teacher education that these claims are correct under some circumstances. I have seen the difference in (a) the reactions of our student teachers who participate in PDSs compared to those who participate in more traditional options, (b) what those who hire our graduates say about their performance, and (c) the reactions of teachers to professional development that connects to their daily work and recognizes and builds upon the knowledge they bring to the experience. I am also seeing this difference in my current research of the e-portfolios of graduates from both the PDS and traditional tracks in our elementary education program in terms of their documentation of student teachers' development of culturally responsive teaching practices.

I am very troubled by the claims now being made by some about the benefits of PDSs because of the great variation in what counts as a PDS. In a review of recently published PDS studies that examine the connections between PDSs and student teacher learning that I still am working on, I have seen PDSs distinguished from traditional programs in institutions by such things as a year-long internship instead of a semester of student teaching, holding seminars and sometimes classes in schools instead of on the university campus, and having the university supervisor based in the school instead of coming from the outside. One immediately noticeable factor is that PDS means something different in each case, even with the emerging use of the NCATE PDS standards to describe programs. In the studies that focus on student teacher learning, there is very rarely discussion about (a) student teachers being situated in schools where professional development and school reform is going on or (b) the role of community members in the PDS process.

One issue that troubles me about this research is that the descriptions of what conditions exist in a PDS partnership are mostly brief self-descriptions rather than careful examinations by impartial outsiders of the conditions in a partnership. In my career, I have had the privilege of being involved as a researcher in several multi-institutional case studies of teacher education programs in which a group of researchers went into programs and studied them in depth from the perspective of the multiple stakeholders (e.g. faculty, students, cooperating teachers) involved. Also, as a teacher educator, I have often been on the receiving end of studies of my own programs that were carried out either by researchers or review teams that are part of program evaluations.

In all of these cases, both as an outsider and insider, I have always seen important differences emerge between the way in which programs are described by those on the inside and those who look at the whole program in depth. In my view, we need to move beyond the brief self-descriptions of PDSs that we see in the current research to more elaborated understandings of the ways in which particular aspects of PDSs are implemented in practice.

The NCATE PDS standards have made an important contribution in pushing the field to begin to address issues of quality in PDSs. However, in my view, neither situating a partnership in relation to these standards nor making statements about the mere existence of certain practices in a PDS adequately gets at the dimensions of quality that we need to understand in order to benefit from the research on PDSs.

For example, although professional development schools are at the more advanced stages on the standards or have some of the practices mentioned above, such as school-based university supervisors and seminars and courses for student teachers, there will still be important variation in the quality of implementation of these practices. Depending on how they are implemented, situating university supervisors of prospective teachers in schools and moving methods classes to schools, for example, may or may not be any different from or better than traditional ways of providing these teacher education components.

These two examples are practices that I have seen implemented at the University of Wisconsin-Madison for some time now. I have always seen, and some of our research has shown, variation in the impact of these practices under specific conditions. Sometimes these practices make a big difference in the quality of student teacher preparation and sometimes they do not. We need to understand the difference (e.g. Gillette, 1990). Are we willing to say that any school that is called a professional development school will have the same connection to desired outcomes regardless of the way that these practices are conceptualized and carried out? Are we willing to say that a year-long internship is necessarily better than a semester of student teaching? Are we willing to say that having a university supervisor or a course based in a school is necessarily better than the alternatives?

In teacher education, I believe we have a problem of advocating certain concepts and practices, such as five-year programs, reflective teaching, action research, mentoring, and so on, without always discussing and illuminating the specific conditions of use that existed in studies that show a link to desired outcomes. The message that we are sending is that these practices of action research, reflective teaching, and yes, professional development schools, are necessarily different and better than what went on before. While in some cases this is undoubtedly true, in others it is not true: What is described as something new and innovative is sometimes no different than what went on before. We need to find some way in our research on PDSs to address the aspects of the quality of implementation that are not addressed even with the standards and some of the promising new research that claims to show the benefits of PDSs.

The core values associated with PDSs are too important for us to make ourselves vulnerable to the dismissal of this work by those on the outside who make policies and have the resources that we need to obtain to do our work well. There are a lot of people who do not believe in the value of PDSs or college- and university-based teacher education programs. There are likewise a lot of people who do not see teaching as a profession that requires careful preparation.

There is no doubt in my mind that the shared responsibility for the simultaneous renewal of schooling and teacher education that is fundamental to the work of PDSs is the direction in which the field as a whole needs to continue to move. I began reading John Goodlad's (1970) arguments about this path in my early days as a graduate student in the 1970s, and I have not changed my mind that he was right.

We need to continue to push ourselves to better understand the particular conditions that need to exist for professional development schools to help us achieve a place where the same high quality of education is available to everyone's children.

Chapter 4

Action Research as a Strategy for Preparing Teachers to Work for Greater Social Justice

A Case Study from the United States[1]

Defending Social Reconstructionist Teacher Education

For many years, I have been responding on a regular basis to the criticism that it is inappropriate for teacher educators to encourage their students to think about the social and political dimensions of their work, the various contexts in which their teaching is embedded, and how their everyday teaching practice is connected to issues of social continuity, change, equity, and social justice. My response to critics has always been that in this unequal and unjust society that is stratified by race, language, ethnicity, gender, etc., teacher educators are morally obligated not only to pay attention to social and political issues in the education of teachers, but to make them central concerns in teacher education curriculum from the very beginning (Liston & Zeichner, 1991). The goals of preparing teachers to be advocates for social justice and providing a high quality education for everyone's children (e.g. Oakes & Lipton, 1999) should be top priorities in U.S. teacher education, given the large gaps in achievement that continue to exist in U.S. public schools (Lee, 2002) and the lack of the social preconditions that are needed for educational equity to become a reality (Children's Defense Fund, 2001).[2]

Today, however, in the politically conservative climate of the U.S., where the Bush administration has supported transferring public money in the form of vouchers to private schools and eliminating both state teacher licensing and the requirement that teachers complete college and university teacher education programs (Paige, 2002), advocacy of multicultural education and preparing teachers to be advocates for social justice have been equated with a lack of concern for academic standards (e.g. Izumi & Coburn, 2001; Kanstroom & Finn, 1999) and even with a lack of patriotism.

If we accept the idea for a moment that all pupils in U.S. public schools are entitled to the same high quality of education, and we examine the current status of both schooling and teacher education in this country, we should conclude that a major effort needs to be made to put equity at the top of the teacher education agenda. This is not to blame either teachers or teacher educators for the current inequitable state of affairs that sees so many students pass through our public school system and remain uneducated. Clearly, the roots of these problems go beyond the schools and are connected to broader social, economic, and political forces that exist across the U.S. and the world (e.g. Apple, 2001; Burbules & Torres, 2000).

Despite the origins of educational inequality outside of education, those of us in teacher education have to make choices that either put us on the side of working to change the situation or on the side of helping to maintain it. We cannot remain neutral. Every plan for teacher education takes a position, at least implicitly, on the current institutional forms and social context of schooling (Crittenden, 1973).

In addition to responding to constant attacks on a progressive and/or critical agenda for teacher education, I have also consistently challenged the logic that separates technical issues from moral ones and argues that preservice teacher education should focus only on technical issues. The argument is that once teachers have mastered the technical aspects of teaching and have some experience in the classroom, they will be ready to think about the complex moral and ethical issues associated with their work. I have argued that all teaching issues have both technical and moral dimensions that must be considered simultaneously. Because all technical skills are used to accomplish particular purposes, it is not enough to teach prospective teachers skills alone. We need to be teaching prospective teachers skills of teaching and help them accomplish purposes that are educationally and morally justifiable in a society that claims to be democratic. Student teachers need to examine the purposes and consequences of their teaching from the very beginning of their preparation programs. Unless both the technical and moral aspects of teaching are part of a teacher's education from the very beginning, the moral, ethical, and political aspects of their work will likely continue to be marginalized (Zeichner & Teitelbaum, 1982).

In the 1990s, a critique of social reconstructionist projects in preservice teacher education being inappropriate on developmental grounds once again emerged. For example, Calderhead and Gates (1993) took the position that it is not reasonable to expect prospective teachers to include a critical dimension in their reflections and actions because of the limited time period of preservice programs and the demands posed by critical reflection.

> The aims of preservice reflective teaching programs are quite often highly ambitious and set targets that are probably impossible to achieve with the majority of students in the time available. Becoming a teacher who is aware of one's values and beliefs, able to analyze their own practice and consider its ethical basis and its social and political context involves considerable ability and experience and may well be beyond the capabilities of most student teachers in the time span of a preservice program. (Calderhead & Gates, 1993, pp. 3–4).

While I accept the general notion that we should not expect beginning teachers to be able to do the same things as experienced teachers, I think that it is a mistake to (a) attempt to separate questions of values, ethics, and the politics of teaching from questions of technical competence and (b) postpone the development of ethical and moral competence until some form of technical competence has been achieved. If it is beyond the capabilities of most student teachers to analyze the social and political dimensions of their practice in current teacher education programs, then maybe we need to alter both the criteria that are used to admit students into teacher education programs and the programs and the institutions in which they are located so that we will have greater success in preparing teachers who are committed to and capable of educating all students to high academic standards. Anything less is morally unacceptable in a society that claims to be democratic.

At the same time that we must passionately strive for a teacher education system that truly prepares all teachers to work for a high quality education for all students, we must be realistic about what can be accomplished within the current structures of teacher education in the U.S. No teacher education strategy, including action research, case-based teaching, teaching portfolios, etc., will be powerful enough to overcome the anticipatory socialization that prospective teachers receive prior to entry into a teacher education program without attention to both the ways in which we admit students into our teacher education programs and the institutions in which programs are embedded. While we must not romanticize and delude ourselves about how much we can accomplish with changes to the teacher education curriculum within existing structures, we also must not exhibit moral cowardice and back off from the task of preparing teachers to be advocates for social justice for all children.

Action Research as a Strategy for Social Reconstructionist Teacher Education

For the last 25 years, I have been involved in promoting the use of action research as one of a number of strategies for preparing more culturally responsive teachers who actively work to educate all students to the same high academic standards. The setting for my work has been an 18-week student teaching experience in an elementary teacher education program that focuses on the same social reconstructionist goals (Ladson-Billings, 2001; Zeichner, 1993b; Zeichner & Liston, 1987; Zeichner & Miller, 1997).

Early in the semester, student teachers identify an aspect of their practice that they want to work on. They move through cycles of action and reflection during the semester, culminating in the presentation of their research to their seminar group and sometimes at a regional action research conference.[3] A weekly student teaching seminar provides a forum during the semester for prospective teachers to discuss their research and receive both challenges and support from their peers. Although student teachers identify a focus (e.g. learning how to ask questions to provoke a deeper level of student thinking) at the beginning of the term, the questions almost always change from the beginning to the end of the semester. This shift in the focus of student teachers' inquiries evolves as data are collected; it is a natural part of the process of doing action research. Although the action research provides this central focus for student teachers' professional development during the student teaching semester, the seminar and the journals that student teachers often keep as part of their data collection also provide opportunities for dialogue about other issues. Although student teachers usually present their research findings at the end of the semester and write a research report, our emphasis is on helping students acquire the habits and skills to conduct classroom-based research, not a finished research product. This is because of the brief nature of the student teaching experience in which expecting a full-blown research study to be conducted would be unreasonable (Zeichner, 1999b).

Over the years, colleagues and I have examined and critiqued our use of action research in our teacher education program, continually modifying our approach on the basis of these inquiries (e.g. Gore, 1991; Gore & Zeichner, 1991; Noffke & Brennan, 1991; Noffke & Zeichner, 1987; Schlidgren, 1995; Tabachnick & Zeichner, 1999; Zeichner, 1999b; Zeichner & Gore, 1995). In this work, we have been very candid that the process of action research by student teachers has frequently not resulted in the kind of thinking and acting related to the social and political dimensions of teaching and schooling that we have desired (Gore & Zeichner, 1991; Zeichner & Gore, 1995). We have also noted examples of action research that have led to a broadening of student teacher thinking to include the social and political dimensions of their teaching and an analysis of the social conditions of their practice (Gore & Zeichner, 1991). Some have used our candidness about our work to dismiss the idea of social reconstructionist teacher education projects entirely or those efforts that begin with student teachers reflecting about their own practice. Some critics have proposed another approach to the development of critical consciousness by teachers that begins with reflections about others' practices.

For example, McIntyre (1993), stressing the limited role of reflection on one's own practice in preservice teacher education, has taken the position that we need to start by helping student teachers analyze other people's experiences before they move to an analysis of their own experiences. McIntyre (1993) concluded:

> It does not seem that teachers or student teachers are led, through reflecting on their own practice, and especially through action research on it, to take a critical view of the structural or ideological context in which they are working. Nor, I think, that it should surprise us: reflecting on one's own practice, and especially engaging in action research, leads one to emphasize one's own agency, and if things go wrong, the logic of the study leads one to explore alternatives for one's own action, not explanations for quite different directions ... It is through theorizing about others' practices that student teachers are helped to gain a critical

perspective on the contexts within which they are working, and it is on the basis of such an understanding that they are encouraged to introduce this level of reflectivity into their reflections on their own practice (pp. 46–47).

The use of action research as an instructional strategy in preservice teacher education is based on a different relationship between the personal theories of teachers and public academic theories. With action research, the task is viewed as helping prospective teachers develop the practical theories of teaching that guide their practice (Handal & Lauvas, 1987). While recognizing the importance of both public and practical theories in teacher education programs, each perspective offers us a different starting point. While McIntyre (1993) would have us initially emphasize public theories in the education of teachers to be applied later to one's own teaching experience, in an action research approach, one would initially emphasize helping student teachers reflect on their own experiences and later introduce public theories once the student teachers' inquiries are underway. Although the Wisconsin student teaching program in elementary education follows a series of courses and practicums in which there is a great deal of emphasis on public academic theory, within the student teaching program itself, the emphasis is on the further development of personal practical theories and the strategic introduction of public theories to inform and enlarge student teachers' reflections. Below is an example of this "inside-outside" theoretical stance of action research in this student teaching program that has been taken from one of the action research seminars for student teachers that Bob Tabachnick and I led as part of a reform initiative in science education (Tabachnick & Zeichner, 1999).

In this project, students were introduced to the idea of action research and the assumptions about theory, practice, knowledge, and learning, etc. that underlie it the semester before their student teaching. During this time, they also interacted with local teachers and student teachers that had been engaged in action research. They began to plan the action research project that they would undertake the following semester while student teaching. The action research in this project followed a common action research spiral of planning, acting, observing, and reflecting (Zeichner & Noffke, 2001), although students began their research in different phases of the spiral. During the 18-week student teaching semester, we all met biweekly for two hours in a seminar and focused on student teachers' research projects. Each student teacher identified (and often reshaped) their own research questions, kept research journals that they shared regularly with one of the two faculty facilitators who responded in writing to their entries, and orally presented their research findings to the whole group at the end of the semester. The seminar meetings were largely spent discussing data brought to the meetings by the student teachers and issues raised by their research. The group consisted of both elementary and secondary science student teachers. (For more information on the nature of the seminar, see Tabachnick and Zeichner, 1999.)

Rachel's Action Research: Dealing With Independent Times in the School Day

Rachel was one of nine student teachers in this action research seminar for student teachers led by Bob Tabachnick and I. Her action research project illustrates how student teacher concerns (e.g. dealing with disruptive students) that first appear to be unconnected to issues of equity and social justice can be developed with the assistance of teacher educators to lead to an exploration of the social and political dimensions of teaching. This case also illustrates how public academic theories produced outside of a student teacher's specific situation can be integrated into the process of inquiry already initiated by a student teacher and lead to new insights related to promoting greater educational equity for low-income pupils of color.

During a seminar meeting, Rachel and another student teacher working at the same elementary school were discussing ways to engage several "disruptive" students in more productive activity in their classrooms. This kind of classroom problem posed by student teachers is often defined in the literature as one of classroom management or discipline, a survival problem located in students and unconnected to the social and political aspects of teaching. After a lengthy discussion of the situation in these two classrooms, it became clear that all of the students who were seen as disruptive in the classroom were children of color from the local neighborhood. About 30 percent of the students in each classroom were neighborhood children. This particular school is involved in a district integration plan that mixes students from the surrounding neighborhood, which includes predominately low-income families and many families of color, with children from a more distant neighborhood that is mostly white and middle class.

Tabachnick and I took this opportunity (of only low-income students of color being identified as disruptive) to initiate a discussion of issues of race and social class in teaching, and we directed the student teachers' attention to the work of those like Ladson-Billings (1990) and Villegas (1991), who have explored the idea of culturally responsive teaching. We also directed the students toward an examination of the cultures of their own classrooms and schools and how these related to the cultures and the cultural resources in their students' homes and communities. Before we made this intervention, there had been some evidence in the student teachers' comments that we needed to try to move the discussion from how to deal with disruptive students to a deeper level, considering the cultural aspects of the situation.

> What I notice is a lot of different communication styles. I mean you can stand out in the hallway at my school or out on the playground and listen to how different kids interact and there's a lot of confrontation that goes on among the neighborhood kids. Whether it's something they bring in, I mean just general, even like "hi how are you doing" at the beginning of the day. It's sort of like, I mean there's just something harsh about it to my ears because it's not my culture. It's not the way that I would greet

somebody. And I think that a lot of the interacting that goes on in the classroom is a foreign culture to me. (Student teacher comment, March 3 seminar).

As a result of this discussion, some of the students suggested readings related to the cultural aspects of teaching and learning and about some of the examples of schools that have successfully adapted themselves to accommodate and utilize aspects of the various cultures of their students. During the seminars, student teachers began to question how students came to be classified as "disruptive." Our aim had been to draw our students' attention to the role of race and social class in a teaching situation when they had been overlooked. We did not attempt to deny their problem, as is often done by "progressive" teacher educators when the problem appears to be a technical one, but we tried to help them reframe it in a way that considered more aspects of the situation than before.

> You have the classroom, half and half, half African-American and half white children, and you've got different cultures going on. So one child says one thing and this story starts to take place and they don't understand each other's cultures because this doesn't happen in one family and that doesn't happen in another. So I think that maybe we have the tendency of course to take our own side and say that the other one is disruptive (student teacher comment, March 3 seminar).

I have frequently argued that the so-called "critical" domain of reflection is right in front of student teachers in their classrooms and that the place to help them enter into a process of reflection about the social and political dimensions of their teaching is by starting with their own definitions of their experiences (e.g. dealing with "disruptive" students) and then facilitating an examination of all of the different aspects of these experiences, including how they are connected to issues of equity and social justice. The experience is an inside-outside one that is experientially grounded (Zeichner, 1999b).

The "disruptive" behavior of a group of African-American students in her fourth-grade classroom was only one aspect of Rachel's action research. The broader issue dealt with her concern that these six students were not accomplishing much of anything during the two daily independent activity periods, when students had many choices about what to work on.

> I am frustrated by what I view as a system in our classroom that does not support those who are unable or unwilling to motivate and direct themselves in this open atmosphere. I appreciate the freedom and respect for children that are evident in our classroom and I am impressed by the creativity and interest of many of the students, yet I feel that several students are getting lost in the shuffle. They seem to wander around during independent times, talking to other students or hanging out in the bathrooms

or library. At the end of the period, they rarely have anything to show for their time and cannot describe or explain what they did in their journals. I have also noticed that in some instances when these students are asked to sit at their desks and work on a specific writing, math or other assignment, they can focus on the work and can do a fairly good job (Rachel journal entry, January 30).

Over the course of the semester, Rachel's action research project dealt with how to engage this group of six students of color more actively in academic work during independent activity times. Rachel and her cooperating teacher gradually provided a more explicit structure for those class periods and closer monitoring of student work. Rachel was especially concerned about two particular boys (in the group of six) who had been working for several months in constructing a football field and had apparently not learned very much while doing so.

We have two kids who have been doing a project since before I came ... It's a football field that they've built. Like it's a piece of wood with two pieces of wood nailed on the sides and they've painted it and painted stripes on. And that was basically what happened during independent activity time for them between January and last Thursday when they finally got to the point of getting magnets. So there is a magnet on the top and they cut out little football guys and a magnet on the bottom, and like these two guys try to go from end to end on the field, which is a really cool thing. I'm not knocking it. But yesterday during independent activity time, we played with it a little while, ok yah it works. It's cool. They had it working for a couple of days. And we started talking about why does it work. And you know, well it's because of the magnets. When it got down to it, they didn't know anything about magnets and couldn't even spell magnets. They made this really cool thing and that's an accomplishment. It's not an accomplishment though that should have taken three and one-half months ... By the end of yesterday, I at least had them looking at a book about magnets and how they work (Rachel comment, April 21 student teaching seminar).

During the semester, Rachel had been struggling with her cooperating teacher's emphasis on providing a positive affective classroom environment and her own concerns that students were wasting valuable time that could have been spent on academic learning. During one seminar discussion, I drew a contrast between Rachel's concern with her students wasting time and not doing much of anything academically and the action research focus of another student teacher in the group who worked in an upper middle-class middle school. In the upper middle-class school, the student teacher's research focused on how to stimulate greater creativity and problem-solving strategies among her students. This led to a discussion of the different kind of education that is provided in public schools to students who come from different social class and ethnic backgrounds. This discussion further encouraged Rachel to examine how her classroom situation and her own behavior as a student teacher might be contributing to the problem she had identified.

Rachel continued to struggle with the tension that she perceived in her situation between challenging children academically and keeping things peaceful in the classroom.

> I don't want to come across like I think she's a bad teacher. I don't. I think she's a wonderful [cooperating] teacher. She's very focused on the affective side of these little kids. We have a real mixed group. We have kids with incredibly different abilities, both social and academic ... And she's done a wonderful job of bringing these kids together and having them, you know, emotionally secure. I mean they do a great job together except for the daily pencil fight ... My teacher feels that the atmosphere is more important than the content. So I don't know (Rachel's comment, April 21 action research seminar).

At the same time that Rachel was struggling with the tension between building a cohesive classroom group and challenging children academically, she read two articles written by Lisa Delpit that had been posted in the teachers' lounge for a teacher study group in the school (Delpit, 1986, 1988). Among other things, these articles emphasized teachers' responsibilities to teach students who are excluded from the culture of power and questioned the cultural appropriateness of some allegedly progressive and learner-centered teaching practices, such as process writing and open classrooms. Reading these papers that directly addressed the dilemma that she was experiencing at that time caused Rachel to rethink some of her earlier interpretations of the behavior of the six students as disruptive and question how the teacher's and student teacher's practices may have been contributing to the problems they were facing with the six students.

> I have been observing and questioning a few of the students about whom I have concerns. I have approached and questioned D. several times when she has been sitting for five or ten minutes before starting her work, asking why she has not started yet. She often replies that she doesn't know what to do. I had been attributing the problem to her failure or inability to listen when instructions are given, or simply to her desire not to do the work. After reading the Delpit article, I wonder if her problems may not lie in not understanding the directions given. Although they seem to be given very clearly in my mind, I cannot be sure that D. is hearing and understanding the instructions in the same way that I and some of the other students understand them (Rachel journal entry, January 30).

Reflections on the Action Research Seminar

There were a number of instances during the semester when we gave student teachers materials to read that directly addressed issues that they were working on in their action research. The readings were intended to stretch their thinking in the same way that the papers written by Lisa Delpit provoked Rachel's thinking. From our experience working with student teachers, we have discovered that this experience of strategically feeding public knowledge into student teachers' action research inquiries is much more effective in challenging student teachers' thinking and actions than asking them to read articles that stand apart from their school experiences. There is a lot of evidence that student teachers often resist the efforts of teacher educators to help them teach in more culturally responsive ways (e.g. Ahlquist, 1991). In the particular student teaching seminar discussed in this chapter, we did not have a syllabus that laid out the topics and readings for each week in advance. The weekly agenda was determined by where the student teachers were in their action research studies. This open format reflected our desire to maintain student teacher ownership of their inquiries—an element that is often identified as a key feature of action research that has a transformative effect on teachers (Angelotti et al., 2001; Zeichner, 1999b). Clearly, we had our own ideas about what ideas were important for the student teachers to think about and we tried to find ways to direct our students' attention to these ideas when opportunities were presented to us in seminar discussions and journal dialogues.

This more student-centered approach is in contrast to a more deliberate attempt by teacher educators to control the topics of discussion and the student teachers' action research. Literature shows that when teacher educators try to do this, the experience of doing action research is less transformative (e.g. Robottom, 1988). Because of our commitment to an ethic of care and our fidelity to our students as people, we rejected the idea of assigning topics for action research. However, the issue of determining whether doing an action research project has helped a student teacher become more culturally responsive and an advocate for social justice for all of his or her students cannot be determined from an analysis of the topics of the research alone. As Rachel's case illustrates, it is the quality of the thinking that goes on in the research rather than the topic that determines whether or not the research has a social reconstructionist impulse in it. There is a great deal of impression management that goes on in teacher education programs. Student teachers display behavior that matches what they think their teacher educators want to see, but they remain internally committed to something else (Zeichner & Gore, 1990). It is our belief that letting student teachers maintain the ownership and control of their action research projects minimizes this kind of strategic compliance that lacks internal commitment. This does not mean that teacher educators should be neutral and back off from pushing their students to think harder about the difficult issues of equity and injustice that exist in schooling and society and become advocates for greater social justice. It does not mean that anything that student teachers produce in their action research should be acceptable to their teacher educators. It does mean though that teacher educators need to be careful not to attempt to indoctrinate student teachers toward particular beliefs. It is the development of a critical consciousness on the part of student teachers and the cultivation of their capacity to examine and learn from their practice in a way that includes attention to the social and political dimensions of their work that is important.

Finally, the labeling of the action research projects of student teachers based solely on their topics and research questions reinforces the distinction between technical and critical that has been so unhelpful and has kept the social and political dimensions of teaching at the margins of the discourse in teacher education in a number of countries. All action research projects potentially have both technical and critical aspects that need to be explored and developed (Zeichner, 1993c). Nothing is to be gained by devaluing student teachers' initial desires to focus on what might be perceived by academics to be purely technical issues. Denying the student teacher's perspective in such a way will lead to covert or overt rejection of the message of their teacher educators.

Conclusion

It is difficult to accept the argument that student teachers are not developmentally ready to consider the kinds of social and political implications of their teaching that Rachel confronted in her action research. Although she could have spent her time devising better ways to control or motivate these allegedly deviant students or blaming their parents or home situations for their behavior (both of which are a common response of student teachers), Rachel made some progress in seeing the situation in a deeper way. She considered its cultural aspects and also made some progress in actually improving the situation for the six children who were the focus in her study. Rachel did not accomplish miracles during her 20 weeks of student teaching. As a vulnerable student teacher, she had very little formal power in the situation. She was working in the classroom of another teacher, who was evaluating her student teaching. There was some disagreement about what students would be doing and how much structure and direction should be provided to students by the teachers.

It is important not to romanticize what can be accomplished by action research or any other instructional strategy that is used in preservice teacher education. Action research is not a panacea for the sorry state of U.S. teacher education with regard to issues of equity and diversity. However, it does provide a way of engaging student teachers in analyses of their own teaching practice that can become the basis for deepening and broadening their thinking to include attention to the social and political dimensions of their work. Action research can do this in a way that minimizes the degree of strategic compliance by student teachers and begins to build the genuine commitment of student teachers to work for social change in their classroom work.

Postscript on Action Research in Preservice Teacher Education

Action research has been a part of preservice teacher education programs in the U.S. for at least 45 years (Beckman, 1957; Perrodin, 1959). In the last decade, action research has progressed from "being present" in some teacher education programs to becoming a common practice in North American teacher education programs (Cochran-Smith & Lytle, 1999). We have reached a point where almost all programs claim that they use some form of action research with their student teachers. Most of these efforts involve student teachers working individually on their own research projects (e.g. Ross, 1987), while others engage teams of student teachers and their cooperating teachers (Angelotti et al., 2001; Cochran-Smith, 1999; Rock & Levin, 2002) or teams of teacher education students and a university professor (e.g. Moore, 1999) in conducting joint or related research projects, oftentimes within school–university partnerships (Clift et al., 1990). Frequently, claims are made about how conducting action research impacts teacher education students. For example, Rock & Levin (2002) claim that doing action research has increased their students' understandings of their own teaching theories, problematized their entering assumptions and beliefs, and developed a greater understanding of and appreciation for the pupils' perspective. Kosnik (1997) presents stories by graduates of her program in which the students make claims about the tremendous impact that doing action research had on them, such as helping them become more learner-centered in their practice, skillful at assessing and evaluating their pupils, etc. Very little evidence beyond the testimonials of teacher education students is presented, however, in support of the claims made about impact. Kosnik (2000) correctly notes that even if certain effects can be documented during student teaching, it is difficult to disentangle the impact of action research from the influence of other features of the teacher education program.

It is not always clear that student teachers have actually studied their own practices, which is a necessary condition for action research (e.g. Fueo & Neves, 1995; Pucci, Ulanoff, & Faulstich, 2000). First, they may research an aspect of their field placements, including issues of inequity, without problematizing their own teaching practice or classroom and social situation. Second, the conditions under which action research has been conducted in teacher education programs are often very unclear in the descriptions of using action research in preservice teacher education. Frequently, there is some statement of teaching research skills to student teachers, then the students formulate research questions and move through cycles of some version of the action research spiral of planning, acting, observing, and reflecting, then the students attend meetings or seminars where their evolving research studies are discussed. In one case (Fueo & Neves, 1995), students are taught and asked to use a specific research methodology that involves hypothesis testing and the identification of independent and dependent variables. Mostly, the specifics of how student teachers were introduced to and supported in conducting action research are left unclear, although it is frequently stated that (a) student teachers identify their own research questions and (b) student teacher ownership is key to the success of the research (Angelotti et al., 2001). In some cases a specific goal is described for the action research, such as in Valli's (2000) attempt to have her students link their action research projects to schoolwide improvement efforts.

Very rarely is anything related to the development of teachers who work for social justice mentioned in conjunction with the use of action research in preservice teacher education. In addition to our work at Wisconsin, the most notable exceptions to this absence of the political in action research in preservice teacher education are the work of Cochran-Smith (1999) and Cochran-Smith and Lytle (1993) at the University of Pennsylvania several years ago and the current work of Jeremy Price at the University of Maryland (Price, 2001). One can also find isolated cases of action research by student teachers that have an emancipatory intent. For example, in one of the four student teacher action research projects presented by Keating et al. (1998), there is a clear focus on increasing educational equity. As Price (2001) states, merely including an action research requirement in a teacher education program does not indicate anything in particular about intent or purpose. It all depends on how action research by student teachers is conceptualized and supported by teacher educators. A reading of the literature on action research in preservice teacher education (e.g. Dana & Silva, 2001; Feldman & Rearick, 2001; Freisen, 1995; Poetter, 1997; Ross, 1987; Stubbs, 1989) clearly indicates that the democratic and political impulse historically associated with action research is not often present. Instead, teacher learning and development is stated as the major goal of the work, whether or not this greater reflectiveness on the part of the teacher and the new knowledge he or she produces through action research contribute to the goal of a high quality education for everyone's children. This does not mean that the teacher educators involved do not care about providing a better education for everyone's children. It means that they do not explicitly discuss or provide examples of research that illustrate emancipatory intent when presenting their work with action research in their programs.

It is time that more of the teacher education community in the U.S. faced up to the challenge of educating teachers to teach all students to high academic standards. On the one hand, to retreat from this complex endeavor on the basis of developmental inappropriateness or ignore it all together is morally unacceptable. On the other hand, to make claims that miracles have been wrought within the current structure of teacher education, schooling, and society by some isolated instructional practice is a naïve or dishonest position. We need to acknowledge the complexity of the work of preparing teachers to teach everybody's children and recognize that, at least for the foreseeable future, we will fall short of our goals. We must, however, keep issues of equity and social justice at the forefront of the teacher education agenda. Unless we do this, we will help sustain and strengthen the very oppressions and injustices that we say outrage us. Action research offers much potential as an instructional tool for teacher educators who want to work toward a better education for all students within the context of a social reconstructionist-oriented teacher education program.[4]

Chapter 5

Action Research
Personal Renewal and Social Reconstruction[1]

Introduction

This chapter focuses on the issues of action research and several different kinds of change: practitioner development, institutional improvement, and social change. Although at times I refer to action researchers as practitioners and to reform in a general sense, because of my background as a teacher and teacher educator, my specific examples focus on teachers and schools. My concern is with the extent to which the continually expanding international action research movement can be counted on to contribute to the processes of change in several different ways: (a) in terms of its ability to promote individual practitioner development and a higher quality of human service work (i.e. teaching, nursing, social work, etc.); (b) in terms of its potential effects on the control of the knowledge or theory that informs the work of these practitioners; (c) in terms of its influence on institutional change in the immediate settings in which these practitioners work (i.e. schools, hospitals, social work agencies, etc.); and (d) in terms of the impact of action research on the making of more democratic and decent societies for all who live in them (i.e. its connection to issues of social continuity and change).

Each day more and more people realize the tremendous power of action research and join the action research community. Although I count myself among them and spend a great deal of my professional life either engaged in research about my own educational practice or supporting the action research of teacher educators, student teachers, and teachers, I raise several issues in this chapter that challenge the uncritical glorification of action research that has become common in recent times.

There are those who see action research and the empowerment of practitioners associated with it as ends in themselves, unconnected to any broader purposes. It is often asserted or implied, for example, that if practitioners are further empowered and more reflective and research their practice, they will necessarily be better practitioners. It is likewise asserted or implied that the knowledge that is produced through their inquiry will be necessarily worthy of our support, regardless of its nature or quality.[2] This view ignores the fact that this greater intentionality and power exerted by practitioners may help, in some cases, to further solidify and justify practices that are harmful to students, patients, and clients and may undermine important connections between institutions and their communities (Zeichner, 1991a).

This uncritical glorification of knowledge generated through practitioner research is, I think, condescending towards practitioners and disrespectful of the genuine contribution that they can make to both the improvement of their own individual practice and the greater social good. I argue that we need to take action research much more seriously than is the case with its uncritical glorification. We should take a harder look than is sometimes the case at the purposes toward which it is directed, including the extent of the connection between the action research movement and the struggle for greater social, economic, and political justice throughout the world. What I have to say in this chapter is an elaboration of these ideas about the need for action research to move beyond giving a greater voice to practitioners in the design and improvement of their own and their colleagues' work. Important as this may be, it is not enough.

When I use the term "action research," I am using it in a very broad sense as a systematic inquiry by practitioners about their own practices. There has been a lot of debate in literature about what is and is not real action research, the specifics of the action research spiral, whether action research must be collaborative or not, whether it can or should involve outsiders as well as insiders, and so on (e.g. Elliott, 1991; Kemmis & McTaggart, 1988; McKernan, 1991; McNiff, 1988). I choose not to enter into these debates here in order to not affirm my allegiance to this or that guru or camp of action research. A lot of this discourse, although highly informative in an academic sense, is essentially irrelevant to many of those who actually engage in action research. As Somekh (1989) has argued,

> This proliferation of theory about what constitutes action research serves to remove it from the reality of schools and classrooms. What has it to do with busy teachers for whom the validity of their research lies in its ability to answer their own practical questions about teaching and learning? (p. 5).

There are many different cultures of action research and it seems to me that an awful lot of time and energy is wasted in arguing over who are the "real" action researchers and who are the imposters.

Also, although I will reveal my biases in this chapter regarding the direction that I think the action research movement should take, I do not want to adopt the now familiar distinction among technical, practical, and critical or emancipatory action research (e.g. Carr & Kemmis, 1986; Grundy, 1982) because I think this classification creates a hierarchy that devalues practitioners. Much of what I have to say in this chapter could be interpreted as placing me in the socially critical camp of action research, which sometimes has been linked with critical social science. While it is true that I share many of the political commitments of those who identify themselves as oppositional to the status quo in terms of the poverty, alienation, powerlessness, and suffering that is a daily reality for an increasing number of people in many countries, this link with critical social science and critical theorists in universities has alienated many in the action research community, in part by creating the perception that the critical is somehow above and beyond the world of practitioners in the macro-world, and that practitioners' struggles in the micro-world in which they live daily are somehow insignificant in the larger scheme of things.[3] Here, with regard to teachers, terms such as "individual" and "classroom" take on negative meanings. Teachers are criticized for focusing their research within their classrooms and for not trying to reform schools and society more directly through their action research.

In this chapter, I argue that these separations between technical and critical and micro and macro are distortions, and that the critical is, in reality, embedded in the technical and micro-world of the practitioner. Every classroom issue has a critical dimension. Individuals or small groups of practitioners, such as teachers, may not be able to change unjust societal structures through their classroom action research, but they can and do make real and important differences in terms of affecting the life chances of their students.[4] While it is important for at least some teachers and other practitioners to be engaged in efforts aimed more directly at institutional change and community action, we should not criticize teachers for concentrating on the arena of the classroom. Most teachers will continue to focus on the classroom no matter how much they are criticized for doing so by critical theorists in the universities.

The reality, though, is that the political and the critical are right there in front of us in our classrooms and other work sites. The choices that we make every day in our own work settings reveal our moral commitments to social continuity and change, whether or not we want to acknowledge it. We cannot be neutral. Part of my argument is that, while we should not ignore efforts to change structures beyond the classroom, the classroom is an important site for what has been called socially critical action research, or action research that is connected to the struggle for greater educational equity and social justice.

Before I get into the substance of my argument, I would like to make a few comments about my own links to the action research community over the years. I was introduced to the idea of action research as a teacher in an inner-city elementary school in New York State in 1970. The school that I entered as a new teacher had undergone a great deal of racial conflict in the years just before I came. The largely African-American parents of the students had, as part of the community control movement that was sweeping the U.S. at that time, negotiated an arrangement with the school authority that gave them an official role in the governance of the school. At the time that I entered the school, the staff and parents were just beginning a series of organizational development workshops facilitated by a local university professor who employed an action research framework to address the numerous problems that had plagued the school, including the academic failure of many of the African-American students and the community's extreme alienation from the school. During these early years of my teaching career, I began to see the potential of action research for contributing in important ways to remaking of the school as an institution, improving school and community relations, and promoting an educational experience of high quality for everybody's children. Not surprisingly, we certainly did not solve all of our problems in these years, but we made a lot of important progress that significantly changed the quality of life in the school.

Like many teachers at that time, I had been educated to believe that the answers to problems of practice resided in the research and theories that emanated from universities. As a student teacher, I had been taught to believe that real research—"with a capital R"—was conducted by university academics, and it was my job as a teacher to implement the results of their findings. My own experiences as a participant in the action research community within my school and my growing awareness, from reading works by John Goodlad, Francis Klein, Seymour Sarason (Goodlad & Klein, 1974; Sarason, 1971), and others about the failure of most, if not all, projects that attempted to reform schools from the outside and ignored the expertise of those who worked in them, inspired me to enroll part time in a graduate degree program which emphasized action research and organizational change in schools. My life as a graduate student was combined with my continued participation in school-based action research, and I continued to work in schools in some capacity throughout all of my graduate studies.

Ironically, despite all of my experience as a practitioner of action research, the thesis for my graduate degree was not an action research study, but a study of the social relations among children in other people's classrooms. Although action research had become an important part of my life, in 1976 it was still not considered appropriate to accept an action research study as a thesis for a graduate degree. It still is not acceptable today in many universities in the U.S. with which I am familiar, despite all of the progress we have made in broadening definitions of educational research.

For the last 15 years, I have been employed at the University of Wisconsin-Madison, coordinating a student teaching program and teaching graduate courses in the study of teacher education. During this time, I have been connected to action research in several ways: doing action research on my own practice, supporting the action research of graduate student teacher educators, and supporting the action research of student teachers and of teachers in the local schools. Most of my published research and writing has involved a critical analysis of my own practice. I also spend much of my time supporting both the action research of graduate students who are studying their practices as teacher educators and the research of student teachers and teachers in the local schools.

The intent of this little digression into some of the history of my involvement with action research is to make the point that I have been an active supporter of action research for a long time (22 years). I have put myself on the line many times to defend the right of teachers and teacher educators to take control of our own practices back from the politicians, professional reformers, and school improvement entrepreneurs who still dominate the business of educational reform. Why then would I criticize the practice of action research? My brief response is that although I am committed to the values and principles associated with action research (e.g. its commitment to democratize the research process and to give greater voice to the practitioners in determining the course of policies that affect their daily work), I am also committed to the joining of action research with the larger issue of building more humane and compassionate societies.

Although action research has the potential to play a part in the building of a more just world, it has not always fulfilled this potential. When I go to a meeting of action researchers, I always expect to feel a certain sense of solidarity. I also expect to feel a shared sense of outrage at the conditions under which most of our fellow human beings are forced to live, the growing gap in many countries between the rich and the poor, and the erosion of democratic processes. And most painful of all, I expect to experience a shared contempt for the fact that an enormous number of children in the world now live in conditions of poverty. There are some 30 million of these children in my own country today (Johnson et al., 1991). Despite my expectations of connecting action research with the lessening of these sufferings and injustices within and beyond the school, and despite the origins of the action research movement before the middle of the century in combating race and class prejudice and in community action work (Altrichter & Gstettner, 1993; Noffke, 1989), oftentimes there is not apparent concern over these matters of educational equity and social justice in the action research community today. Sometimes it seems as though action research and the empowerment of practitioners are pursued in ways that are totally oblivious to the current situation of the people in many countries who, by anyone's definition, do not share equally in the rewards of their societies. Sometimes action research seems too self-serving.

The Accomplishments of the Action Research Movement

I would like to focus on some of the real gains I think action research has produced. These are accomplishments that should not be belittled or taken for granted in the least. In the last two decades, the terms action research, reflective practice, and the reflective practitioner have become slogans for educational reform all over the world. On the surface, this international professional education movement can be seen as a reaction against a view of practitioners as technicians who merely carry out what others, outside of the sphere of practice, want them to do; it can be seen as a rejection of top–down forms of reform that involve practitioners merely as passive participants. It involves a recognition that practitioners are professionals who must play active roles in formulating the purposes and ends of their work, as well as the means. These slogans also signify a recognition that the generation of knowledge of good practice and good institutions is not the exclusive property of universities and research and development centers; it is a recognition that practitioners have theories too and they can contribute to the knowledge that informs the work of practitioner communities.

Although there is the danger that these sentiments can lead to unthinking rejection of university-generated knowledge—and I think this would be as big a mistake as the dismissal of practitioner knowledge—there is a clear recognition that we cannot rely on university-generated knowledge alone for individual practitioner development and institutional improvement. Externally produced knowledge can often be important in helping us gain perspective on a situation or link our efforts to the work of others (Rudduck, 1985). There are valuable things to be learned from university-generated theories, but this external discourse must feed into a process of inquiry that is initiated from the ground up.

From the perspective of the individual practitioner, this means that the process of understanding and improving one's work must start from reflecting on one's own experience, and, as Winter (1989) has argued, that the sort of wisdom derived entirely from the experience of others—even other practitioners—"is at best impoverished and at worst illusory" (p. vii). The slogans of reflection and action research also signify a recognition that the process of learning to be a teacher, nurse, midwife, or social worker continues throughout one's entire career. No matter what we do in our practitioner education programs, and no matter how well we do them, at best we can only prepare practitioners to begin practice. There is a commitment by teacher educators and other practitioner educators to help prospective and novice practitioners internalize, during their initial training and early years of practice, the disposition and skill to study their work and become better at it over time. There is a commitment to help practitioners take responsibility for their own professional development.

Action Research and Individual Professional Development

The first area of change that I want to examine is the issue of whether or not action research has facilitated the development of individual practitioners. The evidence overwhelmingly indicates that action research has been successful. Literature in education is filled with personal accounts of how teachers feel that their classroom practice, and in some cases their professional lives, have been transformed through action research. They say that it has helped: boost teachers' confidence levels (Webb, 1990); narrow the gap between teachers' aspirations and realizations (Elliott & Adelman, 1973); teachers understand their own practices and students more deeply and revise their personal theories of teaching (e.g. Kemmis, 1985b); and teachers internalize the disposition to study their teaching practice over time (e.g. Day, 1984). This kind of evidence led Grundy and Kemmis (1988) to conclude that:

> The first-hand accounts of teachers and students who have been involved in these projects reveal that action research has often been a major and significant experience in their personal or professional development and often a uniquely transforming experience. In short there is plenty of evidence in print and in people to justify a claim for action research based on performance rather than promise (p. 331).

In my own personal experience in facilitating action research, I have often been overwhelmed by the responses of teachers and teacher educators to the opportunity to have their own issues drive their professional development. Very few of the teachers that I have worked with, or I have seen my colleagues in the Madison schools work with, have found action research to be less useful than the conventional kinds of staff development they have experienced. Importantly, most teachers I know who have experienced action research continue doing it beyond their initial encounter with it and bring others on board. Action research groups are multiplying like rabbits in the Madison schools and it is becoming very difficult to keep up with the demand for facilitative support. There is little doubt that teachers find it enormously intellectually valuable and that they feel it enhances the quality of their teaching.

In the U.S. there is still, unfortunately, a dominance of staff development and school improvement programs that ignore the knowledge and expertise of teachers. They primarily rely on the distribution of prepackaged and allegedly research-based solutions to school problems, often at great expense. An example of this is the enormous popularity of Madeline Hunter's instructional improvement programs in the United States (Gentile, 1988). Selling educational solutions and gimmicks, which I have come to refer to as "snake oil" staff development, is still big business in the U.S., despite all of the teachers who have had the experience of action research and other grassroots forms of staff development.[5] When teachers have the experience of action research, the overwhelming majority come to the conclusion that they are on to something that matters, something that is "for real."

Whether this sense of personal renewal has actually been accompanied by a higher quality of teaching and learning is another issue. On the one hand, some claims have been made over the years that better teaching is associated with teachers who research their practice. For example, Elliott and Adelman (1973) claimed with regard to the Ford Teaching Project that action research leads to an improved quality of work—pupils of teachers who have engaged in action research demonstrate superior performance in areas addressed in the research.

Cochran-Smith and Lytle (1992) in the U.S. have gone even farther. They make the sweeping generalization that action research has fundamentally transformed the nature of instruction in the classrooms of teacher researchers:

When teachers redefine their own relationships to knowledge about teaching and learning, they reconstruct their classrooms and begin to offer different invitations to their students to learn and know. A view of teaching as research is connected to a view of learning as constructive, meaning-centered, and social .... Teachers who are actually researching their own practices provide opportunities for their students to become similarly engaged ... what goes on in the classrooms of teacher-researchers is qualitatively different from what typically happens in classrooms (p. 318).

Philadelphia-area schools have presented us with many convincing examples of this phenomenon in recent years. I have also watched this occur in the Madison schools where some teachers use action research as a tool to help them revise their teaching approach to one that is more meaning-centered and responsive to students (Brodhagen, 1992). It does not always happen though. I have also seen teachers use action research to more effectively implement behaviorist management systems and other kinds of teaching that are very unlike what Cochran-Smith and Lytle describe. Action research is undoubtedly satisfying for teachers and helps them do what they want to do better, but what they want to do covers a wide range of alternatives, including those outside of the world of constructivism. It seems to me that whether or not the changes teachers achieve through action research can be considered improvements is an issue that has to consider the merits of what is achieved and whether it is worth achieving in the context of education within a democratic society. Cynthia Ellwood (1992), an experienced action researcher in the Milwaukee, Wisconsin schools, has argued that action research can sometimes lend greater legitimacy to practices that intensify inequities. I agree.

For example, there are still at least some teachers who believe that different races have different intellectual capabilities and certain races have a natural lower ability level or are incapable of learning (Tomlinson, 1989). John Goodlad (1990) recently concluded in his national study of preservice teacher education in the U.S.:

> The idea of moral imperatives for teachers was virtually foreign in con-cept and strange in language for most of the future teachers we inter-viewed. Many were less than convinced that all students can learn; they voiced the view that they should be kind and considerate to all, but they accepted as fact the theory that some simply cannot learn (p. 264).

Are we willing to accept any changes that are produced through the research of teachers as necessarily good? Despite all of the good things that have been achieved in the classrooms of teacher researchers over the years, large num-bers of children continue to be left out of the rewards generated by teacher development and school improvement efforts. They will continue to be left out until there is more explicit concern with the equitable distribution of outcomes in relation to these improvements.

Action Research and School Change

The second area in which educational action research can potentially have a transformative impact is with regard to the institution of the school. It has become very common in recent years to criticize teachers for taking too narrow a view of action research, emphasizing personal renewal at the expense of social reconstruction. This argument, which has been eloquently set forth by Lawn (1989), Holly (1987), Nixon (1987), and Kemmis (1992), among others, is that the emphasis by teacher researchers on classroom action research has ignored the structural conditions that shape their actions within the classroom. Action research, which is felt to have the potential to disturb the deep structures of schooling, is criticized for failing to change institutions. For example, Stephen Kemmis (1986) has concluded that "Educational action research has been captured and domesticated in individualistic classroom research which has failed to establish links with political forces for democratic educational reform" (p. 51).

Lawn (1989) and others have taken a similar view and called for "schoolwork research" that addresses those aspects of their work that define it and create the contradictions with which they have to work (i.e. job definition, resources, colleague relations, and supervision).

While I support the general view that at least some educational action research should focus at the institutional and community levels, I think that there are several serious problems with the calls for schoolwork research as they are typically presented. First, and most serious, is the denigration of the teacher that is perceived by many teachers to be attached to these criticisms of narrowness. One of the hidden texts in these arguments, as perceived by many teachers, is that "There are bigger and more important things going on beyond your limited world of the classroom. I can see them, why can't you? Stop wasting your time with the trivial matters of trying to improve the learning of your students. If you really want to improve that learning, take on the institution and conditions will be created that will make these improvements possible." Lawn (1989) argues:

> Teacher research must include the possibility of dealing with schoolwork issues if it is to emancipate ... how foolish it would be to restrict the boundaries of what we consider their work to be. This will not be emancipatory for teachers (p. 159).

Although there is a lot of merit to the argument of focusing on the social and institutional context in which practice occurs,[6] I am uncomfortable with the negative portrayal that is often presented of those teachers who choose to maintain a focus on classroom research. As I have said above, most teacher researchers will continue to engage in studies within their classrooms or in groups of classrooms without taking on the institution of the school or the structure of teachers' work. I think it is possible to encourage and support schoolwork research without denigrating classroom research. Also, as I will argue below, I think that within the scope of classroom action research it is very possible to establish links with political forces for democratic reform, as Stephen Kemmis urges us to do. One does not necessarily have to move out of the classroom to connect action research with the struggle for educational equity and social justice.

Despite all of the criticisms of teachers for the narrowness of their research efforts, I think that there are many examples of situations where groups of teachers have engaged in action research that has resulted in important changes at the institutional level, such as changes in school and school authority policies. There are highly publicized cases. One such instance is the efforts of the Boston Women's Teachers Group in the U.S. to educate other teachers about the structural contradictions in their work and the misplacement of blame in such terms as "teacher burnout" (Freedman et al., 1983). There are also many lesser known cases where teacher research has moved beyond the level of the classroom and affected school and school authority policies. In fact, I would argue that as teachers pursue issues within the classroom, their attention is naturally drawn to the institutional context in which the classroom is located.

In one case that I was personally involved in recently, a group of Madison elementary school teachers approached me to help them conduct a study about the complexities of their work that could be used in negotiations between the teachers' union and the school authority to gain more released time during the school day for elementary teachers to talk to one another. After we sat down and developed a set of orientating categories to structure the research, a group of us from the university, including faculty and students, followed teachers around for complete days and carefully documented all of the various activities in which they were engaged. We were the data collectors.

A small group of teachers and I then met to discuss the information we gathered. The teachers then planned an organized presentation to the local school board to educate them about the nature of the elementary teachers' work. The result was that several members of the school board commented publicly that they were very surprised by all of the tasks in addition to teaching that elementary teachers had to do, and by the intense pace of a teacher's day in an elementary classroom. The teachers eventually won their battle to secure additional release time. They got an extra hour per week. This result was not tremendous, but it was important. During the process, over 200 teachers came together to actively support the cause. I think that these small victories matter. There are many of them throughout the action research community.

As Allison Kelly (1985) of the UK has argued, a focus on these small victories can enable teachers to break out from the determinism that says, "It's too big for me, there's nothing I can do," and to avoid the disillusion that frequently comes from not having reformed the world all at once. Action research can be an important link in a larger effort toward social reconstruction. We must be able to recognize the importance of each small accomplishment along the way.

Action Research and the Control of Knowledge

Another area in which it is claimed that the action research movement can potentially be subversive and where it has made a significant contribution to change is with regard to the control of the educational knowledge that informs the work of practitioners and policy makers. One of the features of educational action research that was stressed by Lawrence Stenhouse, and continues to be stressed by some today, is making practitioners' research public so that other practitioners can benefit from the inquiries of individuals or groups, and so that teacher educators, university researchers, and policy makers can incorporate the knowledge produced through these action research inquiries into their courses, which are taken by prospective and practicing teachers, and into the deliberations through which educational policies are formed (e.g. Stenhouse, 1975).

As a result of the continuing growth of teacher research communities and their publications, some, like Cochran-Smith and Lytle (1992) in the U.S., have argued that the discourse about schools and schooling has been widened to include the knowledge and perspectives of teachers. Although this has been somewhat true, particularly in the area of English and language arts education, there are real limits to the degree the discourse has been widened. For example, when it comes to the issue of educational research, or more specifically research on teaching, Lytle and Cochran-Smith's (1990) earlier statement about the place of teachers in the educational research hierarchy is still, unfortunately, in my view, an accurate description of what exists today:

> Conspicuous by their absence from the literature of research on teaching are the voices of teachers, the questions and problems they pose, the frameworks they use to interpret and improve their practice, and the ways they define and understand their work lives (p. 83).

Even today, with the growth of teacher research communities throughout the world and the relatively easy access to teacher-generated knowledge, we still see a general disregard for the craft knowledge of teachers in the educational research establishment, which has attempted to articulate what is referred to in the U.S. as a "knowledge base" for teaching, minus the voice of teachers (Grimmett & MacKinnon, 1992). For example, in the most recent edition of the American Educational Research Association's *Handbook of Research on Teaching* (Wittrock, 1986), which is supposed to describe the state of the art knowledge about teaching, there are 35 chapters and over a thousand pages about such topics as teaching mathematics, social studies, classroom management, and bilingual education. However, there is not a single chapter written by a classroom teacher and there are few, if any, references to anything a teacher has written. The same is true for *Knowledge Base for the Beginning Teacher* (Reynolds, 1989), which is a very influential publication in the U.S., and most other books of its kind that are under the editorial control of university academics. The fact that many teachers do not have time to write is no excuse for this, because there is a lot of material that has been published by teachers that could have been drawn upon. The guardians of the knowledge base in education have become more willing to tolerate action research, but when it comes to defining what real educational research is, action research does not seem to count.

As I mentioned earlier, most universities in the U.S. that offer doctoral degrees would probably not accept an action research study as a PhD thesis today. Even at my own university, which is generally considered to be one of the more progressive in the U.S., there was some resistance to my proposal to award graduate credit to teachers and principals who were enrolled in school-based action research groups in the Madison schools. We now have both teacher research and action research interest groups within the American Educational Research Association. At least a few classroom teachers are among the 8000 or so researchers at the annual conference who come and present papers, but their status and significance in the organization is clearly marginal.[7] In many ways, action research has not managed to alter the balance of power between academics and practitioners when it comes to defining what counts as educational research.

When it comes to the question of the degree to which the knowledge generated through action research is incorporated into the courses offered by colleges and universities to prospective and practicing teachers, I do not think the picture is any brighter, again with the possible exception of English and language arts education. Although I see the rapid growth of practitioner research groups throughout the school systems of the U.S., I do not see any noticeable changes in the rest of the teacher education enterprise, including the courses that both prospective and practicing teachers take in colleges and universities. If I were to examine the course syllabi at my own university, I would not find too many instances where course readings would include the voices of practitioners and the knowledge generated through action research.

This is an issue that I have been personally working on during the last few years, thanks in part to Bridget Somekh, Coordinator of CARN. At a research conference in Boston three years ago, one of my graduate students presented a paper that she and I wrote about the use of action research with our student teachers. During the session, Bridget raised questions about the degree to which we were making use of the knowledge that was produced each semester by our student teachers, about how to help students become more active learners, about how to begin teaching based on what students already know, about how to assess student understandings, and so on. While we frequently used our students' action research studies as examples to demonstrate what student teachers can do with action research, we had been doing very little to use the knowledge that was generated in these studies.

My awareness of this contradiction bothered me a great deal and I began to ask more questions about the degree to which my other graduate courses (most of which praised the value of action research and even engaged students in action research) incorporated the voices and practical theories of practitioners. What I found was that despite my use of readings about action research, which challenged the hegemony of knowledge produced in the academy, the voices in these papers and books were mainly academic ones and not those of P–12 practitioners. Despite my commitment to action research, my actual practice undermined my intended message to students. Were my student teachers really learning about the role of teachers as knowledge producers and reformers if they were never assigned to read anything written by a teacher or another student teacher?

In the last few years, there have been many changes with which I have been struggling toward the goal of trying to find a more central place for practitioner-produced knowledge in my work with student teachers and teachers. I am trying to do a better job of incorporating the voices of teachers and students into these courses. For example, we have recently made much use in our student teaching program of *Rethinking Schools*, a publication produced bimonthly by a group of teachers in Milwaukee, Wisconsin. This newspaper raises critical perspectives about many school practices, such as ability grouping, standardized testing, monocultural curriculum materials, and the use of popular packaged programs (e.g. Assertive Discipline from a variety of perspectives, including the school administration, teachers, parents, students, African-Americans, Hispanic-Americans, Native Americans, Asian-Americans, and so on). These kinds of readings help student teachers see the many sides of an issue and hear many voices. Although we are not trying to eliminate the writing of academics from our courses, we have clearly tried to create more of a balance between practitioner- and academic-generated knowledge in our curriculum. I think that this example of my personal struggle with the contradictions between my practice and my rhetoric is a good demonstration of how, even when there is an expressed commitment to the notion of teacher as researcher in teacher education, the commitment sometimes does not go far enough.

There is also the issue of the degree to which the action research movement has affected the course of educational policy making. Here, despite some evidence that more institutional resources are being allocated to support teacher research groups by some school authorities, the overall course of educational policy making in the UK and the U.S., with regard to both teaching and teacher education, seems to have disregarded teachers and teacher educators altogether in recent years. The UK has its recent Educational Reform Acts (e.g. Gilroy, 1992). In the U.S., we have had a similar intensification of efforts to wrest control of decision making from those who do the work of teaching and teacher education (Apple, 1986). Both teachers and teacher educators in many countries have far less control over what they do today than they did a decade ago. One response in the action research community to the recent efforts to centralize control over school curriculum, assessment, teacher education, and so on has been to urge action researchers to fight to take control of education back from the bureaucrats and politicians. But, to date, in the antiwelfare economic climate in which many governments have sought to rationalize public spending and integrate public policy more fully with industrial needs (Hewitson et al., 1991), we have largely been ineffective.

Action Research and the Struggle for Social Justice

There are some who have criticized the call for action researchers to intervene in the social, economic, and political processes of a society. Here, the concern has been that a militant group of people, including many male university academics, are attempting to hijack the action research movement to accomplish goals contrary to those of the mostly female group of action researchers. These so-called "agitators" of the movement are perceived as well intentioned but naïve about the complexities of practitioners' work. In a widely read polemic, Gibson (1985) has compared them to Salvation Army tambourinists. Elliott (1991) has called them dangerous radicals.

Although I have been somewhat critical in this paper of the way in which the call for social responsibility has often been made to action researchers, I think it would be a big mistake to believe, as some apparently do, that we can somehow be neutral participants in relation to issues of social continuity and change. As I have stated several times in different ways, I believe that we cannot help but intervene in these matters, even if we choose to focus our action research within our immediate work settings, such as the classroom.

Furthermore, educators who work in societies that claim to be democratic have certain moral obligations to intervene in ways that contribute to situations in which those with whom we work have the potential to more fully live the values inherent in a democracy. For example, in a democratic society, all children must be taught so that they can participate intelligently as adults in the political processes that shape their society (Gutmann, 1987). This is not happening now in most countries by any stretch of the imagination. This is an international problem that affects most of humankind, and has had its most visible effect on the poor, ethnic minorities, and immigrant groups throughout the world, in both highly industrialized and less industrialized countries. This problem affects Moroccan children in Belgium and the Netherlands, Turkish children in Germany, Pakistani and Afro-Caribbean children in the UK, Hmong, Latino, and African-American children in the U.S., hill tribe children in Thailand, Quechua children in Bolivia, Basarwa children in Botswana, and many, many more.

Currently, in the U.S. and other countries, there is overwhelming evidence of a growing crisis of what Jonathan Kozol (1991) has referred to as *Savage*

Inequalities. Race, gender, social class, language background, religion, sexual preference, and so on continue to play strong roles in determining access to quality education, housing, and health care and rewarding work that pays a decent wage. Such determinants continue to affect the incidence of a whole host of outcomes such as malnutrition, child abuse, childhood pregnancies, violent crime, and drug abuse. A black male child who was born in California in 1988 is three times more likely to be murdered as he is to be admitted to the University of California (Ladson-Billings, 1991).

I am not suggesting, as some of our recent government policy makers have, that these and other problems (such as the crumbling of a country's economy) have been caused by the schools. Schools did not cause these problems, and school reform alone cannot solve them. I am suggesting, though, that we need to play a conscious role in whatever spheres we choose to work, examining the social and political implications of our own actions and acting in ways that promote the realization of democratic values.

For action researchers, this means that what has frequently been sensationalized as socially critical action research should not be considered an exotic tangent in the action research movement. It should not be considered something that is engaged in only by those who go to graduate school and become literate in the latest critical or postmodern social science theories or those who pay homage to certain currently fashionable university theoreticians. All action researchers should, at some point along the way, consider and act on the social and political implications of their practices. This does not mean that they should consider these things every waking minute, or that once they do, the way to the achievement of a more democratic situation is clear, because it is not. It does mean, though, that there needs to be more public concern among action researchers for what we can do as educators and human beings to lessen the pain and suffering that surrounds us every day.

A few years ago, Gaby Weiner (1989), who was then at the Open University, wrote a controversial paper in which she described what she saw as two separate segments of the teacher research movement in the UK: the mainstream movement and the gender research movement. The mainstream movement, according to Weiner, concentrated on issues related to the professional development of teachers and emphasized the process of reflective inquiry rather than the outcomes of the research. In contrast, she saw that the gender researchers emphasized the outcomes of action research and were committed to increased social justice within a professional development framework. Both groups of action researchers, according to Weiner, were concerned with the liberation and emancipation of teachers. Both groups were concerned with creating conditions where teachers, and not academics and external researchers, could develop educational theory grounded in classroom practice. However, only the gender researchers, she felt, connected their efforts explicitly to questions of equity and social justice. In her analysis of the statements of 75 action researchers in the 1984 CARN bulletin, Weiner found only one mention of a gender-related topic. She claimed that gender as a substantive classroom issue was largely ignored by mainstream teacher researchers. She expressed the hope that in the future, teacher research would embrace the dual aims of increased self-knowledge and social justice.

I think that Weiner is right in her call for a focus in action research on both personal renewal and social reconstruction. There is a moral obligation to do so in a world such as ours.[8] Despite Weiner's pessimistic conclusions regarding the lack of attention in teacher research to social justice issues, there have been, and continue to be, teachers who have acted on the social and political implications of their practice in their action research, including both classroom research and school work research.

In addition to the more widely publicized and the large-scale efforts, such as the Girls into Science and Technology project (Whyte, 1985) and Sex Differentiation project (Millman & Weiner, 1985) in the UK in the 1980s, there are many examples of teachers who, by themselves or with a small group of colleagues, have connected their research to the dual aims of personal renewal and social reconstruction. I have known both student teachers and teachers in Madison who have done this in their classroom research, exploring alternative forms of assessment and student grouping practices and pursuing race and gender equity in relation to such areas as science and computers (Cutler-Landsman, 1991; Gore & Zeichner, 1991). I have also seen this occur in other parts of the U.S. (e.g. Fecho, 1992; Langston Hughes Intermediate School, 1988).

At the time of writing (1993), a group of 11 of our student teachers at the University of Wisconsin-Madison were engaged in action research that focused on finding out more about the communities from which their students came and the cultural resources that their students brought to school (i.e. what students already knew and could do), so that their teaching could be more culturally responsive and equitable across lines of race and social class. They were to examine their classroom and school cultures in relation to the various cultures of their students and think about how policies and practices in their classrooms and schools affect children from various backgrounds.[9] These kinds of research projects, although admittedly not the majority of classroom studies, can serve to expose the real but often hidden connections between the micro and the macro. They can help us see how what we do every day as teachers is necessarily related to issues of social continuity and change.

Conclusion

My hope is that we can begin to give more attention as an international community of action researchers to connecting our research and facilitation of research to the achievement of both personal renewal and social reconstruction. I have alluded to the segmentation that currently divides us. On the one hand, we have the glorification of personal renewal and empowerment as an end in itself and the neglect of social responsibility. On the other hand, the call for social reconstruction and social justice is sometimes set forth in a manner that crushes the individual and denigrates those removed from the specialized language of social theory in the university. I have argued that this is too self-serving. We need to learn how to transcend these tribal wars that continue to divide us and become more of the united group that CARN promotional materials describe us to be.

None of what I have said in this paper about more vigorously exploring the social and political implications in classroom action research should be construed as a call to back off from either the kind of school work research and community action work which directly confronts institutional policies and structures or the kind of work that directly challenges the gatekeepers of what is considered real educational research. These efforts should be encouraged and supported, but not at the expense of classroom action research and the dignity of teachers. No matter where we choose to focus our research efforts—in the classroom, school, university, college, or larger community—we all need to continue to speak out against the policies that we view as educationally unsound or morally bankrupt. We also need to become, or to stay, connected to larger social movements that are working to bring about greater social, economic, and political justice on our planet. Although educational action research can only play a small part in this broader struggle, it is an important part. As an action research community, we need to have a greater public social conscience and become more explicitly connected to the struggle to bring about a world in which everybody's children have access to decent and rewarding lives. We all ought to ask ourselves every day, "What am I doing in my involvement with action research to help move us closer to this kind of world?"

Chapter 6

Action Research in Teacher Education as a Force for Greater Social Justice[1]

In this chapter I revisit one of the major themes I addressed in the keynote talk that I gave at the 1992 CARN conference in Worcester, UK. In my 1992 talk, "Personal transformation and social reconstruction through action research" (Zeichner, 1993), I explored the idea of what it means for action research conducted by primary and secondary school teachers to contribute to greater social, cultural, political, and economic justice in a society. I criticized both what I saw as an uncritical glorification of action research because of the alleged personal and social benefits that were often implied to be inevitably associated with doing it and academics' criticisms of teachers for not directly seeking to change the structures of schooling and focusing their efforts mainly within their classrooms. Educational action research does not necessarily promote a more humane and just school or society, and it can (and has been) used to legitimate ideas and practices that are harmful to individuals and societies. However, I argued that it is possible for teachers to do socially critical action research (Tripp, 1990) at multiple levels: in their classrooms, schools, and the society at large.

In this chapter, I discuss initial teacher education and explore the issue of how action research in initial teacher education can serve to support the realization of greater justice in an unjust and often inhumane world. Teacher education is a logical focus for my analysis because it is the sphere in which I work. I also want to focus on teacher education rather than on teaching because of what I see happening to change it in fundamental ways in many countries throughout the world. First, I discuss what I see going on, and what disturbs me about what I see. Second, I address the question of how I think educational action research can contribute to overcoming some of the obstacles that I identify that have prevented teacher education from contributing to the building of more just and humane societies. Third, I share several different kinds of examples of what I see as action research that supports greater social justice.

There are many interesting theoretical debates in the academic literature among advocates of different conceptions of justice (e.g. between advocates of distributional theories and relational theories),[2] but I am not going to get into a philosophical exploration of the different meanings of social justice here.

In several ways, action research has become a central part of teacher education all over the world. Most teacher education programs now require student teachers to conduct action research studies as part of their preparation programs (Grossman, 2005; Price, 2001). Many teacher educators study their own practice through some form of practitioner inquiry as part of the relatively new but rapidly growing self-study movement in teacher education (e.g. Loughran & Russell, 2002). I also discuss the need for more teacher educators to engage in participatory action research in collaboration with people in schools and communities.

I use the term action research in a broad way to include forms of practitioner inquiry that do not necessarily follow the classic action research spiral. In recent years, a variety of different approaches to practitioner inquiry, including action research, participatory action research, critical practitioner inquiry, critical participatory action research, lesson study, the scholarship of teaching, teacher research, and self-study (Anderson, Herr, & Nihlen, 2007; Cochran-Smith & Donnell, 2006; Zeichner & Noffke, 2001), have been used in teacher education programs. My focus is on all of these various forms of practitioner inquiry. There are examples in each form of inquiry that have emancipatory goals and accomplishments associated with them.

Teacher Education Under Attack

No one will have the freedom to seek better teaching and stronger education ... until the intellectual stranglehold exerted by the teacher education cartel is broken (Holland, 2004, p. xix).

Today, teacher education around the world is in trouble. My perception of this situation is highly influenced, of course, by my location in the land of George Bush and his government's efforts to privatize public education and deprofessionalize the work of teaching (e.g. Baines 2006; Raphael & Tobias, 1997). However, I am pretty confident that what I describe below is true, in some form, in many countries throughout the world because of the wide influence of the neoliberal and neoconservative thinking that is guiding efforts to dismantle public education and teacher education in the U.S. and elsewhere (Carnoy, 1995; Compton & Weiner, 2008; Freeman-Moir & Scott, 2007; Hypolito, 2004).

A variety of policies are beginning to emerge that seem directed at taking control of education away from teachers and teacher educators, and eliminating—under efficiency arguments—the very mechanisms that can help teachers to effectively increase education quality (the professional character of teaching with all that it brings, such as a deeper knowledge of the subjects they will teach. A deeper knowledge of how to teach those subjects to an increasingly diverse population, critical thinking, cognitive growth, among others) (Tatto, 2007, p. 13).

There are several characteristics of teacher education in many parts of the world today. On the one hand, there have been several major trends occurring in programs that provide the initial education of teachers. These include commodification of the work of preparing teachers and making teacher preparation subject to market forces, excessively prescriptive accountability requirements from government bodies that seek to control the substance of the teacher education curriculum, consistent and painful cuts in the budgets of public institutions charged with the education of teachers, and attacks on efforts to educate teachers to teach in socially just ways (e.g. preparing them to engage in multicultural or antiracist education). I focus my comments on what is happening in the U.S. because that is the situation with which I am most familiar.

Many of these pressures on teacher education are a result of the spread of neoliberal ideas and policies about markets, privatization, deregulation, and the private versus public good from the world of elementary and secondary education into teacher education (Hinchey & Kaplan, 2005). According to Robertson (2008) these policies have three central aims:

> (1) The redistribution of wealth upward to the ruling elites through new structures of governance, (2) the transformation of educational systems so that the production of workers for the economy is the primary mandate, and (3) the breaking down of education as a public sector monopoly opening it up to strategic investment by for-profit firms (p. 12).

What we are seeing in the U.S. is the tremendous growth of alternatives to traditional college- and university-based teacher education. These alternatives include many new for-profit companies that have gone into the business of preparing teachers. These alternatives are actively supported by the federal government. (Our former Secretary of Education said in a major report on teacher quality that he thought participation in a teacher education program should be made optional.)[3] They are also supported by state policies in certain parts of the country that have actively encouraged alternatives to college- and university-based teacher education.[4]

The encouragement of alternatives to university hegemony over teacher preparation in and of itself is not necessarily bad. What is important to note about the alternatives being encouraged, though, is that they are closely linked with a technical view of the role of teachers and efforts to erode whatever professional autonomy that teachers still have left. A number of scholars from different parts of the world have done a very good job of carefully documenting the transformation of the occupation of teaching worldwide to what has been called "the new professionalism." The new professionalism accepts the view that decisions about what and how to teach and assess are largely to be made beyond the classroom rather than by teachers themselves (e.g. Furlong, 2005; Robertson, 2000; Smyth et al. 2000; Tatto, 2007). The same ideas that have resulted in the new professionalism for teaching have now entered the world of teacher education to try and ensure that teachers are prepared to assume their limited roles as educational clerks who are not to exercise their judgment in the classroom (e.g. Johnson et al., 2005).

There is evidence that many of the programs in the U.S. that are not college- or university-based focus on meeting only the minimum standards set by governmental bodies (e.g. Baines, 2006). Evidence suggests that the goal of such programs is to prepare "good enough"[5] teachers to teach children of the poor. They are to teach by obediently following scripted curriculum and instructional practices that are allegedly supported by research (to raise standardized test scores). In reality, such programs line the pockets of friends of the government who own the companies that make the materials.[6] This approach serves to widen the gap between who gets to learn to be thinkers and authentic problem solvers and who is forced to learn out of context and interact with knowledge in artificial ways (Kozol, 2005).

These attempts to further deprofessionalize teaching through scripting the curriculum, instructional methods, and standardized tests at every grade level continue to ensure that spots will be available for the teachers produced by the growing number of alternative teacher education programs. In many places, teacher professional development has become product implementation. It is aligned with standards and standardized tests and is increasingly conducted by those employed by the testing companies and publishers who produce and sell the materials that are promoted by the government. Money that used to be available in schools for more teacher-initiated and -controlled professional development, like action research groups and study groups, is largely disappearing from American public schools (Randi & Zeichner, 2004). Professional development has shifted from a professional model that focuses on the learning of individual teachers to an institutional model that focuses on getting teachers to conform to institutional mandates (Young, 1998).

What is happening in public schools today has served to drive many good people who are not willing to put up with the continued erosion of the dignity of the work of public school teaching that is associated with these changes out of teaching and actively undermine the goal of improving the quality of learning for all students (Goodnough, 2001; Ingersoll, 2003). Teachers have become easily replaceable technicians in the eyes of many policy makers. The continual openings for the products of the new alternative programs ensure higher profits for the investors in the new teacher education companies. There is a lot of money to be made if teacher education in the U.S. can be privatized.

The solution to the teacher quality problem, according to some, is to deregulate teacher education and open the gates to individuals who have not completed a teacher education program prior to certification (e.g. Walsh, 2004), rather than to improve the conditions in public schools that are driving teachers out. Andrew Rosen, president of Kaplan College, which is part of one of the major for-profit teacher education companies to enter the U.S. teacher education market in recent years, stated the following in an online conversation about teacher education that clearly illustrates this stance:

> Teaching is less lucrative and is rife with work environment issues that many deem not to be worthy of investment ... by reducing the barriers for bright-minded professionals, we can increase the population of qualified candidates (Rosen, 2003).

Most of these new alternative programs use a learn-while-you-earn model in which the teacher candidates are fully responsible for a classroom (usually of poor children of color) while completing their minimalist program.[7] The standards to get into these programs are often very low, sometimes only requiring "a heartbeat and a check that clears the bank" (Baines, 2006, p. 327). The Education Trust has closely monitored the achievement test scores and other educational opportunities made available to various groups of learners in public schools. They have consistently found that if you are poor, and particularly if you are poor and a student of color (i.e. African-American, Latino, Native American, Asian-American), you are many more times likely in many areas of the country to be taught by inexperienced teachers, teachers who have not completed a full-scale teacher education program, or teachers teaching outside of the fields in which they were prepared (Peske & Haycock, 2006; Darling-Hammond, 2004).

Most teachers going into the field still enter it through traditional college and university programs (Spellings, 2006). However, in some parts of the U.S. (e.g. Texas and California), nearly as many teachers now enter through an alternative route, which is often one of the "fast track" programs that provide minimal preparation to teach (Feistritzer & Haar, 2008). An extreme form of a fast track program is offered by the American Board for the Certification of Teacher Excellence, which is a private group supported by the Bush administration with noncompetitive awards totaling 40 million dollars so far. It certifies teachers who pass two paper and pencil tests without having to complete any traditional or alternative teacher education program in seven states.

Another aspect of current developments in U.S. teacher education is the continuing cuts in state government financial support for public universities, where the majority of teachers in the U.S. are still prepared. As the states have had to address increased health care costs for the elderly, build prisons to house the minorities and other poor people whom the public schools have failed to educate, and make up for the shortfalls in federal support for various programs in public elementary and secondary schools that the states are obligated by law to provide (e.g. programs for special education students),[8] they have reduced funding to public universities (Lyall & Sell, 2006).[9] As the demands on university teacher educators have increased with expanding accountability requirements, their resources have gone down.

For example, in my own state of Wisconsin, state appropriations to the University of Wisconsin system's 13 campuses, adjusted for inflation, decreased by 22 percent or $223 million dollars between 2000 and 2007. The public contribution to my so-called public university in Madison is currently down to approximately 19 percent of the total budget (Clark, 2007). The rest of the money needed to run the university has to come from research grants, private gifts, and student tuition. There is hardly any difference anymore between a public and private university in the U.S. This pressure to reduce the size of teacher education in universities by starving the education schools that prepare teachers serves to support the growth of alternative programs and the corporatization of teacher education.

Yet another aspect of current developments in U.S. teacher education is the increased and often excessive accountability demands that are placed on teacher education programs by state governments and national accrediting bodies. In nearly every state, teacher education graduates are required to (a) pass a series of standardized tests to enter and complete their programs and (b) demonstrate mastery of a set of detailed teaching and subject matter standards. Teacher educators are required to spend inordinate amounts of time submitting their programs to states or to a national accrediting body for approval. Teacher educators prepare detailed assessment plans showing how each course in their programs is aligned with state standards and performance indicators showing exactly what tasks student teachers are required to do to meet the standards.

As the associate dean for teacher education at my university, I spent three months last year, on an essentially full-time basis, preparing the reports to our state education department on our teacher education programs so that the state could review our programs for their compliance with state certification laws. While some forms of accountability for teacher education institutions are reasonable and necessary, in a growing number of states, current demands for teacher educators to rationalize their programs have gone beyond the realm of reasonableness and are beginning to interfere with teacher educators being able to accomplish their goals.

For example, recent studies in Maryland and California have shown that, while teacher educators in some situations have been able to meet the increasingly prescriptive program approval requirements while still maintaining intellectual control over their programs (Kornfeld et al. 2007; Rennert-Ariev, 2008), precious resources have been spent on meeting requirements that teacher educators feel have not enhanced the quality of their programs. These resources could have been used for other things that would contribute to improving program quality, such as strengthening school–university partnerships. Rennert-Ariev (2008), who conducted the study in Maryland, found the practice of what he calls "bureaucratic ventriloquism" where "superficial demonstrations of compliance with external mandates became more important than authentic intellectual engagement." (p. 8).

With these requirements, a whole new industry in e-portfolios has emerged. A few companies (e.g. Live Text, Chalk & Wire) aggressively market portfolio systems to colleges and universities so that they can provide the necessary data to gain approval for their programs. These portfolio systems have emphasized the bureaucratic aspects of keeping track of student teachers' performance on standards and, for the most part, have failed to take advantage of the potential in portfolios to deepen teacher learning (Ayala, 2006; Bullough, 2008). Several of the portfolio companies and the two companies that make most of the teacher tests used nationally sponsor the annual meetings of the major national teacher education association, The American Association of Colleges for Teacher Education (AACTE), in the U.S. When people walked into the opening session of the AACTE conference in New York City last February, they first saw two giant screens with the logo of Educational Testing Service (ETS), the maker of most of the tests used in U.S. teacher education programs.

One extreme form of accountability expectations referred to as the "positive impact mandate" is being seriously pushed by policy makers in a number of areas in the country, and there are predictions by some that the so called "results-based" teacher education that will come from using the positive impact mandate will become the norm in the country in a few years. With this requirement, teacher education institutions will be evaluated and ranked based on the value-added standardized test score results of the pupils taught by the graduates of the teacher education programs. This is analogous to evaluating and approving medical schools on the basis of how many of their graduates' patients are helped by their medical care or get sicker. There are several reasons why the positive impact mandate is a bad idea, even if one accepts the ability of value-added assessment to link pupil performance with individual teachers in a way that rules out other explanations for student test performance. First, no other professional school is held accountable for the performance of its graduates after they have left the preparation program. Second, even if one accepts the ability of value-added assessment to link student test performance with individual teachers in a manner that rules out other explanations of student test score differences,[10] the costs involved in implementing this kind of assessment would divert enormous resources away from other teacher education activities that arguably would do a lot more to improve the quality of teacher preparation programs (Zeichner, 2005b). Darling-Hammond & Chung Wei (in press) concluded from their analysis of all of the arguments surrounding this issue that:

> While value-added models may prove useful for looking at groups of teachers for research purposes, and they may provide one measure of teacher effectiveness among several, they are problematic as the primary or sole measure for making evaluation decisions about individual teachers or even teacher education programs. More sophisticated judgments will be needed that take into account analyses of the teachers' students and teaching context, the nature of teaching practices, and the availability of other learning opportunities if judgments are to reflect all of the factors that influence student learning and teacher effects (p. 54).

Recently, the lead story in our national education newspaper, *Education Week*, praised the state of Louisiana for implementing this system for its teacher education programs (Honawar, 2007). If you are familiar with the U.S. school system, you would know that Louisiana spends probably close to the least amount of money on education, health care, and other social service systems in the country. Under the logic of the current government, the states that most support its policies (i.e. Texas, Louisiana, and Misssissippi) are ranked higher in educational quality reports because of their compliance rather than because of the actual quality of their education systems. The states with the highest overall educational quality are usually the ones least supportive of the accountability mandates.

Collectively, the requirements for extremely detailed information about institutional assessment systems, testing, and so on have been forcing teacher educators to spend time on tasks that they do not believe will help them do their jobs better just to appear that they are doing what is expected in order to get approval for their programs. This is time and money that could alternatively be spent on actually improving their programs. Lots of time and money is currently being spent on tasks in U.S. teacher education institutions that have no relation to improving program quality (Johnson et al., 2005).

A final aspect of current teacher education in the U.S. is the attacks stemming from neoconservative views on the proper content for a teacher's education. These attacks have focused on the increased emphases on (a) multicultural education in American teacher education programs and (b) preparation of teachers who can contribute to eliminating the achievement gaps between students from different ethnic, racial, and social class backgrounds (which have not only persisted in elementary and secondary schools, but have grown larger under current government policies). These attacks equate foci on multiculturalism and social justice with a lowering of academic standards and blame university teacher educators and teachers for the continued problems in educating public school students who are increasingly poor and of color. These attacks on multicultural education divert attention from the real influences on the problems in public schools, including the underfunding of public education, lack of access to affordable housing, transportation, and health care, and jobs that pay decent wages.

However, as pointed out by Wilson & Tamir (2008), the objection of at least some of the critics is not to the idea of social justice or multiculturalism per se, but to (a) what they perceive as the closed mindedness of teacher educators to see any value in perspectives other than their own and (b) what they define as an "aggressive multiculturalism" (Hess, 2001), which leads to the exclusion of multiple perspectives and positions on issues from the teacher education curriculum.

One example of the criticism of social justice and multicultural education efforts by external groups is the successful 2006 effort to force the major U.S. accrediting body in teacher education, NCATE, to drop the term "social justice" from its accrediting standards for teacher education programs (Wasley,

2006). Another aspect of this assault on social analysis in teacher education is an effort to define social foundations courses as superfluous. For example, Walsh and Jacobs (2007), in their critique of college- and university-based alternative certification programs, asserted that educational foundations courses are of little practical value to teacher education candidates and should be eliminated.

Another aspect of the critique of education schools involves the construction of an oversimplified distinction between teacher- and learner-centered instruction and the creation of a caricature of teacher educators as advocates of an unrestrained form of learner-centered instruction: "Teacher educators are lumped together as a unified bloc of subject matter-deficient worshipers at the alter of progressive ideals who only care about process and never about content" (Wilson & Tamir, 2008, p. 908).

For example, in a report on teacher education in California that was done by the Pacific Research Institute for Public Policy, Izumi & Coburn (2001) quote Florida State University psychologist K. Anders Ericksson, who describes college and university teacher educators as "radical constructivists" who act in extreme ways that few teacher educators would actually support:

> Radical constructivists recommend educational settings where students are forced to take the initiative and guide their own learning. Many radical constructivists even discourage the teacher from correcting students when their reasoning and ideas are invalid because such criticism may jeopardize their self-confidence in their independent reasoning and challenge their self-respect (p. 9).

Every Program is a Social Justice Program

While all of these forces (e.g. cuts in resources, privatization, increased accountability, and attacks on multiculturalism) are affecting teacher education from the outside, inside college and university teacher education programs, teacher educators are claiming to have programs that prepare teachers to teach for social justice, provide everyone's children with a high quality education, and work against the forces that are leading to increased inequality and suffering in the world today. Social justice teacher education has become a slogan—like reflective teaching was in the 1980s and 1990s—and it is hard to find a teacher education program in the U.S. that does not claim to make social justice a central part of its mission in preparing teachers. These days, action research frequently appears in teacher education literature as a social practice used in socially just teacher education programs. It is often implicitly assumed that having student teachers do action research or teacher educators study their own practice will necessarily be a force for promoting greater social justice.

In the remainder of this chapter, I address the issue of what it means to do action research in a way that acts as a force for greater social justice. While I give examples of action research by individual student teachers and teacher educators within their own classrooms, and think that this work is a necessary and important part of social justice teacher education, I also want to stress the importance of going beyond individual studies toward action research as a more social or collective process in public spaces, similar to Stephen Kemmis's emphasis in his recent writing on what he calls "critical participatory action research" (Kemmis, 2007). I also want to suggest that action research in teacher education that promotes greater social justice has to be extended outside the academy to involve people in schools and communities who are also working for greater social justice. I argue that at least some of the action research that needs to be done in today's hostile environment for teacher education, and public education in general, needs to be connected to broader social movements for social justice in a way that has not been typical.

Action Research in Teacher Education

There are several different types of action research that exist in teacher education programs. These include both forms of self-study by teacher educators and the use of action research as a requirement or option for student teachers. Rather than critiquing examples that I do not think support greater equity and justice, I focus on a few that I think do. I discuss teacher educators' self-studies first.

Self-Study Research of Teacher Educators

Self-study research by teacher educators has grown tremendously in the last decade in many parts of the world. Just in the last few years, we have seen the publication of a 1,500 page handbook (Loughran et al., 2004), numerous collected volumes of self-studies, and a journal, *Studying Teacher Education*. Although, as Mo Griffiths and several colleagues recently pointed out, the possibilities are rich for self-study to address issues of equity and justice (Griffiths et al., 2004), many, if not most, teacher educator self-study projects published so far have not explicitly focused on these issues. Although they have played a positive and important role in the professional development of teacher educators and led to a greater sense of community among teacher educators, improved teaching in many teacher education classrooms, and sometimes promotion and tenure, for the most part, they have not directly and publicly challenged the toxic environment that I described earlier.

Working on Their Own Practice

One type of self-study by teacher educators has involved teacher educators in trying to better understand and improve their efforts to transform the attitudes, beliefs, and practices of their preservice teacher students with regard to issues of race, gender, social class, sexual preference, and other aspects of difference in which the lack of justice prevails. This research has included efforts to develop a greater correspondence between one's professed beliefs as an educator working for social justice and one's practices (which are sometimes inconsistent with one's expressed beliefs) or efforts to attempt to better understand student teacher resistance to the intended emancipatory actions of teacher educators (see Schulte, 2004).

Laurie MacGillivray's (1997) study of her basic reading and study skills class for preservice teachers at the University of Southern California is an example of this kind of research. Laurie, a white teacher educator who describes her orientation as critical feminist, carefully studied her own life history and documented her interactions with several specific students in her class in great detail. This documentation uncovered several stark examples of her practice conflicting with her professed orientation. In her words, these are instances in which "I ended up reinforcing much of what I had attempted to disrupt" and "my unacknowledged biases and expectations sabotaged my conscious attempts to change the traditional power structures in classrooms" (p. 469). Laurie's reflections on her data led to efforts to confront these contradictions by carefully analyzing her motives and actions and redirecting her teaching to include attention to ways of knowing that she had previously ignored. At the end of her study, she leaves us with a sense of the tremendous complexity of libratory pedagogy in teacher education, along with a sense of new insights and accomplishment.

Teacher Educators Working on Themselves

A related but broader type of self-study research in teacher education that goes beyond an examination of practices or the connection between practices and professed beliefs is when teacher educators work on transforming their own attitudes and beliefs with regard to difference. One example of this kind of self-study is the research by Ann Schulte, now a teacher educator in California, on her practice as a teacher educator when she was a graduate student at my university (Schulte, 2001). Through participation in an action research group with other graduate student teacher educators, graduate courses in her doctoral program, and careful analysis of a journal she kept throughout her years of teaching courses and supervising student teachers in the field, Ann developed a growing awareness of the ways in which her own privileged background as a white, middle class, heterosexual, English-speaking woman and her unconscious biases and prejudices connected to her social locations influenced her teaching of teachers and children. Through this analysis, she developed a greater commitment to and skills in preparing her student teachers to both interrogate their own privileges and unexamined biases and examine how these impact their teaching. Ann engages in self-study to better understand how to engage her students, who have backgrounds similar to her own and represent the majority of people going into teaching in the U.S., in a process of personal transformation. Knowing how she transforms her own thinking helps her more effectively support her students' transformation. Ann's study documents both her own transformation and that of her students, and underlines the importance in social justice-oriented work in teacher education of teacher educators' growth and development.

Examining the Structures in Which Teacher Educators Work

Another type of self-study in teacher education that I think serves to promote greater social justice is when the researchers begin to critically examine the institutional and policy structures within which they work. A recently published study by teacher educators at Sonoma State University, California (Kornfeld et al., 2007) is an example of this kind of self-study. In this study, four teacher educators examined their experience of going through the program approval process by the state education department. This process included detailed requirements for presenting the state with documentation of how all of the various courses in their programs helped students meet 128 elements within the teaching standards prescribed by the state. This study documents the ways in which the new discourses imposed on teacher education institutions in California and an unprecedented level of prescriptiveness from the state affected teacher educators individually and as a community and influenced their ability to maintain the critical stance of their teacher education programs. In the end, what we see in this research is an example of teacher educators subtlety subverting the system rather than rebelling outright. Although faculty had to spend many hours producing documentation that they did not, for the most part, believe to be helpful to them or a fair assessment of their work, they managed to maintain the critical orientation of their programs overall, while succeeding in gaining state approval. While the oppressive system for monitoring teacher education still exists, the publication of this study has enabled other teacher educators with critical orientations to see how they can maintain the direction of their work under the face of external pressures toward technocratic rationality.

Student Teachers Doing Action Research

In addition to teacher educators studying themselves, there has been a great deal of work over the years in which teacher educators involve student teachers in doing action research as part of their teacher education program. As I asserted earlier, I think most initial teacher education programs throughout the world today engage student teachers in some form of action research. I have previously criticized some of what I see as narrow and technical forms of action research that are prevalent in U.S. teacher education and professional development programs (e.g. Zeichner, 1993), but here I want to focus on two positive (rather than negative) examples.

The first example of student teacher action research that I want to present that I think illustrates how student teacher action research can contribute toward greater social justice is a study done by a Namibian student teacher, Veronica Liswani (1999). Veronica, who was a student teacher at the Caprivi College of Education in a secondary school in northeastern Namibia in the late 1990s, conducted a study that sought to investigate the lack of participation by the six female students in one of her ninth-year agricultural science classes.[11] Through a series of interviews with her students, observations of their work in other classes in the school, and a survey of the other teachers in her school, Veronica sought to better understand why the girls did not participate in her class. Based on an analysis of these data, she modified her practice over a three-week period through such things as changing her questioning strategies and providing more opportunities for more work in small, mixed-gender groups. Her actions over this period of time led to increased involvement of the six girls in the science class. It would be easy to dismiss this study as inconsequential because it was done by a student teacher who was not fully responsible for her classroom and the intervention was within the boundaries of her classroom. We also do not know if what Veronica did during this one term altered the life trajectory of her students in any lasting way. This reaction, though, would be a mistake if one understood the context in which the research was done.

Lars Dahlstom, John Nyambe, Chuma Mayumbelo, and several others have written about the use of critical practitioner inquiry (CPI) in Namibian teacher education programs (e.g. Dahlstrom, 2006; Mayumbelo & Nyambe, 1999). CPI, which was introduced right after independence from South Africa, is aimed at shifting the preferential right of interpretation over educational practice from academics mostly in the so-called "north" to educational practitioners within Namibia. CPI in Namibia is contextualized at three different levels when it is introduced to teacher educators and student teachers: (a) a scholastic level, which examines education from a global perspective: (b) a level where policy documents within Namibia are critically examined; and (c) a level where the historical legacy of educational practices is unpacked. Doing action research to promote greater gender equity in one's classroom is important in any context, but especially in one with the historical legacy of colonialism and apartheid like Namibia.

Also, through CPI, student teachers, teachers, and teacher educators are producing studies (like the example above) that are later used as readings in teacher education courses. This alters the political economy of knowledge production in significant ways. Instead of only being the receivers of knowledge from academics in the north, Namibians educators have begun to develop their own indigenous research traditions.

The second example of student teacher action research that I think demonstrates socially just action research is actually a combination of a self-study by a teacher educator and her student teachers' participatory action research projects. I want to share this work written by Alice McIntyre (2003), a teacher educator in Massachusetts, because it is an example of action research that takes student teachers out into the communities in which their students live. McIntyre chose participatory action research as the frame for this project because of its explicit focus on "social change within communities of struggle and conflict" (p. 29). Her goal was to help her student teachers become more culturally competent, able to work successfully in urban schools, and committed to being personally engaged in social change to help create the social preconditions needed for successful public school systems.

The focus of this research was the collaboration of 11 prospective teachers, four other graduate students (13 of whom identified as white), and 24 black and Latino students who attended the same Boston area school. In the process of collaborating with the students on a participatory action research project that focused on how to get the substantial amount of trash in their neighborhood cleaned up, the prospective teachers gained new insights into the lived experiences of urban youth. They gained a deeper understanding of both the community and how urban poverty, racism, and the lack of resources for families and communities mediate students' education in pubic schools. They also uncovered and reexamined some of their own prejudices and biases about urban communities and their people. They began to more clearly see how their own privileges and biases "may have prevented them from engaging in teaching-learning experiences with students living in low income communities" (McIntyre, 2003, p. 33).

Conclusion

Now that I have presented a variety of examples of specific studies, I want to return to the question of what it means to do action research that supports the realization of a world in which there is greater justice in the kind of hostile environment for public education that I described earlier. Clearly, one part of this answer, for me, is that there is a variety of kinds of action research that make a contribution. The studies of individual teacher educators and student teachers which are initiated with, or develop along the way, explicit goals that are centered on promoting greater justice are important, even though they often do not go directly beyond the classrooms of the action researchers. Many of these studies are connected though to a community of other action researchers who interact with and challenge and inform the work of individual action researchers.

Another kind of action research that is needed in the struggle for a better world is action research by teacher educators that directly challenges the ideas and structures that are forced on teacher education by the advocates of the neoconservative and neoliberal agendas for schools and societies. Attempts by teacher educators, such as the Sonoma State University researchers, to subvert the mindless and narrowly conceived efforts of policy makers through action research are important because just working within the boundaries of our classrooms, although important, is not enough.

Today, in the U.S., I see too few efforts like these that challenge the way in which issues have been framed by policy makers. Too many teacher educators, including those who say they have social justice-oriented programs, accept the economic and technical rationality that prevails without working to open up a dialogue to reframe the debates and work to give the policy makers the data that they demand.

Like the example from Boston, studies in which action research transcends the academy and involves students and their communities need to be a part of action research in teacher education during these dangerous times. Because the attacks on teacher education are really just one part of a larger assault on public education and democracy itself, a participatory action research model is needed. Teacher educators need to collaborate with public school P–12 educators, parents, and community members in order to do research that contributes to the protection of the civil liberties and institutions which are central to democratic and just societies.

There are many opportunities for teacher educators to join with elementary and secondary school colleagues, parents, students, and community members in doing participatory action research that works against the neoliberal and neoconservative attacks on public education and democracies. For example, recently in my city, educators, students, and community members presented the school district with carefully prepared data and arguments against the school board policy of allowing the military to recruit students in Madison schools into the army. The federal education No Child Left Behind Act requires school districts to give military recruiters student contact information. If school districts do not comply, the penalty is a loss of all federal funding. One week, the protests focused on the display of military recruiting signs in the gymnasiums and stadiums where high school sporting events are held. Compliance with this type of display is not required by the law. The large signs said "Are you army ready?" and listed a phone number to call in order to enlist. The school district, which is in debt every year, in large part because of the failure of the federal government to provide the money that it is supposed to provide in order to carry out federal education mandates, received $17,000 from the military for allowing them to display the signs. At the time of writing, the school district had not agreed to take down the signs, but the discussion continued.

Another example of where teacher educators, elementary and secondary school educators, students, and community members have come together within a participatory action research framework is to challenge the underfunding of public education. We have recently seen an uplifting example in British Colombia, Canada of successful efforts to challenge the reduction of resources for public schools and teachers through careful documentation by students, parents, and educators of the impact of cuts in public school budgets. As a result of these efforts, the government restored the money to the schools that it had cut (BCTF, n.d.).

These broader efforts of participatory action research in which teacher educators join with students, teachers, and citizens to defend the integrity of public schooling and teachers' work (as well as other efforts to provide access

to affordable housing, transportation, jobs, and so on) are intimately connected to the future of teacher education. Attempts to defend college and university teacher education that are isolated from broader struggles for social
justice in schooling and the society will be seen as self-serving—we academics
do live relatively privileged lives—and will fail. The real struggle is over both
the future of the public versus private good in the U.S. and many other countries and the survival of democratic societies.

A strong and well-supported system of public education and teacher education is essential to the realization of a society in which everyone has access
to what is needed to live a life with dignity. Benjamin Barber (1997), a promi-
nent political theorist and scholar of democracy, has argued in response to the
attacks on public education in the U.S.:

> In attacking … public education, critics are attacking the very foundation
> of our democratic civic culture. Public schools are not merely schools for
> the public, but schools of publicness: institutions where we learn what it
> means to be a public and start down the road toward common national
> and civic identity. They are the forges of our citizenship and the bedrock
> of our democracy … Vilifying public school teachers and administrators
> and cutting public school budgets even as we subsidize private educa-
> tional opportunity puts us in double jeopardy: for as we put our children
> at risk, we undermine our common future, at the same moment in con-
> straining the conditions of liberty for some, we undermine the future of
> democracy for all (p. 22).

Action research by teacher educators and student teachers can play an important role in the struggles to provide access to a life with dignity for everyone's
children, but it does not necessarily do so. It is urgent that we work to better
link our (action research) efforts to implement teacher education for social
justice with the struggles of those in other spheres of society who share our
hopes for building a more just and humane world.

Chapter 7

Beyond the Divide of Teacher Research and Academic Research[1]

This chapter explores ways to bridge the separation that currently exists between the worlds of teacher research and academic research. On the one hand, many teachers currently feel that educational research conducted by those in the academy is largely irrelevant to their lives in schools. On the other hand, many academics dismiss the knowledge produced through teacher research as trivial and inconsequential to their work. I argue that our vision of educational research should include both knowledge produced by teachers and knowledge produced by those in the academy. Our vision should take the position that the processes of teacher development, school reform, and teacher education can greatly benefit from occasions when knowledge crosses the divide that currently separates teacher knowledge from academics, and academic knowledge from teachers. I discuss two specific examples that illustrate instances in which academic knowledge and teacher knowledge have improved teaching, as well as the assumptions regarding voice, power, ownership, and status which make them successful cases. One case deals with the teaching of mathematics in elementary school; the other is concerned with the teaching of language minority students. I also discuss several ways in which knowledge produced by teachers and others who work in schools can potentially benefit academic research and teacher education programs in colleges and universities.

This chapter discusses issues of power, privilege, voice, and status in educational research, as well as the need to bridge a separation that currently exists between the worlds of teacher research and academic research. Currently, we have a situation where many teachers feel that educational research conducted by those in the academy is largely irrelevant to their lives in schools. Teachers, for the most part, do not look to educational research conducted by academics to inform and improve their practice (Cookson, 1987; Doig, 1994; Gurney, 1989; Mitchell, 1985).

Conversely, many academics in colleges and universities dismiss teacher research as trivial, atheoretical, and inconsequential to their work. Most academics who are involved in the teacher research movement around the world have marginalized the process of school-based inquiry by teachers as a form of teacher development, but do not consider it as a form of knowledge production (Noffke, 1994). It is very rare, for example, to see citations of teacher-produced knowledge in the writings of academic researchers, such as in the series of Handbooks of Research on Teaching, or to see the use of teacher-generated knowledge in teacher education programs (see Zeichner, 1995). This is the case despite the fact that teacher research is easily available in many places and especially in some subject areas, such as Language Arts Education. It is also rare to see teachers being asked to give keynote addresses at educational research conferences attended mostly by university academics.

Most of the involvement of academics in the teacher research movement has been to produce academic literature about teacher research in an academic discourse (e.g. Carr & Kemmis, 1987; Kincheloe, 1991; Winter, 1987) or to produce manuals and textbooks for teachers about how to do research (e.g. Altrichter et al., 1993; Kemmis & McTaggart, 1988), and not to use the knowledge that teachers have generated through their research to inform their own work in the academy. Also, university researchers generally have not used the process of action research to study their own practices.

Whether or not academic research has ever influenced thinking and practice in schools or teacher research has ever influenced thinking and practice in the academy is not the issue. I think that it is easy to find specific examples of both cases (Clifford, 1973). For example, in U.S. schools one can clearly see the effects of the research of both Jeanine Oakes (1985) and others on the negative effects of tracking and ability grouping (e.g. Wheelock, 1992), and Bob Slavin (1983) and others on cooperative learning. The quality of the implementation of these reforms aside, there is clear evidence in at least a few cases, that research conducted by academics in colleges, universities, and research and development centers has stimulated certain reform impulses in schools. There is also evidence that the major changes in the teaching of writing that Nancy Atwell and numerous other teachers worked out through research conducted in their elementary and secondary school classrooms (e.g. Atwell, 1987) have influenced both the way in which writing is taught in colleges and universities and the way in which teacher education students are taught how to teach writing in teacher education programs.

My point is that there is a perception by both teachers and academics that their inquiries are essentially irrelevant to one another. And, despite isolated examples of instances where teacher research and academic research have crossed the borders that divide them, they have essentially been irrelevant to each other. For the most part, educational researchers ignore teachers, and teachers ignore the researchers right back (Evans et al., 1987). Despite the so-called revolution in teacher research around the world today in which there is a lot of talk about teachers as producers of knowledge (Richardson, 1994), a view of educational research that sees (a) research as an activity conducted by those outside the classroom for the benefit of those outside the classroom (Nixon, 1981) and (b) educational theory as what others with more status and prestige in the academic hierarchy have to say about them and their work (Elliott, 1991) is still dominant among classroom teachers. The political economy of knowledge production and utilization, which has accorded a high status and rewards to certain forms of knowledge production used by academics and not to others used by teachers (Carter, 1993), has even led to a situation in which teachers sometimes deny the legitimacy of their own knowledge that they have generated through school-based inquiries.

One of the main reasons for teachers' skepticism about educational research is the use of a specialized language among academics which makes sense only to members of particular subcommunities of academic researchers. On the whole, the more abstract your work, the higher your status in the academic hierarchy; the more useful and applicable to practice your work, the lower your status (Somekh, 1993). This tendency toward mystification in academic research on education is not true just of the positivist research that has been criticized in recent years by a new generation of qualitative researchers. Some of the new wave of critical, feminist, and poststructuralist educational research is also largely inaccessible to classroom teachers and most academic educational research, qualitative or quantitative, does not recognize the teacher's role in the generation of knowledge about teaching and learning (Lytle & Cochran-Smith, 1994). Many teachers can readily point to instances in which they have felt excluded from the dialogue by the language of university researchers (Carter, 1993; Doig, 1994). Because of the fact that most teachers are women, even what might be considered cutting-edge educational research within current academic circles, despite a rhetoric to the contrary, has sometimes unwittingly joined other social science research in devaluing and silencing women's perspectives on the social world (Luke, 1992).

Susan Threatt (1994), a high school social studies teacher in northern California, recently commented on her feelings of being silenced and exploited in her relations with university researchers:

> Despite my excitement at having other people to talk with—people with unique perspectives and interesting and sometimes valuable information—in some ways at this point, these relations seem to me to have a colonial flavor to them. ... It seems to me that someone else is having the discussion that we need to have for ourselves and that someone else benefits in an economy that rewards their making sense of our work (pp. 231–232).

Another reason for teachers' lack of enthusiasm for academic research on education is the frequency with which they can see themselves portrayed in the literature in an exclusively negative light. It is not uncommon for teachers to read in the academic literature about all of the atrocities that are going on in schools to ruin children and to keep the poor oppressed. Teachers have been referred to as technocrats, sexists, racists, and incompetent in their subjects and entrenched in mediocrity (Noddings, 1986). Teachers on the other hand, feel that academic researchers are largely insensitive to the complex circumstances with which they are faced in their work and frequently feel exploited by university researchers. Probably as a group, teachers are no more sexist, racist, and incompetent than academics.

Despite the persistence of an exploitative relationship between schools and academic researchers, I see a bright spot on the horizon. Specifically, that some academic researchers are becoming increasingly uncomfortable with their position of safety that comes from only studying the work of others and about being in the position of uncovering the faults of schools and teachers for their own personal gain.

Recently, a graduate student who had just finished her thesis for her master's degree came to see me. She had done an ethnographic study in a local secondary school which had uncovered all sorts of horrible activities going on in the school. She was so troubled by what she found that she felt that she could not share the findings of her study with the staff of the school. In preparing for her doctoral dissertation, she wanted to talk with me about investigating some form of educational research that does not merely exploit teachers' weaknesses for the purpose of gaining academic capital. I talked to her about the paradigms of participatory research and action research (e.g. Elliott, 1991; Parks et al., 1993) which, although not free of exploitative tendencies (Griffiths, 1990; Johnston & Proudford, 1994) are less likely to reproduce the undemocratic social relations that have dominated academic educational research to date.

In my 19 years as a university professor, I have seen many graduate student researchers (as well as some faculty researchers) go into schools primarily to expose the horrors of the educational system. What has bothered me most about these studies is not the illumination of the ways in which schools help reproduce social and economic inequalities. (What is exposed often does exist and needs to be vigorously combated.) What is most disturbing about some of these studies is the lack of honesty in the relationships between those who open their lives to academic researchers and the researchers themselves—in Nell Noddings' (1987) terms, this is the wronging of teachers as persons.

I have also been troubled by the lack of effort to actually do something to try and change the problems that are uncovered. Not only are teachers rarely engaged intellectually by researchers with the issues involved in the research projects or in the process of data analysis and interpretation, they are often told nothing at all about the findings of the research. As a classroom teacher 20 years ago in a school in close proximity to a research university, I often had the experience of letting graduate students or faculty come into my inner-city classroom to conduct their studies. Once their data were collected, I never heard from them again.

> Because the reward structures of a career in research are organized around the publication of 'findings,' many researchers heave a great sigh of relief as they mail their technical reports off to funding agencies or

receive cherished letters of acceptance from refereed journals. Often, for the career educational researcher, that work is finished and it is time to go on to another study (Florio-Ruane & Barak-Dohanich, 1984, p. 725).

Despite the fact that academia does not usually reward faculty for taking the time to deliberate with teachers about the meaning and significance of their work, some university educational researchers are doing this (sometimes with risk to their careers and reputations). Susan Florio-Ruane and JoAnn Barak-Dohanich (1984) of the Written Literacy Project in East Lansing, Michigan have proposed a very useful model for teacher and academic researcher deliberations over the findings of research conducted by academics in schools that actively involves teachers in the interpretation of research and its significance for their practice. Some university researchers are beginning to feel a moral obligation to take the time to engage in these dialogues across speech communities.

The second bright spot with regard to the usual pattern of "hit and run" educational research, which merely uses teachers as objects of study, is the growing reluctance on the part of school staff to tolerate a passive role for themselves in academic educational research. Also, they have less patience with situations in which most of the rewards go to the academic researchers. For the last several years, I have been a university representative to the external research committee of the Madison Metropolitan School District. This committee reviews and must approve all research carried out in the school district that is initiated outside of the district. This includes all studies conducted by faculty and graduate students from my university. I have seen a growing trend in this committee, which I have actively supported, to reject research proposals that do not clarify what the school district will gain from the study beyond the perfunctory submission of a written report which is then filed on a shelf to gather dust. It has often amazed me how some (quantitative as well as qualitative) researchers seem to feel that they have the right to muck around in schools (especially ones serving poor kids of color) merely for their own personal benefit, often taking time from students and teachers to fill out surveys or to participate in interviews. My colleagues in the Madison schools are starting to insist on the promise of some clear benefit to the district in proposed research. They have initiated several dialogues with researchers who frequently use the schools for their studies to discuss ways in which the district can become more actively engaged with the research issues. We are hoping to see more research proposals that include plans to involve school staff and/or parents in discussions of research data and findings, and proposals that include teachers as co-investigators who participate in analyzing data and formulating the conclusions of the research. We are also hoping to initiate discussions with academic researchers to share with them the kind of problems and issues the school district is interested in having researched.

Although I am pleased with these developments, the building of more ethical and democratic social relations among university researchers and teachers in research studies initiated by academics alone, or in collaboration with teachers, will not in itself eliminate the exploitation of teachers in educational research because, as Jim Ladwig (1991) has pointed out, "The conditions of teachers' work contribute to reinforcing a separation of teachers and their work from educational research and allow for conditions of exploitation to occur" (p. 112).

Ladwig argues that even in research projects billed as collaborative efforts between academics and teachers, the university researchers continue to gain a larger share than teachers of the cultural capital that is distributed for doing research. Ladwig calls for changes in the structure of teachers' work that will reward them for their involvement in conducting educational research, either their own action research or collaborative research with university researchers. One example that he gives of this restructuring is boosts on the pay scale for involvement in research and/or publication.

So too do the structures in universities that discourage faculty from engaging with teachers in discussions of the meaning and relevance of their research or in the labor-intensive activities of collaborative research need to be changed. While I agree that these and other similar changes are necessary to truly eliminate the exploitation of teachers by academic researchers, I also think that much can be done immediately to raise the ethical standard and level of democracy in academic research conducted in schools. Doing this, I believe, will also help increase the value of this research to schools.

Mike Atkin (1994), the former Dean at Stanford University and the University of Illinois, two of the most prestigious research institutions in the U.S., recently summarized the current condition in which academic educational research largely proceeds almost independently of what happens in schools and the world at large:

> I have come to believe that educational research as we view it today is not an enterprise that makes much of a difference on actual educational events, either in classrooms or in forums where decisions are made about the directions and workings of the educational enterprise (p. 104).

I would like to make some of the dimensions of this problem a bit more concrete by sharing two stories of events from my recent experience that highlight the tensions between academics and teachers around issues of educational knowledge production.

Story 1: What About the Faculty of Education?

Currently, I am working in a local elementary school as part of a new experimental teacher education program, "Teach for Diversity," that is designed to prepare elementary teachers for working across lines of race and social class. I am spending more time than usual in this one local elementary school, which has become a professional development school associated with our program-leading seminars with student teachers, observing and conferring with the student teachers about their teaching and action research projects, meeting with teacher study groups, and helping build new school–community linkages. As the university liaison to the school, I have a mailbox and the use of an office at the school. I attend staff meetings and sit in the teacher's room. Although I have been in and out of schools regularly as a coordinator of a school practicum for the past 19 years, being in school on a more regular basis and being perceived as more or less part of a school staff has given me a different perspective on the academy.

One August, I sat in on the first staff meeting of the school year and listened to teachers talk to each other about what they did during their summer break. A whole group of teachers from the school had been part of a science scholars program, sponsored by the Center for Biology Education at my university, in which elementary and secondary teachers spend part of a summer working in research laboratories with university scientists. The teachers then implemented what they learned in their classrooms the following year that they initiated during the summer. The teachers who participated in this program were extremely enthusiastic about their experiences and encouraged other teachers to sign up for the program the following year. As I listened to all of this excitement about teachers being involved in courses on butterflies, caterpillars, genetics, bottle biology, issues of science and racism, and so on, I could not help thinking about the lack of attention in this lengthy conversation (that included praises for other experiences, as well) to my own Faculty of Education, which is located less than two miles from the school. This situation seemed especially ironic to me because this particular school has one of the highest percentages of poor students of color in the city of Madison and has frequently been singled out by the school district and the media as a problem school because of the low standardized test scores of the pupils and problems in the surrounding community with violent crime and drugs. Despite the fact that many of my colleagues are known throughout the world for their research related to issues of equity, social justice, and schooling, these teachers, for the most part, did not feel connected to this body of scholarship (including my own). They did not see it as offering them much guidance in dealing with their daily struggles to educate all students to high academic standards.

The Faculty of Education at my university has more than once been ranked number one in the U.S. for the scholarly production of its researchers. With a few exceptions—one of which I will speak about shortly—this did not mean much in the context of this particular elementary school. Inside the walls of the academy, it is easy to get carried away with the importance of our scholarly endeavors. We often fail to acknowledge, however, that it is us and our careers, and not the world beyond, which receives most of the benefit from this work.

One possible interpretation of the situation in the elementary school that I work with is that the staff are closed minded, anti-intellectual and do not want to push themselves to think and act in new ways. Some teachers, like some professors, are undoubtedly uninterested in challenging their current ways of acting in the world. This would not be a very accurate portrayal in this situation, though, because the teachers in this school are extremely active in signing up for various school-sponsored and grassroots professional development activities, such as action research groups and university-sponsored activities like the science scholars program, where they feel they are treated as knowledgeable adults instead of empty vessels. The school has been involved in many new school district initiatives designed to increase the quality of learning for poor students of color, and several teachers have written and received grants to support innovative classroom projects. This is an intellectually alive staff that, in many ways, feels unconnected to the conversations about educational research that occur in the hallways and classrooms of my department.

In my view, something is terribly wrong when a dedicated and innovative group of teachers such as this feels so disconnected and alienated from the scholarship generated in academic educational research. They are not looking for easy answers or recipes for instruction and are willing to be intellectually challenged and stretched, but they want to be recognized for what they know and can do, which they feel is not usually the case when they interact with university researchers.

Story 2: Where are the Professors?

For the past several years, Bob Tabachnick and I, together with several colleagues from the Madison Public Schools, have organized a regional action research conference where student teachers, teachers, principals, and teacher educators who have been involved in an action research group during the year come together to share their work. During this time, we have tried very hard to entice our colleagues at the university to attend this conference to hear practitioners of teaching and teacher education present their work to one another. For each conference, despite the attendance of approximately 200 teachers and student teachers, we have been largely unsuccessful in getting our university colleagues to attend (with the exception of the graduate student teacher educators who come to present their own action research). It is relatively easy to generate a large audience when some noted university researcher passes through Madison and presents a seminar on our campus. When it comes to the voice of teachers, however, not many in my Faculty of Education have wanted to make the time to listen. Teacher research is tolerated as an interesting and less oppressive form of professional development for teachers, but few seriously treat the knowledge that teachers generate through their inquiries as educational knowledge to be analyzed and discussed.

These two stories underline one of the major problems that I see in educational research throughout the world today. Despite some of the exciting breakthroughs (i.e. both academic and teacher research in opening up possibilities for new forms of inquiry) that have occurred in recent years, teachers generally do not see much value in the scholarship of academics, and academics do not see much value in the research of teachers. The worlds of teacher research and academic research rarely intersect. Although both of these stories discuss a setting that I am familiar with, namely my own university, I think the patterns of mutual disinterest that I have described are typical for research universities and schools, at least in the U.S.

Beyond the Divide

There are many things that I think need to be done to restructure the social relations and political economy of knowledge production in educational research. Here I discuss several examples of crossing the divide between teachers and academics in educational research. Because of my location as a university researcher, and therefore part of a system that helps to maintain the exclusion of certain epistemic communities (e.g. teachers), I focus on what I think educational researchers in the academy ought to be doing. The first set of examples have to do with instances in which university researchers have gone into schools to conduct research with classroom teachers—projects which I think point us toward a new ethical standard for the conduct of academic researchers with teachers in educational research. The second set of examples describe several cases where attempts are being made to incorporate teacher-generated knowledge into universities, including into teacher education programs.

Academic Research and Academic Researchers in Schools

More often than not, knowledge presented to teachers generated through academic educational research is presented in a reified form, which does not invite teachers to engage with it intellectually. Strangely, educational research has been very uneducational. It is often simply presented as given or used as the justification for the imposition of some prescriptive program for teachers to follow. For example, despite ambitious visions for schools and teachers that have been set forth by policy makers and academics in this era of school restructuring, much of the staff development for teachers in Wisconsin and throughout the U.S. ignores what teachers already know and can do and relies primarily on the distribution of prepackaged and allegedly research-based solutions to school problems, often in the form of skill-training and at great expense, by some entrepreneur of staff development. The selling of educational solutions and gimmicks, which I have come to call "snake oil staff development," is still big business in the U.S., often consuming precious school district resources that could otherwise be used to build on and extend the expertise of teachers, supporting genuine rather than bogus staff development (Slavin, 1989; Stover, 1988).

The slogan of "research says," according to Judith Little (1993) of the University of California, has increasingly become a means for exercising institutional authority over teachers rather than for informing teachers' judgments (also see Meyers, 1986). In the two examples below, research findings, or the methodological expertise of university researchers, were used as the starting point for conversations with teachers about the ideas involved with the research and not as the final word for teachers to merely accept or reject. While these projects have not greatly altered the ways in which institutional rewards are distributed to teachers and academics for their participation in research, they have involved a more democratic environment within the research where both teachers' and academics' expertise informs the process of making schools more educative environments for all students.

Cognitively Guided Instruction in Mathematics

The first example of where I think more academic researchers in education need to be headed in their relations with teachers is a project entitled Cognitively Guided Instruction in Mathematics (CGI), directed by Elizabeth Fennema and Tom Carpenter from the University of Wisconsin-Madison (Fennema et al., 1995). This elementary school mathematics project began in the late 1980s with a series of workshops conducted with grade one teachers in local schools. Teachers' involvement with the CGI project begins with receiving information based on research by cognitive scientists in mathematics education about the development of children's thinking in well-defined mathematical domains. This research-based knowledge about how children solve particular kinds of mathematical problems provides teachers with a structured body of knowledge that enables them to conduct ongoing assessments of their students. Unlike most staff development programs in the U.S., CGI does not provide specific curriculum materials or instructional activities for teachers to use. Teachers, who are treated as thoughtful professionals, are given the opportunity to decide how to relate the knowledge on student learning to what they already know about teaching and figure out how to make use of it in their classrooms. The academic researchers then study with teachers how the teachers use the research information. A pedagogy of CGI instruction emerges from teachers' collaborative action research on their use of the research findings. This action research includes the testing of the claims made by the academic researchers about student learning in a wide variety of classroom and school contexts.

Unlike other staff development programs in the U.S., which have merely put teachers in touch with the findings of academic research, which teachers often detest, the CGI project has become enormously popular among teachers in Madison area elementary schools, including those in the school in which I work. The program has also spread to teachers across the U.S. Today, several hundred teachers in Wisconsin, California, New York, Texas, and Washington, DC are engaged in conducting action research on CGI. I think that the key reason for the success of this program, aside from the academic accomplishments by children in CGI classrooms that have been documented in numerous case studies and experimental research (e.g. Carpenter & Fennema, 1992), is the respect for teachers and their knowledge that is part of the program. When working with educational researchers from the university, CGI teachers mostly feel that what they know and can do is recognized and respected, and that the academic researchers are interested in learning how teachers make use of their research. This is an experience of ownership and dignity that is vastly different from most of teachers' experiences in organized staff development activities.

Documenting Funds of Knowledge in the Community

The second example of a research program that I think illustrates how both teacher knowledge and academic knowledge can inform efforts to improve schooling is a project, directed by Luis Moll at the University of Arizona, which has sought to develop innovations in teaching that draw upon the knowledge and skills found in local households in Mexican-American communities in Tucson (e.g. Moll et al., 1992). The assumption by Moll and his colleagues (1992) is that "By capitalizing on household and other community resources, we can organize classroom instruction that far exceeds in quality the rote like instruction these children commonly encounter in school" (p. 132). They argue that mobilizing funds of knowledge in the community for classroom instruction represents a positive and more realistic view of households as containing many cultural and cognitive resources with great potential utility for classroom instruction. This view contrasts sharply with the prevailing view of working-class families as somehow socially disorganized and intellectually deficient.

Moll and his colleagues have developed a research approach that is based on understanding households and classrooms qualitatively, using a combination of ethnographic observations, open-ended interviewing strategies, life histories, and case studies that, when combined analytically, can portray the complex functions of households within their sociohistorical contexts.

The research project consists of workshops for teachers in the conduct of qualitative research (e.g. methods of observing, interviewing, writing field notes, and managing and analyzing data). Following these workshops, teachers and educational anthropologists go together into the homes of the teachers' students and conduct ethnographic analyses of household dynamics. They seek to understand the funds of knowledge which exist in the community, and how household members develop social networks to use this knowledge. According to Moll and his colleagues (1992), funds of knowledge are "Historically accumulated and culturally developed bodies of knowledge and skills essential for household and individual functioning and wellbeing" (p. 33).

In the particular Mexican-American community that Moll and the teachers have studied, funds of knowledge include such things as knowledge of farming, carpentry, construction, herbal medicine, child care, midwifery, and cooking. Following the documentation of the funds of knowledge in the community, teachers and academic researchers meet together in after school study groups to discuss the funds of knowledge in relation to classroom practices and figure out how to mobilize this knowledge for classroom instruction—how to develop ethnographically-informed classroom practices. Moll and his colleagues, including the co-researching teachers, have presented several case studies of how teachers have developed classroom practices that use the knowledge gained in the community. These case studies include asking students to write about topics in community living (e.g. construction), developing theme studies based on activities in the community (e.g. the making of candy), and using parents to share their expertise in instructional situations (Moll, 1992; Moll et al., 1992; Moll & Greenberg, 1990).

In this research project, using Moll's language, there is an exchange of funds of knowledge between academic researchers and teachers. The academics provide teachers with knowledge about research methods, including assistance with the analysis and interpretation of data, and the teachers provide researchers with expertise about the school context, curriculum, and instruction. Access to information is facilitated by the fact that the teachers have special status in this community, and in some cases only the teachers have had knowledge of Spanish, which is the language of many of the parents.

Here, as in the CGI Mathematics project, teachers and academic researchers come together as colleagues in genuine mutuality. There is not absolute equality since the teachers and researchers bring different funds of knowledge to the collaboration, but there is a parity in the relationships; each side recognizes and respects the contribution of the other. In both cases, teacher knowledge and academic knowledge have informed the process of school reform. Most importantly, both projects have been able to document learning among children that many think is not possible for children of the poor.

Collaborative Research

Not all collaborative research projects involving teachers and academics have involved the kind of genuine mutual respect for teachers that is present in these two projects. This is sometimes due to the inability of individuals to break away from old patterns of hierarchy, and sometimes because of the circumstances of collaborative research (Feldman, 1993; Meyer-Reimer & Bruce, 1994; Oakes et al., 1986). Some so-called collaborative research projects still leave teachers in the position of second-class citizens (in a caste system) who participate under ground rules set mainly by supposed academic "experts." This is not surprising since most of the experience that teachers and university researchers have had in relating to each other has been as professors and students. Teachers, who are frequently conditioned by their experience of being relatively powerless in both the hierarchical structure of schooling and as students in the academy, often defer to academics, some-times even in matters where the teachers might have more expertise (Meyer-Reimer & Bruce, 1994). It is not easy to give up old patterns (Gitlin et al., 1992). It is also not surprising, given the real pressures on academics (but not on teachers) to not only publish, but to stand on new ground, distinguishing themselves from their colleagues (Ladwig & Gore, 1994). This aspect of the work context of university researchers encourages academic entrepreneur-ship and the silencing of teachers, even in supposedly collaborative ventures. I think that we need to look very closely at the specific character and quality of research collaborations in order to determine if there is really any change from the usual pattern of dominance by academics. Collaborative research is one important way to cross the divide between academics and teachers, but not just any collaborative research will do so.

Teacher Research and Teachers in the Academy

For academic researchers, the other side of bridging the divide between teacher and academic research is to treat the products of teacher-initiated inquiry seriously as educational knowledge within the academy. Susan Lytle and Marilyn Cochran-Smith of the University of Pennsylvania have recently argued about the need for a different epistemology in educational research that regards inquiry by teachers as a distinctive and important way of know-ing about teaching (Cochran-Smith & Lytle, 1993). They argue that teachers are uniquely positioned to provide a truly insider or emic perspective on teaching that is not possible for others to gain. Whether or not we want to recognize it, there is a tremendous amount of inquiry that has been conducted by teachers on their own practices throughout the world in the last decade. This research, while often receiving facilitative support from university researchers, is not collaborative research with academic researchers; it is research of another genre.

In March, 1994, I attended a meeting in Washington, DC that was organ-ized by the U.S. Department of Education. It was a meeting of people who are actively involved in coordinating groups in the teacher research movement in the U.S. Out of the 80 or so participants, there were only 13 university aca-demics. I came away from this three-day meeting genuinely amazed at how much activity there is in teacher research across the U.S. Most of the teacher research is never publicized beyond local sites and takes place with little or no university involvement. Several new national journals of teacher research have just been initiated,[2] and the U.S. Department of Education, as well as several major educational foundations, are making plans to invest in a sub-stantial way in teacher inquiry. When I talk about the world of teacher research, I am speaking about a very strong and rapidly growing community in which teachers are the dominant actors.

Several years ago, at a meeting of the American Educational Research Association in Boston, Jennifer Gore presented a paper that she and I wrote about facilitating action research by student teachers in the Wisconsin elementary teacher education program (Gore & Zeichner, 1991). During the session, Bridget Somekh, the coordinator of CARN in the UK, raised a question about the degree to which we were making use of the knowledge that was produced each semester by our student teachers. While we frequently used our students' action research studies as examples of research by student teachers, we had done very little to utilize the knowledge that was generated in these studies.

My awareness of this contradiction bothered me a great deal. I began to ask more questions about the degree to which my other courses (most of which engaged my students in action research) incorporated the voices and perspectives of teachers. In my examination, I found that, despite the fact that the readings in my courses were mostly positively oriented toward teacher research and reflective practice and challenged the hegemony of academic researchers over the production of educational knowledge, the voices in the readings were mainly those of academics, not teachers. Despite my expressed commitment to teacher research, my actual practice undermined my intended message to my students. Were my students really learning about the role of teachers as knowledge producers if they were never assigned to read things written by teachers?

Since this revelation about the shortsightedness of my commitment to action research by teachers, I have been working very hard to figure out how to make teacher knowledge a more central part of both my teaching of graduate courses and my work in teacher education. This has included both trying to achieve more of a balance in the readings in my courses between teachers' and academics' voices and attempting to organize and make more accessible the large number of action research studies that have been completed in the last decade by teachers in the Madison Area Action Research Network. The Madison Area Action Research Network project includes the development by Robin Marion, a Wisconsin graduate student, of a set of research abstracts and a local database that will enable people to order copies of particular studies or studies done on specific topics, video records of teachers talking about their research, plans for a cable television show on action research (which includes a teacher talking about her research each week), and the facilitation of interested teachers' efforts to publish their work in one of the new journals of teacher research.

In our teacher education program we have tried to make more use of the publications of teachers in our curriculum. For example, in the student teaching portion of the program with which I am associated, we have frequently asked students to read texts produced by a group of teachers in Milwaukee, Wisconsin. Through a quarterly newspaper, *Rethinking Schools*, and several special topic publications (e.g. Bigelow et al., 1991, 1994), this group of teachers has both raised critical perspectives about many school practices, such as ability grouping, standardized testing, monocultural curriculum materials, the dumbing down of instruction for poor students of color, and included the voices of teachers, students, and parents from many cultural and economic backgrounds. We have also initiated a teacher lecture series in which a P–12 teacher comes to the university to give a series of talks to prospective teachers and the rest of the university community each semester. The first lecture on the challenges of teaching in urban schools was given in February, 1994 by Rita Tenorio, a kindergarten teacher in Milwaukee and one of the editors of *Rethinking Schools*.

Another fascinating project along these lines is an attempt in Philadelphia by Fred Erickson of the University of Pennsylvania and a group of Philadelphia teachers to develop archives of the work of teachers in urban schools using hypermedia. These archives include such materials as video-tapes of teaching episodes, interviews with teachers, students, and parents, excerpts from teachers' journals, and samples of student work. All of these materials are designed to create and deepen conversations about how and why teachers do what they do. This group of researchers is particularly con-cerned about documenting teaching practices that many people think are not possible in inner-city schools like those in Philadelphia. This project goes far beyond my modest attempts to develop better access to the written products of teachers' research and brief video interviews and has much potential for bringing teacher knowledge into teacher education programs for discussion and analysis.

These attempts to use the products of teacher research within the academy should not be interpreted as an uncritical glorification of teacher knowledge. Uncritical glorification of knowledge generated through teacher research is condescending toward teachers and disrespectful of the genuine contribution they can make both to the improvement of their own individual practice and to the greater social good. Just as academic research can further practices in schooling and society which are undemocratic and in some cases morally rep-rehensible, so too can teacher research strengthen and legitimate practices that are harmful to students. For example, the recent book *The Bell Curve*, which argues under the guise of science that the poor in the U.S. are poor because they are stupid and that African-Americans are genetically inferior to whites (Herrnstein & Murray, 1994), is an example of how bad and morally corrupt academic research can become.

There is good teacher research and bad teacher research, just as there is good and bad academic research. For example, "At worst, teacher research might reduce itself to an uncritical documentation of a teacher's prefer-ences—a selective gathering of evidence to support a preconceived end" (Bissex, 1987, p. 16).

There is a great deal of work going on in the U.S. right now among teacher researchers to try to work out criteria that can be used to fund and publish the inquiries of teachers. Because teacher inquiry is often very different than academic research, these criteria will not necessarily be the same as those used in the academy. When I select teacher research for use in my teacher educa-tion program, in addition to the quality of the work itself (e.g. whether it is clearly presented, truly problematizes an issue, uses evidence to support conclusions, etc.), I also look for teacher knowledge that expresses particular points of view.

The overall goal of my teacher education program is to educate teachers to be thoughtful and reflective practitioners who are committed to educating all students to the same high standards. We want to engage our students in deliberation about different perspectives on a wide variety of educational issues in relation to their own practice (see Liston & Zeichner, 1991). Some of the teacher research studies that we read in my graduate seminar on action research, in which we study the epistemological dimensions of teacher research, have raised important issues related to teaching about AIDS and issues of sexuality in the classroom, dealing with racism and sexism in the classroom, teaching language minority students, multiculturalizing the curriculum, and so on. I continue to select readings and learning experiences that expose my students to a variety of perspectives on issues (including perspectives and issues often excluded from U.S. teacher education programs), but I have broadened the base from which I draw these readings to include teacher-initiated inquiries. (Incidentally, "teacher-initiated inquiries" is the term now used for action research in some places in the U.S. because of teachers' opposition to the term "action research").

Conclusion

First, my arguments for a greater interaction between teacher and academic voices in the conduct of educational research, a greater role for teachers in educational decision making, and a higher ethical standard among university researchers in their dealings with schools and in their respect for teacher knowledge, do not reflect a purely instrumental view of the purpose of educational research (i.e. that all research needs to be directly and immediately applicable to school practice). This is an overly narrow view of educational research that is bound to stifle creative thought and to limit our vision. There is a place for scholarship in education that is unrestrained by the demands and pressures of practical utility.

Second, my arguments do not represent support for the policies of economic rationalism that have recently been implemented by governments in Australia and elsewhere (Bartlett et al., 1992; Gilroy, 1992). Such policies have undermined the important role of colleges and universities in teacher education and educational research.

Third, my arguments do not represent a retreat from my belief about the need for educational researchers to acknowledge the partisan nature of all research (Lindbloom & Cohen, 1979) and use their research to further the realization of the goals of an education in a democratic society, which are to promote access to decent and rewarding lives for all students.

In a recent book called *Power and Method: Political Activism in Educational Research*, Andrew Gitlin argues:

That the whole enterprise of educational research both qualitative and quantitative needs to be reconceptualized so that it can more powerfully act on some of the most persistent and important problems of our schools, namely those surrounding issues of race, class, and gender (p. 2).

While I agree with this goal and reject the idea of neutral and impartial educational research—even if we claim to be neutral, other people will use the results of our research in partisan ways—I do not think that it will be achieved by academics exclusively talking among ourselves at educational conferences. Only one of the 16 authors in Gitlin's book is a classroom teacher and the language used in the book is not conducive to dialogue across speech communities. In this chapter, I have argued that I think that we need to cross the boundaries that divide the worlds of teachers and academic researchers in three ways: (a) by engaging with school staff in open discussions about the meaning and significance of the research we conduct ourselves; (b) by engaging in genuine collaborations with teachers in research where old patterns of dominance by academics are really broken; and (c) by supporting teacher-initiated inquiry or teacher action research by taking the knowledge that is produced through this work seriously.

It is critical that the institutional rules that govern the careers of academic researchers be altered to support the above changes. We must figure out ways, as some are trying to today (Lawson, 1990), to both reward university researchers for spending the time with teachers that is needed to develop a common language and shared meanings about research (Duffy, 1994) and encourage the kinds of genuine collaborations that I have tried to illustrate with my examples.

Until these structural changes occur, it will take a great deal of courage for academics to operate in these ways. It will also take courage for academics to begin to openly integrate the products of teacher-initiated inquiries into their teaching, including into their teacher education programs. In many research universities, the closer that one is associated with teachers and schools, the lower one's status; the lower one's status, the fewer resources that are available to support one's research and practice. This has been an enduring problem for teacher educators in many countries. The idea of treating knowledge produced by teachers through their research seriously as educational knowledge to be analyzed and discussed is an idea that will offend many, and there are real consequences in the academy that are associated with spending a lot of time with teachers under the conditions I have suggested.

Teachers and academics are currently isolated from each other and, in some countries, both academics and teachers have been subjected to reactionary government policies that undermine the goals of equity and social justice and ignore discussion, debate, and research evidence of any kind (Gipps, 1993). Given these conditions, we must have the courage to take risks and form new alliances with teachers. Unless we begin to make the kinds of changes that I have suggested (e.g. to begin to establish dialogues about our research with teachers, form genuine research collaborations with teachers, treat teacher knowledge more seriously and with more respect, etc.), academic educational research will continue to be ignored by teachers and by policy makers. I believe that those of us within the academy have an important contribution to make to the production of educational knowledge that informs school reform efforts and the professional development of teachers, but we will only be able to make it if we pursue and develop our common interest with teachers. I hope that we begin to mend our ways and institutions before it is too late.

Chapter 8

Connecting Genuine Teacher Development to the Struggle for Social Justice[1]

This chapter discusses two issues that continue to undermine the authenticity and social value of efforts to promote teacher development. First, it is argued that underneath the rhetoric of many current efforts to empower teachers to take control of their own professional development is a reality in which teachers remain extremely limited in the scope of their power to influence the conditions of their work. Second, it is argued that even when efforts to promote teacher development are not illusory, teacher development often becomes an end itself, unconnected to broader questions about education in a democratic society. I argue for efforts to promote teacher development that are both genuine and connected to the promotion of equity and social justice.

Introduction

This chapter addresses some of my hopes and concerns about the so-called "second wave" of educational reform, which has stressed the need to improve schooling by improving the status, power, and working conditions of teachers in North America. This emphasis on teachers as the most important actors in educational reform has come after belated recognition, by at least some educational reformers and administrators, of the futility of attempting to improve school primarily through greater external prescription of school processes and outcomes.

For the last 25 years, I have worked hard as an elementary school teacher, teacher center director, and university teacher educator, either preparing student teachers to be active agents in their own professional development and the direction of schools or in supporting the efforts of teachers who were already engaged in doing so. It would be very easy for me to spend all of this chapter either delineating the numerous reasons why we should make teacher development, teacher learning, and teacher empowerment absolute priorities in our efforts to improve schooling for everybody's children or describing some of the exemplary schools where this is now a reality.

It is still important to do this. Even today, with all of the talk of teacher empowerment and teacher development, we see a general disregard for the craft knowledge of good teachers in the educational research establishment, which has attempted to articulate a knowledge base for teaching, minus the voices of teachers (Grimmett & Mackinnon, 1992; Lytle & Cochran-Smith, 1990). For example, in the most recent edition of the American Educational Research Association's *Handbook of Research on Teaching* (Wittrock, 1986), which is supposed to be a compilation of our current knowledge about teaching, there are 35 chapters and over a thousand pages on various aspects of teaching, including teaching mathematics, social studies, classroom organization and management, teaching bilingual learners, and so on. Not a single chapter is authored by a classroom teacher, and there are few, if any, references to anything written by a classroom teacher. The same is true of the recent American Association of Colleges for Teacher Education compilation of a *Knowledge Base for the Beginning Teacher* (Reynolds, 1989) and most other books of its kind that are under the editorial control of university academics. As Lytle and Cochran-Smith (1990) of the University of Pennsylvania have put it,

> Conspicuous by their absence from the literature of research on teaching are the voices of teachers, the questions and problems they pose, the frameworks they use to interpret and improve their practice, and the ways they define and understand their work lives (p. 83).

There is a lot of rhetoric in the professional literature about the importance of (a) improving the working conditions of teachers, (b) supporting their efforts to play more meaningful roles in determining the content and contexts of their work, and (c) building collaborative professional environments within schools (e.g. Lieberman, 1988, 1990). Despite this rhetoric, we see efforts (often under the banner of teacher development) that maintain the teacher's subservient position to those who are removed from the classroom with regard to the core aspects of their work, curriculum and instruction. Such efforts deny them any say about the contextual conditions of their work which greatly influence their actions in the classroom (e.g. their time and resources).[2]

For example, much of the staff development in Wisconsin school districts and elsewhere across the U.S. ignores the knowledge and expertise that teachers bring to the sessions. Most of this staff development primarily relies on the distribution of prepackaged (and often expensive) research solutions to school problems by some entrepreneur of staff development, who is often a former university academic or school administrator. The selling of educational solutions and gimmicks is big business today in the U.S. The purchase of such products often consumes school districts' precious resources that could otherwise be used to tap into the expertise of their own staff and support genuine, rather than bogus, teacher development (Slavin, 1989; Stover, 1988).

I do not want to minimize the importance of continuing to struggle in support of teachers' efforts to gain more control of their work, and to make schools places where teacher learning is valued as much as student learning. Despite the importance of these efforts however, I want to focus here instead on some aspects of the teacher development and school restructuring movement that trouble me, even as I continue to do all that I can to serve it. These are aspects of the teacher development movement that I rarely see discussed in literature or at professional conferences. They raise difficult questions that are often uncomfortable for us to face. However, it is important that we think about such questions because they continue to undermine the authenticity and social value of efforts to facilitate teacher development.

I want to focus on two specific issues in this chapter. First, I argue that underneath the rhetoric of many efforts to empower teachers to take more control over their own professional development, teachers often remain under tight control and are limited in the scope of their power to influence the conditions of their work. In other words, not all that we see going on today under the banners of teacher empowerment and teacher development is actually empowering or developing in its effects. I discuss the case of reflective teaching and the reflective practitioner to illustrate my concerns about bogus teacher development.

Second, even when teacher development is a real concern and not a charade, I become concerned when teacher development and teacher empowerment become ends in themselves, unconnected to any broader purposes or questions of equity and social justice. In its extreme form, we see a glorification of anything that a teacher does or says and an outright rejection of anything that is initiated outside of the immediate context of teachers' classrooms. The issue is often who is speaking through their actions or words and not what they are saying.

One example of this in the literature on reflective inquiry in teacher education is the frequent assumption that teaching is necessarily better merely because teachers are more deliberate and intentional about their actions. This view ignores the fact that greater intentionality may help, in some cases, to further solidify and justify teaching practices that are harmful to students. One consequence of this extreme reaction to oppressive forms of staff development and educational reform is that questions related to the broader purpose of education in a democratic society sometimes get lost. Specific aspects of the teacher research movement are discussed to illustrate my concerns.

Reflective Teaching and the Illusion of Teacher Development

Let us examine the problem of efforts to foster teacher development which are illusory. In the last decade, the terms reflective practitioner and reflective teaching have become slogans for reform in teaching and teacher education all over the world. In addition to efforts in North America to make reflective inquiry the central component of teacher education program reforms, we can see similar efforts in such countries as the UK, Australia, Norway, the

Netherlands, Spain, Thailand, and Singapore (Zeichner, 1994). Amid all this activity by educational researchers and teacher educators, there has been a great deal of confusion about what is meant in particular cases by the term reflection. It has come to the point now, where the whole range of beliefs within the education community about teaching, learning, schooling, and social order have become incorporated into the discourse about reflective teaching practice, and the use of the term by itself has become virtually meaningless. I agree with Calderhead (1989) of the UK who says:

> Terms such as reflective practice, inquiry-oriented teacher education, reflection-in-action, teacher as researcher, teacher as decision maker, teacher as professional, and teacher as problem solver, all encompass some notion of reflection in the process of professional development, but at the same time disguise a vast number of conceptual variations with a range of implications for the design and organization of teacher education courses (p. 43).

On the surface, the international movement that has developed in teaching and teacher education under the banner of reflection can be seen as a reaction against a view of teachers as technicians who merely carry out what others, outside the classroom, want them to do. This can be seen as a rejection of top–down forms of educational reform that involve teachers merely as passive participants. It involves a recognition that teachers are professionals who must play active roles in formulating the purposes and ends of their work as well as the means. Reflection also signifies a recognition that the generation of knowledge about good teaching and good schools is not the exclusive property of universities and research and development centers. It signifies a recognition that teachers also have theories too that can contribute to a knowledge base for teaching. Although there is the danger that these sentiments could lead to unthinking rejection of university-generated knowledge—and I think that would be as big a mistake as the dismissal of teacher knowledge—there is a clear recognition that we cannot rely on university-generated knowledge alone for school improvement.

From the perspective of the individual teacher, it means that the process of understanding and improving one's own teaching must start from reflection upon one's own experience. As Winter (1987) of the UK has argued, the sort of wisdom derived entirely from the experience of others (even other teachers) "is at best impoverished, and at worst illusory" (p. vii). Reflection as a slogan also signifies a recognition that learning to teach is a process that continues throughout a teacher's entire career. It involves a recognition that no matter what we do in our teacher education programs, and no matter how well we do them, at best, we can only prepare teachers to begin teaching. During their initial training, there is commitment by teacher educators to help prospective teachers internalize the disposition and skill to study their teaching and become better at teaching over time. This is a commitment to help teachers take responsibility for their own professional development.

Despite all of this rhetoric about the values and commitments associated with the reflective inquiry movement in teaching and teacher education, we get a very different picture when we look more closely at the ways in which the concepts of reflection and the reflective practitioner have been employed in teacher education programs.

Over the last few years, I have been conducting a systematic analysis of the ways in which these concepts have been used by teacher educators in the U.S. I have examined the writings of teacher educators who say that reflective inquiry is a central force in their preservice teacher preparation programs. I have also attended several conferences where these programs have been described. I have also examined a number of the curriculum materials that have been designed to assist teacher educators in encouraging reflective teaching practice by their students, such as the materials on reflective teaching developed at Ohio State University.[3]

As a result of both analyzing all of this material and having discussions with teacher educators from across the U.S., I have come to the conclusion that the ways in which the concepts of reflection and the reflective practitioner have come to be used in U.S. teacher education programs have frequently done very little to foster genuine teacher development. Instead, an illusion of teacher development that maintains, in more subtle ways, the subservient position of the teacher is created. There are four characteristics of the way in which the concept of reflection has been employed in preservice teacher education that undermine the expressed emancipatory intent of teacher educators.

First, one of the most common uses of the concept involves helping teachers reflect on their teaching with the primary aim of better replicating in their practice that which university sponsored empirical research has found to be effective. Sometimes the creative intelligence of the teacher is allowed to intervene to determine the situational appropriateness of employing particular strategies, but more often not. Grimmett et al. (1990) refer to this perspective as one in which reflection serves merely as the instrumental mediator of action. It clearly falls within the social efficiency tradition of reform in teaching and teacher education (see Liston & Zeichner, 1991) in which the source of knowledge for reflection is external to the practice being studied. What is absent from this very prevalent conception of reflective teaching practice is any sense of how the practical theories that reside in the practices of teachers—knowledge in action if you will—are to contribute to the knowledge base for teaching.

Ironically, despite Schon's very articulate rejection of this technical rationality in his presentation of the case for an epistemology of practice in several very influential books (Schon, 1983, 1987, 1991), theory is still seen by many to reside exclusively within universities, and practice is still seen to reside only within elementary and secondary schools. The problem is still wrongly cast by many as merely one of translating or applying the theories of the universities to classroom practice. The facts that (a) theories are always produced through practices and that (b) practices always reflect particular theoretical commitments either are not grasped or are deliberately ignored.

There are many instances of this in contemporary teacher education programs. I refer to just one example here, the definition of a reflective teacher in the graduate teacher education program at the University of Maryland, a program which bills itself as one of the cutting-edge reflective inquiry programs. According to a recent description of the program by faculty (McCaleb et al., 1992),

> a reflective teacher is a teacher who has command of the knowledge base for teaching. This teacher can: explain the core ideas emanating from the knowledge base and cite appropriate best practices associated with them; cite key pieces of research associated with the knowledge base and provide thoughtful critique of the research; execute effectively (at a novice level) selected best practices which grow out of the research in simulated and laboratory settings and in real classrooms and engage in critical reflection and intellectual dialogue about the knowledge base and understand how the various ideas are connected and how they interact to inform (situationally) a particular teaching/school event or episode ... (pp. 57–58).

The definition goes on, but I think the emphasis is clear. Although here, and in many other similar programs, we see language that emphasizes the empowering effects of reflecting upon an externally generated knowledge base of teaching and a clear message to teachers that they should engage in thoughtful and critical use of the research by engaging in problem solving, decision making, critical analysis, and so on, the fact is that this conception of reflective practice denies teachers the use of the wisdom and expertise embedded in their own practices and the practices of their colleagues. They are merely to fine tune and/or adapt knowledge that was formulated elsewhere, by someone unfamiliar with the teachers' particular situations. The relationship between theory and practice is seen as one-way instead of dialogic. In a dialogic relationship, theory and practice inform each other.[4]

Second and closely related to this persistence of technical rationality under the banner of reflective teaching is limiting the reflective process to considering teaching skills and strategies (i.e. the means of instruction), and excluding from the teacher's purview defining the ends of teaching (i.e. its ethical and philosophical dimensions). Here again, teachers are denied the opportunity to do anything other than fine tune and adjust the means for accomplishing ends determined by others. Teaching becomes merely a technical activity. Important questions (e.g. what should be taught to whom and why) that relate to values are defined independently and relegated to others removed from the classroom. This instrumental conception of reflective practice, which officially limits teachers to carrying out the values of others, ignores the inherent ethical quality of reflective teaching practice. Elliott (1991) of the University of East Anglia has articulated very clearly how it is impossible to define in a final way the ends of instruction prior to and independent of teaching practice and why, if one is truly concerned about teacher development, one must reject the kind of means-end thinking that limits teachers to technical concerns.

> Improving practice ... necessarily involves a continuing process of reflection on the part of practitioners. This is partly because what constitutes an appropriate realization of value is very context bound. It has to be judged afresh in particular circumstances. General rules (e.g., curriculum outlines) are guides to reflection distilled from experience and not substitutes for it. What constitutes an appropriate realization of a value is ultimately a matter of personal judgment in particular circumstances. But since personal judgments are in principle infinitely contestable, practitioners who sincerely want to improve their practice are also under an obligation to reflect continuously about them in situ. Values are infinitely open to reinterpretation through reflective practice; they cannot be defined in terms of fixed and unchanging benchmarks against which to measure improvements in practice. The reflective practitioner's understanding of the values she attempts to realize in practice are continually transformed in the process of reflecting about such attempts ... Thus values as ends cannot be clearly defined independently of and prior to practice. In this context, the practice itself constitutes an interpretation of its ends in a particular practical situation. The ends are defined in the practice and not in advance of it (pp. 50–51).

One of the clearest examples of limiting teachers to instrumental reasoning while claiming to liberate them can be found in the so-called "reflective teaching" materials developed at Ohio State University and disseminated throughout the world by the U.S. Association of Teacher Educators and Phi Delta Kappan (Cruickshank, 1987).[5] On the one hand, these materials speak very eloquently about the empowerment of teachers through reflective teaching:

> The point is that teachers who study teaching deliberately and become students of teaching can develop life-long assurance that they know what they are doing, why they are doing it, and what will happen as a result of what they do. Foremost, they can learn to behave according to reason. To lack reason is to be a slave to chance, irrationality, self interest, and superstition (Cruickshank, 1987, p. 34).

On the other hand, when teachers use these materials in teacher education programs, the content of what is to be taught is provided to student teachers in 36 reflective teaching lessons, 32 of which it is actually claimed are "content-free." Not surprisingly, what results from this structure and the discussion questions that are provided with the materials is a lot of thinking about and discussing teaching techniques and strategies divorced from ethical questions related to what is being taught.

A third aspect of the recent proliferation of the teacher education literature and programs with material related to reflective teaching is a clear emphasis on focusing teachers' reflections inwardly at their own teaching and/or on their students, to the neglect of any consideration of the social conditions of schooling that influence the teacher's work within the classroom. This individualist bias makes it less likely that teachers will be able to confront and transform those structural aspects of their work that hinder the accomplishment of their educational mission. The context of the teacher's work is to be taken as a given and unproblematic. Now, while teachers' primary concerns understandably lie within the classroom and with their students, it is unwise to restrict their attention to these concerns alone. As Scheffler (1968) has argued:

> Teachers cannot restrict their attention to the classroom alone, leaving the larger setting and the purposes of schooling to be determined by others. They must take active responsibility for the goals to which they are committed and for the social setting in which these goals may prosper. If they are not to be mere agents of others, of the state, of the military, of the media, of the experts and bureaucrats, they need to determine their own agency through a critical and continual evaluation of the purposes, the consequences, and the social context of their calling (p. 11).[6]

We must be careful here that teachers' involvement in matters beyond the boundaries of their own classrooms does not make excessive demands on their time, energy, and expertise, diverting their attention from their core mission with students. In some circumstances, creating more opportunities for teachers to participate in schoolwide decisions related to curriculum, instruction, staffing, budgeting, and so forth can intensify their work beyond the bounds of reasonableness, making it more difficult for them to accomplish their primary task of educating students (see Zeichner, 1991a). It does not have to be this way, of course, but it can be, unless efforts are made to incorporate their participation in schoolwide decision making into their work, rather than adding it.

A fourth and closely related aspect of much of the material in the reflective teaching movement in preservice teacher education is the focus on facilitating reflection by individual teachers who are to think by themselves about their work. There is very little sense in a lot of the discourse on reflective teaching of reflection as a social practice, where groups of teachers can support and sustain each other's growth. The definition of teacher development as an activity to be pursued by individual teachers greatly limits the potential for teacher growth. The challenge and support gained through social interaction is important in helping us clarify what we believe and gain the courage to pursue our beliefs.

One consequence of this isolation of individual teachers and of the lack of attention to the social context of teaching in teacher development is that teachers come to see their problems as their own and unrelated to those of other teachers or to the structure of schools and school systems. Thus, we have seen the emergence of such terms as teacher burnout and teacher stress, which direct the attention of teachers away from a critical analysis of schools as institutions to a preoccupation with their own individual failures. If we are to have genuine teacher development in which teachers are truly empowered, then we must turn away from this individual approach and heed the advice of those like the teachers who were members of the Boston Women Teachers Group in the 1980s. (This was a group of teachers who conducted their own research related to the institutional aspects of teachers' work.) These teachers argued that:

> Teachers must now begin to turn the investigation of schools away from scapegoating individual teachers, students, parents, and administrators toward a system wide approach. Teachers must recognize how the structure of schools controls their work and deeply affects their relationships with their fellow teachers, their students, and their students' families. Teachers must feel free to express these insights and publicly voice their concerns. Only with this knowledge can they grow into wisdom and help others to grow (Freedman et al., 1983, p. 99).

A statement by one of the 25 elementary teachers who was interviewed in their research illustrates how concern for the institutional context of schooling can serve to strengthen teachers' commitment to their educational mission. The comments refer to a discussion about the attempts of a school district to reduce teaching positions.

> Probably for the first time in my school we have not talked specifically about the kids and subject matter and school problems. We've been talking about political things and how it affects our personal life too. I think it's taught me a lesson that you cannot hide your head in the sand. I'm not just fighting for me either. Yeah I'm fighting for my job, but I'm also fighting for the kids too. I think it's going to help my awareness of things and help me maybe stick through it a little bit. That I'm not alone in this and I've got other people to talk with and see how it's going to affect other people. I think it has already made me mentally, and in action, make more of a commitment to my work (Freedman et al., 1983, p. 299).

In summary, when we examine the ways in which concepts of reflection and reflective practitioner have recently been integrated into preservice teacher education programs—at least in the U.S., but I suspect to some extent in other countries as well—we find four themes that undermine the potential for genuine teacher development: (a) a focus on helping teachers better replicate practices suggested by research conducted by others and a neglect of the theories and expertise embedded in their own and other teachers' practices; (b) a means–end thinking which limits the substance of teachers' reflections to technical questions of teaching techniques and internal classroom organization and a neglect of questions of curriculum; (c) a facilitation of teachers' reflections about their own teaching while ignoring the social and institutional context in which the teaching takes place; and (d) an emphasis on helping teachers reflect individually. All of these practices help create a situation in which there is merely the illusion of teacher development.

Teacher Development and Social Justice

Ironically, another general concern has to do with those situations where these four characteristics are not present. There are clearly many conceptions of reflective teaching and teacher development other than those I have been describing thus far, even though what I have been discussing is still very prevalent in preservice teacher education programs in the U.S. A so-called "second wave" of educational reform has swept across North America in the last several years and has transcended the limitations of what I have been describing. This recent aspect of the reform movement, while coming in the U.S. according to Darling-Hammond and Berry (1988), at the expense of greater regulations of teacher education programs and more detailed teacher certification laws, has clearly focused on genuine and not bogus teacher development. During the last few years, the professional literature and popular press have been flooded with calls for the empowerment of teachers to (a) participate in a more central way in the determination of school goals and policies and (b) exercise their professional judgment about both the content of the curriculum and the means of instruction. Along with these calls for the empowerment of teachers have come proposals for restructuring the institution of the school to become a more professional and collaborative work environment. Teacher empowerment, teacher leadership, teacher collaboration, and school restructuring are clearly the buzzwords of the day (e.g. Barth, 1990; Maeroff, 1988).

If all of this is now happening in the general educational context, one might argue that all that needs to be done is to enlighten the teacher education community to adopt this broader vision. This would make me happier, but not happy. My concern is that the movement to empower teachers and restructure schools has been taken to such an extreme by some that the really important questions about the purposes of education in a democratic society sometimes get lost. Teacher development becomes an end in itself, unconnected to any broader purposes.

Reflection, as Stephen Kemmis (1985a) tells us, is unavoidably a political act that either hastens or defers the realization of a more decent and just society, whether or not it is acknowledged. All teaching actions have a variety of consequences. These include personal consequences (e.g. the effects of classroom actions on students' self-images), academic consequences (e.g. the effects on students' intellectual achievement), and social consequences (e.g. the cumulative effects of school experience on students' life chances) (Pollard & Tann, 1987).

What concerns me is that the teacher empowerment and school restructuring movement, while attending very carefully to the intellectual and personal consequences of classroom and school events, often gives very little attention to how these events are joined to issues of social continuity and change (i.e. issues of equity and social justice). How teachers' everyday actions challenge or support various oppressions and injustices related to social class, race, gender, sexual preference, religion, and numerous other factors needs to be a central part of teachers' reflections, teacher research, and collaborative decision-making schemes. I do not want to reduce student teachers' deliberations to considering only these such factors, but I do want to help extend their thinking to also consider them. It is also important, as Noddings (1987) has reminded us, that in our pursuit of social justice, our commitment to the quality of relationships (i.e. an ethic of care) is not abandoned.

For example, instead of merely talking about such things as teaching for understanding, developmentally appropriate instruction, whole language instruction, and conceptual change teaching, all of which are currently fashionable terms in North America to describe some version of enlightened teaching practice, we need to think very clearly about who is intended to benefit from these innovative instructional approaches. Furthermore, instead of merely discussing teaching and learning for understanding for everybody's children—a currently fashionable slogan in the U.S., thanks in part to the Holmes Group—we need to ensure that everybody's knowledge and everybody's cultural heritage is represented in that which we seek students to understand. Unless we take such action, the likelihood is that many students will continue to be bypassed by innovative school practices and continue to be denied, with the complicity of the school, access to decent and fulfilling lives.[7]

The evidence is very strong that we cannot assume a willingness to educate everyone's children to the same high standard, and that even when teachers are well intentioned, their actions will always have the effect of promoting democratic education. For example, there is clear evidence that the empowerment of teachers through school restructuring schemes can serve, under some circumstances, to undercut important connections between schools and their communities as teachers use their strengthened position to more effectively minimize the influence of parents (see Zeichner, 1991).

Let me be clear. I am not suggesting, as some have, that the numerous injustices (e.g. gaps in achievement between students of different races, grouping and labeling practices that create gaps in access to knowledge, school suspension and dropout rates that are highly correlated with race and social class, etc.) that can be found in our public school systems are caused by teachers and schools. Schools have not caused these problems, and school reform by itself cannot solve them.

There is irrefutable evidence in many countries that social class background, gender, and race play strong roles in determining access to a variety of benefits in addition to quality education, housing, and health care and rewarding work that pays a decent wage. Social class background, gender, and race also affect the incidence of a whole host of rotten outcomes such as malnutrition, child abuse, physical and psychological stress, childhood pregnancies, violent crime during adolescence, and drug abuse. Over 13 million children in the U.S., for example, currently live in conditions of poverty, which make them highly vulnerable to many of these factors.[8]

However you look at it, this situation is simply outrageous. However, one can agree that it is an outrageous situation and yet see little connection between what one does as a teacher and these economic and social problems. Or, one can see the connections and feel so overwhelmed by the enormity of the problems that one tries to insulate oneself from them. There were many times during my career as an elementary school teacher in inner-city schools in the north-eastern U.S., that I felt so overwhelmed by all of the problems that my students brought with them to the school door, that I was ready to give up. We cannot give up of course. We must do the best we can within our classrooms and schools, and importantly, we must also link up with those who are struggling in various other sectors of society for the achievement of the social preconditions that will enable our educational efforts to be more successful.

While educational actions by teachers within schools cannot solve all of these societal problems by themselves, they can contribute their share to the building of more decent and just societies. The most important point is that neither teaching nor teacher development can be neutral. We, as teachers at whatever level, must act with greater political clarity about whose interests we are furthering in our daily actions, including our approach to professional development, because like it or not, and whether or not it is acknowledged, we are taking a stand through our actions and words. We should not, of course, reduce teaching only to its political elements, but we need to make sure that this aspect of teaching does not get lost as it often does.

The following is an example of how practices, which in many ways deal with the limitations I outlined earlier, do not go far enough in connecting to issues of equity and social justice. My example deals with teacher research, the "systematic intentional inquiry by teachers into their own school and classroom work" (Lytle & Cochran-Smith, 1990). In preparing for a course on teacher research that I taught at Simon Fraser University recently, I came across an article published in the British Educational Research Journal that documents some of the uneasiness that I have been feeling for a while with the failure of some of the knowledge production by teachers to connect to issues of social justice.

The article is written by Gaby Weiner, then of the Open University, who was involved from 1981–1983 in the Sex Differentiation Project, a teacher research project sponsored by the British Schools Council. The aim of the Sex Differentiation Project was to "establish the eradication of gender inequities in the schools as a mainstream education priority" (Weiner, 1989, p. 42). One of the main aspects of the project was supporting teachers as researchers in both exploring issues in the schools and accumulating examples of practices from the teachers' research, which served to reduce gender inequities.

This is research by teachers that clearly makes the connection to issues of social justice.

The problem is that this kind of teacher research is not all that common, according to Weiner's appraisal of the teacher-researcher movement. In her analysis of teacher research in Britain in the 1980s, she identified two different segments of this movement: the mainstream movement and the gender research movement. On the one hand, the mainstream movement, according to Weiner, concentrated on issues related to the professional development of teachers and placed the emphasis on the process of reflective inquiry, rather than on the outcomes of the research. On the other hand, the gender researchers placed more emphasis on the outcomes and were committed to increased social justice within a professional development framework. Both groups of researchers were concerned with liberating and emancipating teachers and creating conditions where teachers, not academics or external researchers, could develop educational theory grounded in classroom practice. However, only the gender researchers explicitly connected their efforts to questions of equity and social justice. In her analysis of the statements of 75 action researchers in the 1984 Bulletin of the Classroom Action Research Network, for example, Weiner could only find one mention of a gender-related topic. Gender as a substantive classroom issue was largely ignored by mainstream teacher researchers. Weiner expressed the hope that in the future all teacher research should embrace the dual aims of increased self-knowledge and social justice.

Despite some oversimplification of the richness of the teacher-researcher movement, Weiner is right. Much of the research now being produced by teachers fails to incorporate an explicit concern with equity questions of any kind. My own experience confirms Weiner's. In the many teacher research studies that I have read over the years, as well as studies conducted by our student teachers at the University of Wisconsin-Madison, I too have seen a great deal of concern with increased self-knowledge, professional development, and the personal and academic consequences of teaching, but often very little evidence of a connection of the research on issues of equity and social justice to issues related to gender, social class, race, ethnicity, physical handicaps, and so on (e.g. Gore & Zeichner, 1991). Of course, this is not solely a problem of teacher research; university-initiated educational research is equally lacking. What needs to happen, especially with teacher research and other forms of genuine teacher development, is for teachers to extend their inquiries to consider how their actions challenge and support the access to and achievement of a high quality education by all students.

There are many examples of teacher research that exemplify just what I propose. For example, recently a group of eight elementary school teachers in the Madison Metropolitan School District conducted studies in their own classrooms that focused on ways to improve the school experiences of students of color. In one of these projects, for example, Ellen Ranney, an elementary teacher of English as a Second Language (ESL), explored the impact on her students of various ways of teaching English as a second language both inside and outside of the regular classroom. In Madison, like many other cities in the U.S., there are serious problems with achievement gaps between minority and majority students. The teachers' studies will be fed into an overall plan for dealing with these problems. This group was so successful that the school district agreed to sponsor two more groups the following year; a group of middle school teachers and a group of principals. Much of this work is focused directly on promoting greater educational equity throughout the school district[9].

In my course at Simon Fraser University, we read about a similar project at a middle school in Fairfax, Virginia (Langston Hughes Intermediate School, 1988). We also read about a project by Donna Cutler-Landsman, a Madison-area elementary teacher who sought to promote greater gender equity in science education in her sixth grade classroom[10]. All of these research projects were completed by full-time classroom teachers at little extra cost to their school districts. In all of the projects, greater equity was an explicit concern.

While I strongly agree with those who argue that the voices of teachers need to be at the center of the dialog and debate surrounding current educational reform and research on teaching (e.g. Miller, 1990), we have to ensure that teacher development does not become an end in itself. Teacher development needs to be genuine, not fraudulent, but it also needs to be a means toward the education of everybody's children. It needs to support teachers' efforts to reflect on and change the practices and social conditions that undermine and distort the educational potential and moral basis of schooling in democratic societies.

I conclude by quoting from a talk that was given at Simon Fraser University 11 years ago at a Summer Institute in Teacher Education by Lawrence Stenhouse of the UK, who devoted most of his career to furthering the cause of genuine teacher development. In his lecture called "Artistry and Teaching," Stenhouse clearly set forth both the conditions that must be realized in order to foster genuine teacher development and the supportive roles that must be assumed by people who claim to want to see it happen:

> Good teachers are necessarily autonomous in professional judgment. They do not need to be told what to do. They are not professionally the dependents of researchers or superintendents, of innovators or supervisors. This does not mean that they do not welcome access to ideas created by other people at other places or in other times. Nor do they reject advice, consultancy or support. But they do know that ideas and people are not of much real use until they are digested to the point where they are subject to the teacher's own judgment. In short, it is the task of all educationists outside the classroom to serve the teachers. For only they are in the position to create good teaching (Ruddick & Hopkins, 1985, p. 104).

I would add that it is only teachers who are in the position to create good teaching for everyone's children. Those of us who say we are concerned about genuine teacher development need to ensure that the connection to "everyone" is not forgotten.

Contradictions and Tensions in the Professionalization of Teaching and the Democratization of Schools[1]

> As teaching seeks to elevate its status and prospects, it must attend to a broader set of concerns. Professionalism alone is not enough. There must be a social vision animating reform that encompasses but is not limited to the interests of teachers. Educational reform must embrace equity goals, must honor the rights of parents and communities, must promote tolerance for diversity, and responsiveness to clients (Sykes, 1989, p. 270).

The "Second Wave" of Educational Reform in the 1980s

A so-called "second wave" of educational reform in the 1980s was initiated in 1985 and 1986 with the release of a set of reports that included those issued by the Holmes Group, the Carnegie Task Force on Teaching as a Profession, the Education Commission of the States, the National Governors Association, and the Public Information Network (Carnegie Task Force on Teaching as a Profession, 1986; Education Commission of the States 1986; Holmes Group, 1986; National Governors Association, 1986; Public Information Network, 1985). Unlike earlier reports, such as *A Nation at Risk* (National Commission on Excellence in Education, 1983), which emphasized greater external specification of school processes and outcomes, these new reports stressed the need to improve schools by both improving the status and power of classroom teachers and decentralizing school decision making (Darling-Hammond & Berry (1988).[2]

Since 1986, literature has been flooded with calls for the empowerment of teachers to participate in a more central way in the determination of school goals and policies and exercise their professional judgment about the content of the curriculum and the means of instruction (Bolin, 1989). Along with these calls for the empowerment of teachers, there have been proposals for the restructuring of schools to become more professional and collaborative work environments (Lieberman, 1989; Rosenholtz, Bassler, & Hoover-Dempsey, 1986). Teacher empowerment, teacher leadership, and school restructuring are clearly the buzzwords of the day (Fiske, 1990).[3]

This chapter is concerned with various tensions and contradictions that are associated with these proposals to restructure schools and give teachers greater control over their work. On the one hand, we need to recognize and celebrate the positive aspects of teacher empowerment and school restructuring, such as the role they can play in (a) providing teachers with more stimulating and humane environments in which to carry out their work, (b) tapping the tremendous amount of expertise possessed by teachers, and (c) strengthening a largely female labor force in relation to dominance by a mostly male administration. We cannot have good schools unless classroom teachers are enabled to play central roles in the running of those schools and the development of solutions to the numerous problems that schools face.[4] On the other hand, we also need to recognize several pitfalls that can be associated with these efforts to professionalize teaching, such as the potential for (a) intensification of teachers' work and the diversion of teachers' energies from the school's primary academic mission and (b) deepening the divisions between schools and communities.

Following an analysis of a few of the tensions and contradictions underlying recent efforts to professionalize teaching and democratize schools, I argue for a broad rather than a narrow version of school democracy, one that includes parents, community members, and students in the processes of democratic deliberation within schools. However, as is the case with teacher empowerment, community and student empowerment do not, by themselves, provide simple solutions to our problems. In these times of conservative resurgence, supporting a greater role for communities in running their schools makes schools more vulnerable to the wishes and desires of those who seek to force antidemocratic beliefs onto the public schools (Shor, 1986). Although we need to encourage and support a process of democratic deliberation within schools that includes parents and students as well as administrators and teachers, we need some way of determining the goodness of the choices that emerge from these deliberations. I am personally unwilling to accept any choice that is made just because it emerges out of a process in which all interested parties have participated. First, the fact that all relevant parties have participated does not mean that everyone has had influence in the deliberative process. Recent research has shown that parents and other community members have often been unable to exert meaningful influence on school decision making even when they are formally involved in decision-making processes (e.g. Malen, Ogawa, & Kranz, 1990).[5] Second, we need some way of ensuring that the decisions that emerge from these deliberations do not violate certain moral standards, such as social justice and equity. In the last part of this chapter, I draw on Amy Gutmann's work on democratic education to propose a way of dealing with some of these dilemmas (Gutmann, 1987).

Finally, I argue that calls for teacher empowerment and school restructuring are misleading unless they are connected with efforts to bring about changes in the economic, social, and political structures of society. The problems in our public schools are a reflection of a crisis in these social structures. No organizational arrangement within schools or level of professionalization among teachers will be adequate, by itself, to deal with societal problems of inequity and injustice. To call for the restructuring of schools while remaining silent on the need for broader social and economic change is to lend support to the mistaken view, so successfully ingrained in the public consciousness in recent years, that what is wrong with society is largely the fault of the schools or is amenable to correction by the schools.

Celebrating Teacher Empowerment and Social Democratization

Recent proposals for giving teachers more control over their work and the schools in which their work is carried out have provided us with many good ideas about how to overcome the debilitating consequences of efforts to rationalize and control teachers' work through external mandates and the standardization of practices (Apple, 1987a; Wise, 1979).[6] There is increasing acceptance of the idea that good schools must treat their teachers with what Sara Lawrence Lightfoot calls "respectful regard" (Lightfoot, 1983), allowing them to exercise their judgment in matters related to the instruction of their students and with regard to a variety of curricular and organizational issues that extend beyond their individual classrooms.

> The new reformers argue that decisions about education must be decentralized and professionalized. That is, they must reflect teachers' and principals' best professional judgments on behalf of students rather than adhering blindly to rules and procedures that emanate from higher bureaucratic offices and governmental agencies (Darling-Hammond, 1988, p. 59).

These second-wave reformers have argued that relationships among the adults in a school are critical in determining the character and quality of education for students in a school. They have called for the creation of collaborative work environments in public elementary and secondary schools that encourage continued learning for adults as well as students (Barth, 1989). It is frequently argued that schools that are educative for the adults who work in them will be educative for students (Barth, 1989).

Underlying these calls for greater roles for teachers in the way schools are run are tensions between centralized and diffused authority at two levels: (a) between the schools and authorities external to the schools and (b) within schools, between administrators and staff. There is the view that greater specification and standardization of school practices from a point external to the school (e.g. a state education department or school district central office) is the best way to ensure educational quality within schools. We have seen a lot of this in recent years with efforts to mandate student competency objectives, standardized testing, the use of particular curricular materials, and the use of particular configurations of teaching strategies, such as those advocated by

Madeline Hunter (Gentile, 1988)[7] or by state education departments (e.g. the Florida Performance Measurement System). This view of greater quality through greater standardization across schools conflicts with the currently popular idea of school-based management or the dispersal of authority to individual schools. Within individual schools, we have a similar tension between principals and staffs over the control of school decision making.

Although there have been some challenges to recent efforts to give classroom teachers a greater voice in running schools (Shanker, 1990), the current consensus in mainstream educational literature is to restructure schools by diffusing authority, both to individual schools and to the staff within schools. In addition to the positive impact this strategy is likely to have on the recruitment and retention of teachers (McLaughlin & Yee, 1989), the strengthening of the teacher's position should also be supported for its contribution to reversing the patriarchal relations that have dominated schools for many years. Teaching is not just work; it is gendered work. Work dominated by women has been particularly vulnerable to the kind of rationalization and standardization seen in teaching (Apple, 1986). Greater professionalization of the work of teaching makes an important contribution toward realizing a situation in which schools can be characterized as "gender-just" (Weiss, 1990).

> The very notion of professionalism has been important not only to teachers in general but to women in particular. It has provided a contradictory yet powerful barrier against interference by the state; and just as critically, in the struggle over male dominance, it has been part of a complex attempt to win equal treatment, pay, and control over the day-to-day work of a largely female labor force (Apple, 1986, p. 46).

The Downside of Teacher Empowerment and School Restructuring

Despite the positive aspects of restructuring schools to give teachers more say in how they are run, there are potential pitfalls associated with these plans that must be recognized. A first concern is the danger that involving teachers in school decision making about programs, budget, and staffing will make excessive demands on their time, energy, and expertise, diverting their attention from the core tasks with students (Cooper, 1989). In some circumstances, creating more opportunities for teachers to participate in decisions related to curriculum, instruction, staffing, resources, and so forth can intensify their work beyond the bounds of reasonableness and make it more difficult for them to accomplish their primary mission.[8] There are currently about 20 teachers in the Madison Metropolitan School District, for example, on leave because of stress-related factors that have resulted, in part, from the extra demands being made on teachers there. Many teachers throughout the U.S. are currently experiencing the effects of increased demands on their energies, resulting from prescriptive requirements emanating from state education units and local school districts but also, in some cases, from plans that have been designed with the goal of giving teachers more opportunities to shape the conditions of their work (Apple, 1986; Carnoy & MacDonnell, 1990; Liston & Zeichner, 1991). Teacher empowerment does not necessarily have to lead to a situation in which the achievement of the school's academic mission is undermined or teachers are overstressed, but it can, unless efforts are made to incorporate their participation in schoolwide decision making into their work instead of adding it to their work. Teachers must be given the time and resources to participate in the various noninstructional activities that are increasingly open to them. One way to do this is to provide teachers with time during the school day to engage in noninstructional tasks.

A second concern with an uncritical acceptance of teacher empowerment and school restructuring is that the increased professionalization of teaching can serve, under some circumstances. to undercut important connections between schools and their communities, leading to a greater insensitivity within the school to the legitimate interests of parents and other community members in school affairs. (An example of this would be teachers using professionalism as a weapon to further distance parents and communities from attaining a meaningful voice in school affairs.) The school–community connection is a critical element in the success of schools in our inner cities, where the gap between the culture of the school and the cultures of the community is often the greatest (Bastian et al., 1986).[9] James Comer's (1980) work in New Haven and other similar work has convincingly demonstrated that one key to academic success in city schools, especially for students of color and children of low socioeconomic status, is the positive interaction between community members and school staff that can result from meaningful community involvement in school decision making (Chubb, 1988; Heath, 1983; Lightfoot, 1978).

> The New Haven experience has demonstrated that when parents participate in schools in meaningful, well conceived and well structured ways, they come to identify with the schools' academic concerns. Parents checking homework, working as classroom assistants, volunteering as coordinators of after-school activities, and participating as members of the governmental and management teams give black students immediately recognizable role models. Teachers and parents are seen as being in alliance, working for and believing in common intellectual and social goals. Parents also begin to develop a sense of ownership of the schools and feelings of responsibility for academic success (Committee on Policy for Racial Justice, 1989, p. 27).

Underlying the relations between schools and communities is a tension between professional and communal authority over school affairs. Plans that have given more power to local schools and teachers within those schools have not necessarily created the means for authentic partnerships between communities and schools. In fact, the evidence suggests that meaningful community involvement in school affairs is very rare even when formal mechanisms exist, allegedly to encourage such involvement. First, with regard to schools in low-income communities in particular, Michelle Fine has argued:

> When urban schools extend themselves to parents and initiate the dialogue or relationships with parents and community, these relationships are rarely reciprocal and are never about sharing power. Sessions for parents by school districts, designed to increase parental involvement, may include "how to love the unlovable child," but much less often "your legal rights in a special education placement," or "knowing when your child can and cannot be legally discharged from high school." School-community relations are rarely bilateral in low-income communities (Fine, 1987, p. 103).

Second, recent analyses of the literature on school-based decision making have revealed that although community participation is often a central objective of school-based management plans and opportunities have been created for parents and other community members to be involved in schoolwide decision making, communities have rarely been able to exert significant influence on schools through these mechanisms (Grant, McCarty, & Volpiansky, 1989; Malen, Ogawa, & Kranz, 1990; White, 1989).[10] For example,

> On councils composed of principals, teachers, and parents, professional-patron influence relationships are not substantially altered primarily because principals and, at times principals and teachers control council meetings ... Since professionals can set the agenda, manage the meeting time, disperse the information, and shift politically contentious issues to more private arenas, they essentially control decision processes and ultimately control decision outcomes. Parents are reluctant to challenge this dynamic. As a result, the traditional pattern where administrators make policy, teachers instruct, and parents support is mandated (Malen et al., 1990, p. 54).

According to these analyses, parents and community members approach their involvement in these policy-making bodies as a way to acquire information about the school and provide service to the school, not to make school policy. These councils have rarely addressed central and salient policy issues. They have established themselves in an advisory and supportive capacity rather than the administrative roles they were supposed to assume (Gartner & Lipsky, 1987).[11]

Complementing this marginal role for parents and communities in plans for decentralized school decision making is the almost total lack of attention to community empowerment in the mainstream educational literature that advocates teacher leadership and school restructuring. For example, in Maeroff's (1988) and Bolin's (1989) arguments for teacher empowerment and in Lieberman's arguments for school restructuring and teacher leadership, there is hardly a word said about the specific ways in which parents and communities can gain respected voices in school affairs. Although Bolin asks, "What of student and community empowerment?" she has little to say about it. Likewise, Roland Barth includes parents in his "school as a community of learners," but then only discusses ways that teachers can be incorporated into that community (Barth, 1989). *Tomorrow's Schools*, one of two recent documents of the Holmes Group (1990), displays this same tendency in its assertion that a greater sense of professionalism on the part of teachers should never distance them from parents and others in the community surrounding the school. The report then spends little space discussing how the legitimate interests of parents and communities on the one hand, and teachers and principals on the other, can be balanced to give everyone a meaningful role in school decision making.[12]

There is little doubt that this question of community participation without community influence will have to be addressed before we will be able to make any progress in establishing the strong and authentic school–community connections that are critical for the success of our urban schools (Rosewater, 1989).[13]

> Addressing the deep social problems gripping urban schools without a broad political and social mobilization of the communities they're located in is simply not possible .... When it comes to schools, community mobilization means giving parents real decision making power ..., and not just advisory and supportive roles (Karp, 1990, p. 12).

In addition, the isolation of schools from their communities undermines the sense of civic responsibility that public education should, but rarely does, cultivate among all students (Bastian et al., 1986). There are examples of school-based management where parents and community members play significant rather than cosmetic roles in the making of school policy. For example, both the Institute for Responsive Education and the National Committee for Citizens in Education have developed models of local school governance in school districts across the U.S. in which parents have strong roles. La Escuela Fratney, a two-way bilingual school in inner-city Milwaukee, is an excellent example of how professional educators and a community can work together to shape school reform (Davies, 1989; Henderson, 1987; Peterson, 1990; Williams, 1989). Finally, while it is too early to assess the impact of the "Chicago plan," it is clear that the composition of the 595 local school councils was deliberately designed to overcome the limitations placed on parents and communities in most school-based management plans (see Ayers, 1989; Clinchy, 1989; Karp, 1990). Although these efforts to establish genuine partnerships between communities and their schools need to be applauded, there are potential dangers involved in community empowerment, just as there are with teacher empowerment.

Pitfalls of Community Empowerment

Merely asserting the legitimate rights of parents and the community in shaping school policy is not a panacea. There are several potential dangers in community empowerment in the public schools. First, there is the danger that an emphasis on community empowerment, if taken to the extreme, can lead to the ossification of teacher and administrator roles (i.e. to a denial of their roles in school policy making) (Gutmann, 1987).[14] In asserting the importance of teacher empowerment, Bolin asks an important and difficult question: "What if communities desire and demand teachers who emphasize memorization and drill, absolute obedience to authority, and punitive discipline?" (Bolin, 1989). Do we merely accept the rights of communities to dictate school policy, no matter what is asserted as desirable and no matter how compatible these desires are with the judgments of professional educators about how to best educate everyone's children for citizenship in a democratic society? If we accept this extreme view of community empowerment and the school as a community institution that would have schools be whatever local communities desire them to be (and I think few advocates of community empowerment would go this far), we are opening ourselves up to a variety of demands, some of which will negate teachers' and administrators' visions for their schools.

Second, there is the danger that some of what communities may assert for their schools may be in conflict with principles of a democratic society, repressing particular points of view or discriminating against certain groups of people. Two recent examples in Madison, Wisconsin, under the banner of parent involvement and community empowerment in public education, illustrate this problem. In the first incident, a recently defeated school board member and a group of parents attacked parts of the Madison Metropolitan School District curriculum in multicultural education which, with the goal of promoting the acceptance of all people in the Madison community, provided students with information about homosexuality. This school board member and the parents, with the assistance of Pat Robertson and a national fundamentalist religious constituency, charged the school district with encouraging homosexuality among students—a charge that was later proved to be a distortion—and sought to have all material on this topic removed from the school curriculum. The school district defended the information about homosexuality in its curriculum as consistent with its obligation to promote an acceptance of all people in the local community.

In the second incident, a group of parents at a local elementary school marched into the school with a Christmas tree and a Santa Claus, challenging the school district policy prohibiting the display within Madison public schools of religious symbols that are not used primarily for educational

purposes. Despite some after-the-fact efforts to append an educational purpose to their activities (e.g. attaching a sign to the tree presenting the history
of the Christmas tree), these efforts were seen by the school district staff
and many members of the Madison community as an attempt to force the
celebration of one group's religion on everyone in that school.

Incidents like these have been repeated over and over again in communities
throughout the U.S. under the banner of parent involvement and community
empowerment. Teachers and administrators have understandably reacted
defensively to attempts to remove such things as "secular humanism" from
the curriculum, to force the teaching of creationism, to ban particular books
and children from schools, and to force one particular group's point of view
on everyone's children. Sometimes what communities want for their schools
is clearly discriminatory with regard to certain kinds of ideas and groups of
citizens.

Teachers have often viewed community empowerment as a threat to their
own sense of professionalism. After struggling to achieve a situation in which
teacher empowerment is seen to be legitimate within mainstream educational
circles, why would they not be reluctant to give up that for which they have
fought for so long? Currently, we find ourselves caught up in a situation in
which arguments for teacher empowerment are viewed as a threat to either
administrators' authority or to community empowerment, and arguments for
community empowerment are seen as threats to professional authority and
teacher empowerment.[15] Is there a way out of this situation of polarization?

A Broad View of Democratic Schooling

In contrast to narrow views of school democracy that assert the rights of particular groups in making school policy, we should be aiming for the realization of the school as a democratic community that recognizes the legitimate
rights of all parties to have substantive input into decision making about significant school issues. At the secondary level, this would include students. To
recognize the right of any particular group does not have to mean that the
rights of others are denied. No single group, including state education department, central office district staff, building administrators, teachers, parents,
community members, or students, should be allowed to determine what is
"good education" for a particular school community. In recognizing the
importance of local versus centralized control over individual schools, all
parties at the level of the individual school need to have a respected voice in
deliberations about school policies. This does not mean that states and the
central authorities of school districts do not have a legitimate right to set the
broad parameters for educational policies. It does reflect the view, however,
that the emphasis should be on local control of individual schools to represent
the judgments of local school communities. Ways must be found to create
conditions within schools so that all groups can participate in a meaningful
way in these deliberations. Groups that traditionally have not been involved

in the making of school policies (e.g. teachers and parents) need to be enabled to assume roles that go beyond giving advice and support. As I argued earlier, merely forming groups that include all relevant parties by itself merely serves to maintain traditional authority relationships (Malen et al., 1990). Teacher involvement in school governance needs to be viewed as part of the teaching role and not as an addition to this role. All groups, but especially parents and students, need to be provided with training that will enable them to assert their views in the face of claims of professional expertise.

Despite the dominance of views of school democracy that assert the rights of one constituency to the exclusion of others, there are several examples we can look to for models of school democracy that seek to preserve the legitimate interests of all parties. The Rethinking Schools group in Milwaukee, Wisconsin and the Institute for Democracy in Education in Athens, Ohio are two examples of groups that advocate a broad, rather than a narrow, view of school democracy. Both of these groups, composed primarily of classroom teachers, have stimulated much discussion and debate within public education about the antidemocratic aspects of such practices as standardized testing, ability grouping, behavior management systems (e.g. Assertive Discipline), and certain instructional practices and curriculum materials. Importantly, they have also provided a rich set of resources and ideas about alternative practices that seek to overcome the inequalities that pervade our public schools. We need to learn from the good work these groups are promoting (Peterson, 1990).[16]

The question now arises, however, whether we should be prepared to accept any and all decisions that emerge from these broadly based groups that include all relevant parties merely because everyone has had a voice. Even if it is possible to create conditions within schools for the realization of this idealized version of the school democracy (a question that will be dealt with shortly), should we not have some guidelines beyond full participation by all parties for determining the goodness of the choices that are made?

It is with regard to this important question that I find Amy Gutmann's work on democratic education particularly helpful. Gutmann argues on principle for the broad view of school democracy to which I have lent my support. Importantly, though, she sets forth certain restraints on this democratic process that are intended to preserve the rights of all within a democratic society. These restraints are (a) nonrepression, which prevents the use of education to "restrict rational deliberation of competing conceptions of the good life and the good society," and (b) nondiscrimination, so that no child may be excluded from an education adequate to participation in the political processes that structure choice among good lives (Gutmann, 1987).

This conception of democratic education does not eliminate all of the problems that I have outlined in this article (i.e. there still will be legitimate disagreement over what is discriminatory or repressive). (See Liston and Zeichner's (1991) discussion of educational traditions for examples of how these debates are played out in relation to both teaching and teacher education.) However, it does deal with the kinds of extreme cases of repression and discrimination exemplified by the two examples from Madison as well as with a host of other practices, such as curriculum censorship, a Western white Eurocentric and thus racist curriculum that often excludes the histories and perspectives of women and people of color, gender discrimination that denies boys or girls access to certain educational opportunities, and school choice plans that create elite middle-class enclaves within urban school systems.[17]

Although Gutmann's notions about school democracy and the work of groups like Rethinking Schools in creating genuine school–community alliances justify a certain degree of hope that we will be able to move beyond the limits of special interest politics, we need to be cautious about what can be achieved by reforms within the educational arena alone. Because of the growing gap between the haves and the have-nots in all elements of our society, including education, the potential of educational reform is severely limited unless it is coupled with fundamental changes in the economic, social, and political structures of society.[18] Given these inequalities in schooling and society, the question arises as to whether we can create this idealized version of school democracy even if we are inclined to do so.

The Limits of Educational Reform

There is little question that we are faced with a growing crisis of inequality in every aspect of our society. Race, gender, and social-class background continue to play strong roles in determining access to quality education, housing, health care, and rewarding work that pays a decent wage and affect the incidence of various rotten outcomes such as malnutrition, child abuse, physical and psychological stress, childhood pregnancies, violent crime during adolescence, and drug abuse (see Katznelson & Weir, 1985; Oakes, 1985; Persell, 1977; Schor, 1988). Over 13 million children in the U.S. currently live in conditions of poverty that make them highly vulnerable to these interrelated factors. Nearly half of African-American children, two-fifths of Hispanic children, and one-seventh of white children in the U.S. are poor (Edelman, 1989). This situation is simply outrageous.

Many on the Left in recent years have challenged the ideology prevalent in so-called reports of the state of education in the U.S. that identify an alleged crisis of excellence in our public schools but ignore the crisis of equality in both schools and society (e.g. Apple, 1987b and Ginsburg, 1988). Many of these early reports, such as *A Nation at Risk*, effectively export the crisis in society to our schools, seeking to create the impression that what is wrong with society is the fault of the schools and can be fixed by school reform alone. The educational programs advocated in these early reports stress an elitist concept of meritocracy that is to be achieved through more rigorous academic standards, more standardized testing, and the transmission of a narrowly conceived "common cultural heritage." Although these reports acknowledge a crisis in the U.S. economy, they place the blame for our inability to compete favorably in world markets primarily on the failure of our public schools to produce literate workers.

Several of the so-called second-wave educational reports, such as *Tomorrow's Schools*, go far beyond the simplistic analyses evident in reports such as *A Nation at Risk* by acknowledging the crisis of inequality in schooling and society, advocating an educational program that gives serious attention to the elimination of educational inequalities (i.e. by advocating teaching for understanding for everyone's children, as in *Tomorrow's Schools*). Most of these second-wave educational reports are problematic, however, because they fail to acknowledge the need for, let alone discuss, the kinds of economic, social, and political changes outside of schools that will be needed to complement the democratic educational projects advocated for within schools: the social preconditions for educational reform.

This same limitation applies to proposals, such as the one I have advocated in this chapter, for a broad version of democratic school governance. Despite the desirability of this idealized vision of a democratic school community in which all constituents have a respected voice in making school policy, there is little hope of achieving this ideal without linking this project to efforts in other spheres of society that are directed toward the elimination of inequalities based on gender, race, social class, sexual preference, physical condition, and so forth, no matter how noble our intentions. We cannot create democratic school communities in an undemocratic society.[19] We cannot build "tomorrow's schools" in today's unequal society.

For example, parents who are worried about meeting basic human needs for their families (e.g. physical safety, shelter, food, medical care, child care, and decent jobs) cannot fully participate in the democratic school community, no matter how enlightened the views of professional educators are about the legitimacy of community empowerment, and no matter how much training is offered to members of the general community in the politics of school decision making. The parents and other community members who are the most alienated from their local schools are also the ones who are least likely to have jobs that provide them with some flexibility in their work schedules to become involved in school affairs. Many good ideas for countering these discriminatory aspects of community empowerment proposals exist, including the creation of new jobs within schools for community members as paraprofessionals and the granting of paid released time by businesses for the purposes of involvement in school affairs.

As I argued early on, advocating democratic educational projects without explicitly calling for general social reconstruction serves to strengthen the mistaken view—so successfully ingrained in the public consciousness in these times of conservative resurgence—that the schools are largely responsible for the whole host of rotten outcomes that confront so many of our children. Remaining silent on the need for broader social, economic, and political change only serves to create false expectations about what can be accomplished by educational reform alone. The position that I have supported here is that no school organizational plan or level of autonomy in school decision making for teachers or the community, by itself, will ever be sufficient for dealing with our society's institutional and structural inequalities, which underlie the educational problems in the schools.

This is not to say that I am opposed to changes that seek to counter the drill, drudgery, and bureaucratic superficialities endured by so many teachers and their students, even in public schools for relatively advantaged students. The conditions for teaching and learning in our public schools are indeed in great need of improvement almost everywhere. In working for these important changes within schools, however, we must not lose sight of the most important goal: working to create a more just and decent United States for all of us and our children. Every educational reform must also be evaluated for its contribution to the building of this more just and humane society.[20] I have argued here that merely empowering teachers and/or parents does not necessarily lead us in this direction.

There is little question that the various proposals for school restructuring that are the centerpiece of almost every contemporary report on the reform of schooling and teacher education will require substantial reallocation of national resources. Our government spends roughly 290 times more on defense research than it spends on research on education, and pours billions of dollars annually into the support of such things as weapons systems and tax relief for the rich.[21] There is just no way that we can build schools and a society that will provide everyone with access to decent and rewarding lives without diverting more resources away from such areas as military preparedness and certain tax and economic policies (which have permitted the gutting of social programs of almost every kind during the last decade and continue to permit endless obscene contrasts such as the recent building of the $1.2 billion Taj Mahal gambling casino in the midst of the poverty of Atlantic City) (Goldberger, 1990). Educational reforms can contribute to the creation of a democratic decent and just society, but by themselves they are not sufficient.

Reflections of a University-Based Teacher Educator on the Future of College- and University-Based Teacher Education[1]

Drawing on my 30-plus years as a university teacher educator, I reflect in this chapter about the future of college- and university-based teacher education in the U.S. in light of recent attacks on education schools. I argue that university and college teacher educators should do four things: (a) work to redefine the debate about the relative merits of alternative and traditional certification programs; (b) work to broaden the goals of teacher education beyond raising scores on standardized achievement tests; (c) change the center of gravity in teacher education to provide a stronger role for schools and communities in the education of teachers; and (d) take teacher education seriously as an institutional responsibility or do not do it.

A little more than 30 years ago, I began my career as a university teacher educator as a team leader in the National Teacher Corps supervising Teacher Corps interns in Syracuse, New York. At this time, competency-based/performance-based teacher education was mandated for program approval in a number of states and in all Teacher Corps projects (Gage & Winne, 1975), and the federal government funded the development of a number of competency-based teacher education program models in elementary education that were to serve as exemplars for other institutions across the nation (Clarke, 1969). Preservice teachers in many parts of the U.S. had to demonstrate proficiency on numerous competencies as part of the process of gaining their initial teaching license. These competencies were assumed by many to be based on empirically demonstrated relationships of teacher effectiveness established by researchers between particular teacher behaviors and student achievement test scores, despite evidence to the contrary (Heath & Nielson, 1974). Many of the assessments in teacher education programs were cast in the form of behavioral competencies that could be observed because of the heavy influence of behavioral psychology and systems theory on education at that time (McDonald, 1973).

These efforts to strengthen teacher education and teaching through the articulation of a knowledge base for teaching in the form of teaching competencies was not the only vision for how teacher education programs could be strengthened. At the same time that efforts were being made to expand the professional education component of programs, others were advocating for less emphasis on methods courses, foundations courses, and so forth, and arguing for a greater attention to preparation in the content knowledge to be taught by teachers. Several years prior to my entry into teaching, a series of widely publicized attacks on schools and colleges of education had criticized the allegedly low academic standards in teacher education programs and the weak content knowledge preparation of prospective teachers (e.g. Conant, 1963; Koerner, 1963). These external critics of teacher education programs argued that professional education course work should be reduced and that more time needed to be spent by prospective teachers in studying and mastering the academic content that they would later teach. Special efforts were made by a number of foundations at the time that I went into public school teaching (the late 1960s) to attract liberal arts graduates into teaching through master's level certification programs (i.e. M.A.T. programs) that were firmly grounded in the liberal arts and academic content departments (Coley & Thorpe, 1986).

During this same period, the field of multicultural teacher education began to receive national visibility as the American Association of Colleges for Teacher Education formed a commission on multicultural education. The Association subsequently published several reports, including a survey of member institutions about multicultural education practices and resources related to strengthening the multicultural component of programs (e.g. American Association of Colleges for Teacher Education, 1980; Baptiste, Baptiste, & Gollnick, 1980). In addition, in the late 1970s, the National Council for Accreditation of Teacher Education began to require teacher education programs to meet standards related to multicultural teacher education for national accreditation of an institution's programs (Gollnick, 1991). At this same time, other teacher educators identifying with the historical movement of social reconstructionism advocated for teacher education programs to prepare teachers who could act as agents in the realization of greater social justice in school and society (Giroux & McLaren, 1987; Shor, 1987).

These three visions for improving the quality of teacher education have been identified as the professionalization, deregulation, and social justice agendas for teacher education. They have continued to frame the debates concerning the question of teacher quality and how to strengthen teacher education programs in the U.S. (Zeichner, 2003).[2] Although these three positions on teacher quality and teacher education reform are not mutually exclusive and do not necessarily take the same exact form in different time periods,[3] they do identify different priorities for teacher education programs and imply different policies at the state and federal levels.

Advocates of the professionalization agenda have supported the shift to performance-based assessment based on standards that now exist in almost all teacher education programs as well as the testing of teachers' content knowledge, and have offered proposals for mandatory national accreditation for teacher education institutions.[4] The programmatic consequences of the professionalization position involve efforts to strengthen the professional education and fieldwork components of teacher education programs. Underlying these efforts to articulate a professional knowledge base for teaching through standards and performance-based assessment is a view of teachers as needing to exercise their judgment in the classroom to make the necessary adaptations to meet the learning needs of their students (Sykes, 2004). The recent report of the National Academy of Education Committee on Teacher Education is the latest example of an effort to articulate what teachers need to know and be able to do to begin teaching and make the professional judgments that are needed to meet their students' learning needs (Darling-Hammond & Bransford, 2005).[5]

Advocates of the deregulation agenda have promoted alternative pathways into teaching that minimize or exclude professional education content and emphasize preparation in the content to be taught. Some deregulation advocates have even gone so far as to question the need for teacher preparation and state certification of teachers, calling for a shift to a competitive model that subjects teacher hiring to market forces (e.g. Hess, 2001; Walsh, 2004). U.S. Education Department support for the American Board for the Certification of Teacher Excellence and its Passport to Teaching (a pathway to certification that involves the passing of a professional knowledge and content examination but not participation in a teacher education program) are examples of concrete actions that have resulted from the deregulation critiques.[6] The prevailing view among deregulation advocates is that teacher education courses at colleges and universities add little value to a teacher's effectiveness and what needs to be learned about how to teach can be learned on the job (Walsh & Hale, 2004).

Finally, advocates for teacher education for social justice have emphasized the development of sociocultural consciousness and intercultural teaching and competence among prospective teachers so that they will be prepared to teach the increasingly diverse students who attend U.S. public schools (e.g. Irvine, 2003; Machelli & Kaiser, 2005). They have also stressed the importance of developing a much more diverse teaching force that more accurately reflects the diversity of the population (Villegas & Lucas, 2002). It has come to the point that the term social justice teacher education is so commonly used now by college and university teacher educators that it is difficult to find a teacher education program in the U.S. that does not claim to have a program that prepares teachers for social justice. Most of this work on social justice teacher education in the U.S. thus far seems to focus on the actions of individual teacher educators in their college and university classrooms and has not included the kind of proposals for structural changes in teaching as an occupation and teacher education that have been set forth by professionalization and deregulation proponents (Zeichner, 2003b). An exception to this trend is the call for a greater role for communities in the teacher preparation process (e.g. Murrell, 1998).

As mentioned earlier, these three reform agendas affecting teacher education programs are not mutually exclusive, and individual teacher education programs have been influenced by all of them. For example, some state requirements for performance-based assessment compel teacher candidates to meet standards that address teachers' competence and multicultural teaching abilities. Also, many college and university programs have strengthened teachers' subject matter knowledge preparation and general education in recent years in ways that also enhance teachers' cultural competence and knowledge of different ethnic groups and cultures. For example, at my university we have recently developed a new liberal studies requirement for future teachers which includes a new ethnic studies component and global perspectives requirement. The goal is to provide all teaching candidates with broader knowledge about the histories and cultures of different groups inside and outside of the U.S. Other examples of this overlap among reform agendas could be generated. The point is that the three reform agendas, although emphasizing different aspects of teacher preparation, come together in teacher education programs as teacher educators respond to various local, state, and national requirements, while attempting to assert their own views of how teachers can best be educated.

The Current Situation for University-Based Teacher Education in the United States

Today, with the existence of the No Child Left Behind Act of 2001, Title II of the Higher Education Act, the growth of various fast-track alternative routes to teaching that include little (if any) involvement of higher education institutions, and state policies that have increased surveillance of teacher education programs, university-based teacher education programs continue to supply our nation's public schools with more teachers than any other source in most parts of the country (Spellings, 2005). College- and university-based teacher education, however, has lost much of its credibility in the larger policy community.[7] Tom Payzant (2004), the superintendent of Boston public schools, in a plenary address to the American Association of Colleges for Teacher Education meeting, addressed an important question: Should teacher preparation take place at colleges and universities? The fact that this question is even a topic at a major session at the annual meeting of the major teacher education association in the U.S. is a sign that the future of college- and university-based teacher education is in doubt. Payzant answered this question by laying out the complex and difficult conditions that face urban schools in the U.S. today. He argued that colleges and universities will play a role only if they make some significant changes in how they do business so that the teachers prepared in these programs will choose to teach in urban schools in the U.S. today. He was not very optimistic about the future of colleges and universities in preservice teacher education if we continue our current ways. He then referred to plans in Boston to set up a preservice teacher education programs within the district to supply them with the kind of teachers they need if colleges and universities are unwilling to prepare them. This practice of school district-based preservice teacher education programs has been common practice in large urban districts in the U.S., including in the cities of Los Angeles, New York, and Houston, for some years now.[8]

In addition to the points that Payzant (2004) made about the need for teacher education programs to do a better job of preparing teachers for the realities of urban schools, there is the issue of the need to improve conditions in these urban schools for teachers so that more teachers will be successful. Preservice teacher education can do only so much, and even under the best of conditions, it can only prepare teachers to begin teaching and know how to learn from their teaching. Conditions within the schools must support the continued learning and development of teachers. Currently, although there are some signs of progress in this area as many states have introduced carefully planned induction programs for beginning teachers, the allocation of shrinking school district resources toward providing the expensive testing apparatus required by the No Child Left Behind Act of 2001 has negatively affected professional development for staff in many school districts across the country (Randi & Zeichner, 2004).

On July 31, 2005, *The New York Times* published a feature story in *Education Life* titled "Who Needs Education Schools?" (Hartocollis, 2005). This article reflects the extent to which teacher education has become a debatable topic in the popular press. It includes many of the charges that have been leveled against college- and university-based teacher education programs by their critics. For example, Harocollis (2005) argued that a "flurry of new studies challenges their ideological bias on low admission standards" (p. 25). He referred to one nonpeer-reviewed study by Steiner and Rozen (2004) in which the authors asserted, based on their reading of course syllabi from a few teacher education institutions in literacy education, that many teacher education programs in universities and colleges ignore the practicalities of teaching and indoctrinate their students into a "countercultural" mistrust of the system in which teachers work. Steiner, in a subsequent interview with Hartocollis, asserted that there is an exclusive focus in colleges and universities on the progressivist and constructivist vision: "the theory that it is better for children to construct knowledge than to receive it" (Hartocollis, 2005, p. 25). In addition this caricature of university teacher education programs as hotbeds of progressive opposition to the status quo,[9] Hartocollis referred to unnamed critics who equate a concern for preparing teachers to be able to establish caring learning communities and advocating for social justice with a lack of concern for preparing teachers for the practical aspects of classroom teaching: "It ill prepared them to function effectively in the classroom" (p. 25).

Apart from debates about the accuracy and genuineness of these and other charges leveled against education schools, it is clear that the legitimacy of education schools to engage in preparing teachers for our nation's schools is under question in an intense way. Following are my thoughts about how we as university- and college-based teacher educators should respond to these attacks in a way that will best serve the interests of all children in our public schools. In my view, best serving the interests of all students requires multiple pathways into teaching that include but are not limited to college- and university-based programs.

We need to ensure however, that all programs, no matter what their structure or who sponsors them, have the necessary components to prepare teachers to successfully begin teaching the diverse learners who are in the public schools. I also argue that blaming teachers and education schools for the problems of public education has diverted attention from the need for a greater investment in public education by the society and for the establishment of the social preconditions for educational reform. Those of us who work in education schools or public schools need to improve how we educate students and teachers, but society as a whole needs to invest more heavily in public education and teacher education. Society needs to reallocate societal resources to better support the conditions in the larger community that will make educational success for teachers and their pupils more likely, such as access to housing, health care, jobs that pay a living wage, and so on.

Shaping the Future of College- and University-Based Teacher Education

There are several things that I think university teacher educators and our professional organizations need to do in this climate of skepticism about our work.[10] I address four of these in this chapter: (a) work to reframe the debate about traditional versus alternative programs; (b) broaden the goals of teacher education beyond raising scores on standardized achievement tests and broaden our vision for teachers beyond compliant implementers of teaching scripts; (c) change the center of gravity of teacher education programs so that the connections between universities, schools, and communities in the preparation of teachers are stronger and less hierarchical; and (d) take teacher education seriously or do not do it.

I think that it would be a big mistake, given the numbers of teachers we need to prepare to staff our nation's schools and the actual complexity of teaching and learning, to continue down the current path toward the destruction of university-based teacher education programs. Colleges and universities have an important role to play in this critical task of preparing teachers for public schools in a democracy. However, I do think that we need to make some changes in how we conduct our work in teacher education so that we make a greater contribution to preparing teachers who choose to teach in the schools and fields where they are most needed and who are successful and continue teaching in these schools.

Currently, despite the fact that we prepare more than enough teachers to teach in public school classrooms in the U.S., not enough of the teachers who we prepare are willing to teach in the schools where they are most needed, and even if they do, many are unsuccessful and leave (National Commission on Teaching and America's Future, 2003). The disproportionate distribution of teachers who have completed a teacher education program among students of different racial, ethnic, and social class backgrounds is a significant part of the savage inequalities that persist in our public schools. Those pupils who can least afford it have been taught by the least experienced and prepared teachers who are often teaching outside of the subjects for which they have been prepared (Education Trust, 2000).

Reframing the Debate About Traditional Versus Alternative Programs

First, it makes no sense to defend college- and university-based teacher education programs as if they are necessarily better than alternative pathways into teaching. Although there are clearly many excellent preparation programs among the 1,300 or so institutions of higher education that offer teacher education, there are also some weak ones. Although to some extent national accreditation and state approval of teacher education programs is supposed to play a role in monitoring the quality of programs, I do not think that these processes have always addressed many of the fundamental weaknesses in teacher education programs. There is some evidence that the focus on bureaucratic details and loss of the larger sense of purpose that was a problem when performance-based teacher education was mandated in the 1970s (Zeichner, 2005b) is also a problem today as teacher education institutions are asked to devote a substantial amount of their dwindling resources to the construction of elaborate assessment systems and accreditation portfolios for state and national approval of their programs. It has been asserted by some (e.g. Johnson, Johnson, Farenga, & Ness, 2005) that this focus on the minutiae of teacher education programs has served to trivialize the work and interfere with the broader conversations about the work of teacher education curriculum and program development that should be taking place.

Although I think that there is some value to the quality of programs that has resulted from the movement back to a performance-based approach, I think that there is some truth to the criticisms that the amount of resources that needs to be devoted to obtaining program approval diverts attention and scarce resources from the achievement of the end goal of preparing teachers who can teach all students. For example, if the thousands of dollars that are now being spent on aligning hundreds of courses with standards in teacher education institutions and on preparing elaborate accreditation portfolios were spent on supporting such things as professional development school partnerships, paying cooperating teachers a decent wage for their important role in mentoring student teachers, or funding expert P–12 teachers to spend time on college and university campuses working alongside university faculty in teaching methods and content courses, we might get more quality in teacher preparation than we are now getting from some of the hyperrationalized accountability systems that we have been required to create as part of state and national approval and accreditation processes.

Thus far, research does not clearly demonstrate that meeting the various state and national accreditation standards that are mandated for most programs today makes a difference in terms of the quality of teachers who emerge from these programs (Floden, 2005; Wilson & Youngs, 2005). This is not to say that I think that state and national program approval mechanisms should be eliminated. I think that it is important to have an external audit of the work that we do in our teacher education programs, but I think that things have gone too far in the direction of focusing on details. We should streamline these assessment processes so that they focus on only the major elements of programs that make them effective.

It also does not make sense to me to uncritically glorify alternative certification programs as necessarily better than university-based preparation, as a number of critics and government officials have done (e.g. Fordham Foundation, 1999; R. Paige, 2002). There is a range of quality within both university-based programs and alternatives to these programs. The research on this issue clearly shows that neither traditional nor alternative programs have particular kinds of effects on teacher and student learning because of their sponsorship (e.g. Zeichner & Conklin, 2005). The research indicates that it is the characteristics of the programs rather than who sponsors them that matters in terms of influencing a variety of teacher and pupil outcomes. Although some alternative certification programs provide legitimate preparation for teaching in learning theory, pedagogical approaches, assessment, classroom management, and so forth, others, such as Passport to Teaching, merely put unprepared individuals into classrooms as teachers of record (who often teach the pupils who can least afford it) with little or no prior preparation and continuing support. Such programs should be shut down. We need to begin focusing on the quality of teacher education programs rather than on who sponsors them, whether they are graduate or undergraduate, and how long they last.

Research has begun to identify the program characteristics of effective teacher education programs (Humphrey, Wechsler, & Hough, 2005; Zeichner & Conklin, 2005). These include clear and consistent visions of teaching and learning that guide the program, strong integration between instruction about teaching and clinical practice, and clear articulation of the performance standards by which candidates' teaching is judged (e.g. Darling-Hammond, 2000b). We need to support teacher education programs of all kinds that have these and other characteristics that are shown by research to enable the achievement of desired outcomes, whether they are traditional or alternative, and criticize and/or close down those that do not have them.

We also need to conduct further research to better understand the kinds of programs, teacher education pedagogies, and curricular patterns that best prepare teachers for a broad range of desirable teacher and pupil outcomes, not just pupil performance on standardized achievement tests (Zeichner, 2005c). Educational research has been terribly underfunded compared with resources for research in the sciences and the military (Lagemann, 2000). Teacher education research has received a very small share of the little that has been allocated to educational research. In addition to needed societal reallocation of resources toward education, health care, other social services and public P–12 education, some of the resources now being spent on the construction of elaborate assessment systems in teacher education programs could be better spent on funding carefully designed research to further illuminate the characteristics and practices of effective teacher education programs (Zeichner, 2005b).

Until the mid-nineteenth century, there were debates in the U.S. about whether or not any teacher preparation was necessary beyond knowledge of the content to be taught (Lucas, 1999). Since then, although there have been vigorous disagreements about (a) the proportion of education and noneducation courses that should be present in a teacher education program, (b) how long a program should be, and (c) whether it should take place at the undergraduate or graduate level, very few have argued that no preparation in teaching beyond content knowledge is needed. Although I think that we should embrace the entry of new kinds of alternative teacher education programs into the field and focus on the quality of all (traditional and alternative) programs, there is no question in my mind that programs like Passport to Teaching, which would put people into classrooms without any preparation, should be strongly opposed. The fact that the U.S. Department of Education is actively supporting this program is an outrage in my view.

Broadening our View of the Goals of Teacher Education and of Teachers' Roles

Another necessary priority is to work to reframe the debate in teacher education so that teacher quality is broadened to include outcomes beyond the results on standardized achievement tests. The current policy environment is wedded exclusively to standardized achievement tests as the sole measure of teacher quality and student learning, and it is very possible that someday in the future, teacher education programs will be evaluated based on the test score performance of the pupils of their graduates. The likelihood of this "positive impact mandate" (Hamel & Merz, 2005) becoming a requirement on a national scale in the current political climate seems strong despite both the continued debate concerning the usefulness and validity of value-added models for linking teacher education to pupil test scores (e.g. McCaffrey, Lockwood, Koretz, & Hamilton, 2004) and the enormous expense involved in this task.

Although professional schools in some fields are accredited in part based on the pass rates of their graduates on licensing exams, I am not aware of any other field in which professional schools are held accountable for the performance of their graduates in the field after completion of their programs. Why should teacher education programs be singled out for being required to assess the performance of their graduates as a condition for accreditation? Although I think there are useful ways to build greater accountability into all teacher education programs (both traditional and alternative), such as accrediting programs based on emerging research-supported characteristics of programs that are associated with performance-based assessments of graduated at the end of their preparation, pass rates on licensing examinations, and requirements for use of data from regular surveys of program graduates, I think that it is a mistake to jump on the positive impact mandate bandwagon as I see some teacher educators now doing and to engage in what I consider to be silly practices, such as offering warranties on program graduates.

Also, although it is clear that standardized test scores will need to be part of any conversation about student learning, studies clearly show that the public wants a number of additional achievements from its schools beyond high performance on standardized test scores. For example, in his comprehensive study of U.S. schools in the early 1980s, Goodlad (2004) found that parents wanted a lot more from their schools than the development of basic skills in reading, writing, and mathematics. Goodlad argued that his findings are still true today: "They want and expect attention to personal, social, vocational, and academic development" (p. 371). An exclusive focus on raising standardized achievement test scores does not address other important aspects of learning that the public wants its schools to achieve, such as high-level skills of reasoning and problem solving in the academic realm, social learning, aesthetic learning, and civic learning. It also does not address the negative side effects for many poor students of color and their teachers that have resulted from a narrow focus on test scores, such as a narrowing of the curriculum at the elementary level in high-poverty schools to preparation for the tests, the marginalizing of core academic subjects such as science and social studies, and the scripting of the curriculum—all of which have served to further disadvantage those students who already lacked the same level of resources and programs as students from more economically advantaged school districts (Hursh, 2005; Kozol, 2005; Sirotnik, 2004).

At a meeting in California a few years ago that was focused on research in teacher education,[11] a senior member of the U.S. Department of Education argued that the focus in teacher education needs to be on preparing "good enough" teachers who will be able to raise the standardizes test scores of their pupils. This official did not support the idea that teacher preparation programs need to prepare teachers to be reflective and analytic about their practice and able to make situated judgments to adapt their teaching to particular contexts. He also did not support the view that teachers need to develop intercultural sensitivity and intercultural teaching competence because of the belief that if teachers follow the script that is allegedly based on research, test scores will go up regardless of who the students are. This view of teachers as low-level technicians who are to obediently carry out the plans of those removed from the classroom without exercising their judgment and making adaptations to the specific needs of their pupils is troubling given what we know about the science of learning and the complexity of teaching that requires teachers who are able to do much more than follow inflexible scripts (Darling-Hammond & Bransford, 2005). This limited view of the role of teachers is even more troubling to me because it is likely that it will be other people's children who will be taught by these "good enough" teachers. The children of those who advocate the further deprofessionalization of teaching will continue to be taught by teachers in the most resource-advantaged schools that have completed full-scale teacher education programs at our colleges and universities (Kozol, 2005).[12]

Changing the Center of Gravity in Teacher Education

The New York Times critique of education schools (Hartocollis, 2005) presents one of the main solutions to issues of teacher quality in teacher education programs as providing prospective teachers and novice teachers with more clinical practice and exposure to the practices of experienced teachers. The article quotes several students from one university program in New York City who claimed that their program did not provide them with the practical knowledge needed to teach subjects such as reading and spelling. Although many teacher education institutions across the U.S. include clinical experiences throughout the entire length of their teacher education programs,[13] it is clear from research on learning to teach from firsthand experience in schools (McIntyre, Byrd, & Fox, 1996; Zeichner, 1996b) that more experience in and of itself will not necessarily be educative for prospective teachers or help them to learn how to successfully teach the pupils who are in our public schools.

If we are to take seriously our obligation to prepare teachers to successfully teach all students, then we need, as our critics say, to situate more of teacher preparation outside of the college and university campus and inside schools and communities. However we need to do much more than just send them out there to pick up what they need to learn by a process of osmosis. These clinical experiences need to be as carefully planned as any other college or university course and closely integrated with the rest of the teacher education program (Darling-Hammond, 2000b). A lot of good work has gone on in this area in recent years to help move clinical programs in college- and university-based teacher education programs away from the traditional model in which there is little oversight of what student teachers do and close links to campus-based instruction are the exception rather than the rule.

The building of professional development school partnerships in teacher education and the efforts that have been made by the National Council for Accreditation of Teacher Education and others to address issues of quality in professional development schools have been moving teacher education in the right direction (Boyle-Baise & McIntyre, 2008; Clark, 1999; Levine, 1998). Having served as director for the Madison Professional Development School Partnership for the past eight years, in a time of severe budget cuts both in the Madison public schools and at my university, I know firsthand what a challenge it is for advocates of these partnerships that provide greater coherence in a teacher education program to secure the resources needed to maintain program quality.[14] As resources are being slashed in public institutions of all kinds, it is very difficult, in my view, to justify the use of dwindling resources to build the elaborate accountability systems that I discussed earlier.

We need to continue moving teacher education away from the traditional sink-or-swim model of field experience. We need to move toward a model like the professional development school or partner school in which university faculty and staff provide instruction about teaching contexts and expertise of P–12 teachers informs this instruction and the general planning and evaluation in the teacher education program as a whole.

If teacher quality is going to be enhanced by this work, however, there is one major area where efforts on school and university partnerships in teacher education need to go further than they have to date. Specifically, as Murrell (1998) argued, unless these partnerships are expanded to embrace communities as full partners in the education of teachers, the partnership movement in teacher education will fail to develop the cultural competencies that teachers need to successfully teach everyone's children.

In recent years, there has been substantial development in our understanding of what teachers need to be like, need to learn, and need to be able to do in order to teach in culturally responsive ways to provide a higher quality of learning to more students (e.g. Gay, 2000; Irvine & Armento, 2001; Ladson-Billings, 1995; Villegas & Lucas, 2002a, b). In a number of places where community-based learning has been incorporated into teacher education programs, including in the context of school and university partnerships, there is growing empirical evidence that novice teachers are helped to acquire in some forms of community field experiences the kind of knowledge, skills, and dispositions teachers need to be successful in today's public schools (e.g. Boyle-Baise & McIntrye, 2008; Zeichner & Melnick, 1996).

High-quality clinical experiences like professional development schools need to be supported and closely monitored by teacher education faculty, but they need to be extended out to the communities served by these schools so that novice teachers can develop the sociocultural competence they need to be successful in today's public schools (Moll & Arnot-Hopffer, 2005).

Taking Teacher Education Seriously in Colleges and Universities

Probably the most important thing that we can do to contribute to the preparation of our nation's teachers is to ensure that wherever colleges and universities choose to engage in teacher preparation, this work receives strong support from the permanent faculty and from regular institutional budgets. An additional aspect of this issue is that the research universities that supply colleges and universities with the faculty who staff the vast number of teacher education programs throughout the U.S. need to take the preparation of teacher educators more seriously.

Tom (1997) has argued that teacher education is often treated as a form of financial aid for doctoral students at research universities and the work of teacher education is largely carried out by these doctoral students, who often receive little formal preparation and continuing support for this work. The troubled history of teacher education in universities in the U.S. and the reluctance of tenure-track faculty to pour their intellectual energies into offering the best teacher education programs possible because of the lack of rewards for this work has been well documented by a variety of scholars (e.g. Clifford & Guthrie, 1988; Goodlad, 1990; Labaree, 2004; Schneider, 1987). For some faculty in education schools, teacher education serves as the domestic labor or "keeping house" work (Liston, 1995) that enables them to secure funding for their doctoral students and engage in the more high-status work of research and publication. In other colleges and universities where faculty is more directly involved in teacher education, there is often little or no professional development provided to help them learn how to continually improve their work with novice teachers. The teaching loads of these institutions are often very heavy and the travel budgets for attending professional conferences are often meager. Frequently, supervising students in field placements is farmed out to adjunct staff who have very little connection to the rest of the program and very little decision-making power within the institution (Goodlad, 1990). The teacher education faculty in these institutions receive their graduate education in the research universities where teacher education and the preparation of teacher educators is often not taken very seriously as a component of the graduate program.

For some institutions, teacher education has functioned as a "cash cow," bringing in tuition dollars that have then been funneled away from teacher education to support more prestigious activities (Holmes Group, 1995). Although there are many college and university programs in which the faculty do take teacher education seriously and do a good job, there is still much work to be done within research universities in the preparation of teacher educators and with regard to rewarding faculty in higher education institutions for doing high-quality work in educating teachers and working with schools. One aspect of taking teacher education seriously that has come back into prominence recently is that the activity of teacher education is a responsibility of whole institutions and not just education units.

Although the concept has been around for many years (e.g. Stiles, 1958), it has become common in recent years to talk about the all-university concept of teacher education in which faculty throughout a college or university take responsibility for active participation in discussions and decisions related to teacher education. This concept has been endorsed by a number of influential organizations (e.g. American Association of Universities, 1999; American Council on Education, 1999) and is a central element in several reform networks, such as the Teachers for a New Era project and the National Network for Educational Renewal (e.g. Kirby et al., 2004; Sirotnik, 2001). To secure the broader involvement of faculty throughout institutions in the education of teachers, ways must be found to attract them to this work and reward the high-quality work that they do.

During the past year, I have served as the external evaluator for the University of Wisconsin-Milwaukee Teachers for a New Era project. In my observations of the building of the all-university approach to teacher education in this institution, I have seen a number of examples of genuine commitment by arts and sciences faculty to the task of improving teacher education programs. One thing that particularly struck me in Milwaukee was the way in which some of the design teams composed of education and noneducation faculty have sought to turn the work of reforming teacher education into an intellectually satisfying task. They have gone beyond the technical task of aligning courses with content standards to build in what I have called a study group component. Here faculty have read and discussed conceptual and theoretical issues related to the coherence and integrity of teacher education programs. In the long run, these and other efforts to broaden the commitment of high-quality teacher education beyond schools and colleges of education will have to find ways to modify promotion and tenure systems to include high-quality work in teacher education.

Others have proposed, and in some cases implemented, new institutional structures. These include university-wide councils on teacher education and new ways of organizing faculty, such as the Center of Pedagogy idea that has been used in the National network for Educational Renewal (Patterson, Machelli, & Pacheco, 1999).[15] I believe that these efforts to broaden the institutional commitment to teacher education are critical to the future of college- and university-based teacher education.

One of the biggest challenges that lies ahead in making teacher education a greater priority in many colleges and universities is the continuing budget cuts that public institutions have experienced in recent years. These cuts have come at a time when most public school systems in the U.S. are also in great financial difficulty. In the long run, however, working to build an all-institutional commitment to the importance of teacher education will serve to lessen the negative impact of continued budget cuts. The problem here is, of course, a much broader one than one of education and teacher education because social services of every kind are being slashed as we continue to invest as a society in the building of prisons and jails, corporate welfare, and unnecessary wars at the expense of education, health care, housing, and decent jobs.[16]

Conclusion

The professed goal of educators in the U.S. to provide a high-quality public education to everyone's children is a noble one. College- and university-based teacher education has an important role to play in achieving it. It would be a terrible mistake, in my view, to continue on the path of deregulation, destroying college and university teacher education and lowering standards for entry into teaching. With a need to continually supply our country's teaching force of approximately three million with new teachers who are willing and able to teach the students who are in our public schools, we must have multiple ways for people to become teachers. We need to find ways, however, to maintain high standards in both college- and university-based teacher education and alternative pathways. Efforts that have arisen, such as Passport to Teaching, that would put individuals into public schools with essentially no preparation for teaching should be opposed by all teacher educators, whether or not they are based in colleges and universities.

I have suggested four elements that I feel need to be part of this task: (a) focusing attention on the quality of teacher education programs rather than on who sponsors them; (b) broadening our vision of public learning beyond standardized test scores and our view of teachers' roles beyond following scripts to only raise test scores; (c) connecting teacher education programs more closely to schools and communities and more carefully monitoring the quality of teacher learning in these experiences; and (d) taking teacher education seriously as an important responsibility of higher education institutions or closing down these programs.

Finally, those individuals on the outside of schools and colleges of education who have equated a concern for greater social justice with a lowering of academic quality and a lack of concern for teacher quality need to think more seriously about the purpose of public education in democratic societies. The concern in many alternative and traditional teacher education programs to prepare teachers to work to contribute through their work in classrooms and schools to the realization of a more decent and humane society for everyone's children should be the core principle underlying all forms of teacher education, whether or not they are sponsored by colleges and universities.

This is not a naïve belief that teacher education and teachers can solve the major problems of inequality and injustice that have become structured into the fabric of our society. It is clear that in addition to improvements in teacher education programs, the working conditions in schools, including the provision of high-quality professional development, will need to be strengthened. This is a belief, however, that in their daily work in teacher education programs and schools, teachers and teacher educators can make a difference in the outcomes. "Good enough" teachers should not be good enough for everyone's children, and we need to move beyond the current territorial debates about where teacher preparation should occur, focusing instead on what is achieved by different forms of preparation. In the end, teacher education programs need to incorporate the major interests of all three reform agendas that have been battling with each other (i.e. teaching expertise, knowledge of content, and contribution to the realization of a better society for all). The goal of greater social justice is a fundamental part of the work of teacher education in democratic societies and we should never compromise on the opportunity to make progress towards its realization. As Maxine Greene (1979) has argued,

> The concern of teacher educators must remain normative, critical and even political. Neither the teachers colleges nor the schools can change the social order. Neither colleges nor schools can legislate democracy. But something can be done to empower teachers to reflect upon their own life situations, to speak out in their own ways about the lacks that must be repaired; the possibilities to be acted upon in the name of what they deem to be decent, human, and just (p. 71).

Notes

Preface

1 The National Teacher Corps was a major federal program for preparing teachers to work with students living in poverty. It lasted from 1965–1981 (Rogers, 2002).

2 These strands are similar to the earlier paradigms of teacher education and traditions of teacher education reform that I identified in earlier work (Zeichner, 1983, 1993b).

Chapter I

1 Portions of this paper in an earlier form were presented at the annual meeting of the Association of Teacher Educators in Denver, February, 2002, and at the annual meeting of the American Educational Research Association in New Orleans, April, 2002.

2 There are also efforts in some places to extend performance-based teacher education, a central element of the professionalization agenda, to what has been called evidence-based teacher education. Here teacher education programs become accountable for the learning of the pupils taught by their graduates. This movement has not yet become a major force in teacher education reform in the United States, but it may become so in the future. In the teacher education community, there is a growing amount of attention paid to work sample methodology (e.g. Girod, 2002), an approach to documenting the pupil learning "produced" by teacher education students and graduates.

3 The governor later backed off after an angry reaction from local officials across the state. It is not clear currently how the projected one billion dollar-plus state budget deficit will be managed, and the aid to local cities and towns from the state is not secure by any means.

4 More recently, the U.S. Department of Education has taken up the deregulation banner in the Secretary of Education's first annual report on Teacher Quality (U.S. Department of Education, 2002). This report uses many of the same arguments against university-based teacher education that are found in the reports of the Fordham Foundation. It uncritically endorses the value of alternative certification without paying attention to the tremendous variation in the way in which these programs are conceptualized and implemented.

5 These examples are taken from a draft document under development by one of the workgroups in UNITE. It is available by contacting me at zeichner@wisc.edu.

Chapter 2

1 Based in part on lectures given at the University of Maryland in April 2004 and at the University of Washington in May 2004.

2 An expressed commitment to social justice does not necessarily mean that other goals of teacher education, such as subject matter preparation and teaching teachers to plan, assess and adapt instruction to the varied needs of learners, are ignored (Hansen, 2008).

3 Some elements in the multicultural education literature focus on a celebration of diversity without a commitment to dealing with individual, social, institutional, and societal forces of oppression that undermine access to social and economic justice for large numbers of people in most societies (Kailin, 2002).

4 This conclusion is based on an analysis of published work on social justice teacher education and on an analysis of a sample of conceptual frameworks that were submitted to NCATE as part of their accreditation process. McDonald & Zeichner (2009) were given access to these conceptual frameworks by NCATE.

5 Banks et al. (2005) refer to these practices as "equity pedagogy" and elaborate on them.

6 For an overview of these types of practices see Ladson-Billings, 1999 and Zeichner, 1996a.

7 Conklin (2008) argues that "compassion signals not only developing empathy for others but also brings attention to the social conditions that lead to suffering" (p. 13).

8 INTASC stands for Interstate New Teacher Assessment and Support Consortium, which was a consortium formed in the early 1990s by the Council of Chief State School Officers.

9 During its existence, this project has included programs that focus on the preparation of high school teachers and the preparation of college teachers.

10 Another example of linking teacher education to a broader social movement for social justice is located in Brazil where several universities involve their student teachers in working in the popular education movement as part of their teacher education program. This involves student teachers teaching adults elementary and secondary school subjects usually during the evenings and seminars in which the adults, teacher educators, and teacher education students analyze and critique this practice.

11 See Zeichner & Conklin (2008) for a discussion of this issue.

12 Our analysis here focuses on teacher education in research universities. There are similar problems for teacher education in liberal arts colleges and regional universities, but the situation there requires a separate analysis that is beyond the scope of this chapter. There is also a different set of issues to be discussed for social justice teacher education in early entry alternative certification programs where candidates complete their preservice education while serving as teachers of record.

13 The application of scholarly habits and skills to teacher education program renewal would include such things as carefully examining the literature to see what can be learned from other institutions, and conducting research on one's programs and using the data as input for program renewal.

14 Grossman & McDonald (2008) refer to these as the "pedagogies of enactment."

15 For example, Villegas (2008) cites data that indicates that one in five students attending U.S. public schools today is an English learner. This same problem exists with regard to immigrant students in many parts of the world although the new language they are learning may not be English.

Chapter 3

1 Adapted from a keynote address presented at the annual meeting of the National Association for Professional Development Schools, Orlando, FL, in March 2006 and a lecture given at Beijing Normal University, China in December 2005.
2 See Madison Professional Development School Partnership at labweb.education.wisc.edu/pds.
3 It is not necessary to use a professional development school (PDS) model to involve P–12 teachers in the teaching of program courses. See Beynon, Grout, & Wideen (2004) and Post et al. (2006) for discussions of innovative models at Simon Fraser University and the University of Wisconsin-Milwaukee that involve teachers in teacher education.
4 Andreal Davis is the teacher who has developed this program.

Chapter 4

1 This chapter is a revised version of a keynote address presented at the meeting of the Association of Practical Experiences in Professional Education, Christchurch, New Zealand, in January, 1999.
2 Despite the obvious nature of this assertion, a State Appeals Court in New York recently ruled in a case concerning equitable funding for New York City Schools that the state is obligated by its constitution to provide nothing more than a minimal education that prepares students for low-paying jobs (Worth & Hartocollis, 2002). This statement that the government is not responsible for removing gaps in the quality of education provided to different students has undermined attempts to provide more equitable funding for students in city schools. Also, recently, Russell Whitehurst, the Assistant Secretary of Education and Director of the Office of Research and Improvement in the U.S. Department of Education, argued in a meeting at which I was present that the government is not responsible for preparing high-quality teachers for everyone's children. He argued for an emphasis on preparing "just good enough teachers" who would be "just good enough" to follow the prescriptions dictated by teacher proof curriculum materials. The fact that these teachers would be mostly teaching children of the poor and not children from more economically advantaged families (like his own children) was not a concern to him.
3 Action research has been used by a number of different teacher educators in the program and they all do things somewhat differently. What is described here is what happens when I work with preservice teachers in supporting their research.
4 Also see Diniz-Pereira (2002) for a general discussion of the emancipatory potential of action research.

Chapter 5

1 This chapter is a revised version of a keynote address presented at the annual meeting of the Collaborative Action Research Network, Worcester, UK in September, 1992.
2 See Zeichner (1991b) for substantiation of this assertion.
3 See Whitehead and Lomax (1987) and Grierson and Pamplin (1989) for examples of negative reactions against a perceived imposition of social science categories.
4 As Pollard and Tann (1987) state: "Classroom practice can never fail to have some influence on the development of society at large through the ways in which it impacts the identity and life chances of individuals" (p. 192).

5 Even with regard to action research, the emphasis in the U.S. is often on the application by teachers through their research of an externally derived knowledge base, not on the production of new knowledge by teachers. For an example, see Livingston and Castle (1989).

6 There are also dangers attached to this broadening of the scope of action research, such as increased vulnerability of practitioner researchers to manipulation by administrators and managers (Griffiths, 1990).

7 See Ellwood (1992) for a story about how one classroom teacher felt belittled at a meeting of the AERA even in this period of the ascendancy of teacher research.

8 See Fals-Borda (1992) for a discussion of the moral justification for action research and the responsibility of action researchers toward the poor and underprivileged, who constitute the majority of humankind.

9 This work examining the relationships between home and school cultures is similar in some respects to what both Arville McCann (1990) did in relation to one ethnic minority group (Mirpuri Pakistanis) in a U.K. infant school and Shirley Brice Heath (1983) did in the U.S.

Chapter 6

1 This chapter is a revised version of a keynote address presented at the annual meeting of the Collaborative Action Research Network, Umea University, Sweden in November 2008.

2 See McDonald & Zeichner (2009), North (2006, 2008) and Sturman (1997) for a discussion of some of these conceptions and their relationship to one another in an educational context.

3 Paige (2002).

4 See Zeichner & Hutchinson (2008, pp. 15–29) for a discussion of the evolution of alternative certification policies in the U.S.

5 The term was used by a high-ranking official in the U.S. Department of Education at a meeting held at the Carnegie Foundation for the Advancement of Teaching in June 2002.

6 Two examples of this are the scandal over the Reading First program initiated by a government audit (Grunwald, 2006) and criticisms of the inappropriate use of money in three states to buy educational products from a company owned by the president's brother, Neil Bush (Thompson, 2007). There is strong evidence that the so-called "Texas miracle" on which current policies emphasizing standardized testing are in part based did not produce the kinds of success for students that were claimed by the Bush administration (e.g. Haney, 2000; Valenzuela, 2005).

7 Feistritzer & Haar (2008) report that in 2006, approximately 50,000 individuals were teachers of record in schools across the country while they were still in the process of completing their preservice teacher education programs.

8 For example, between 2002 and 2006, Title I funding was underfunded by 31.5 billion dollars and IDEA was underfunded by 37.6 billion dollars. Retrieved September 8, 2006, from the National School Board Association website www.nsba.org/site/docs/38600/38542.pdf.

9 Feistritzer & Haar (2008) state that as many as one half of teachers certified through alternative routes in 2005 were in just three states: Texas, California, and New Jersey.

10 There is much debate over this issue. See McCaffrey, Koretz, Lockwood, & Hamilton (2004).

11 I worked as a consultant with the Namibian National Institute for Educational Development from 1994–2000 and became familiar with action research studies being done by student teachers in Namibian education colleges.

Chapter 7

1 An earlier version of this paper was presented as a Keynote address at the Annual Meeting of the Australian Association of Research in Education, University of Newcastle, New South Wales, November 1994.
2 For example, *Teaching and Change* is a new journal of teacher research initiated by the National Education Association. This journal and *Classroom Inquiry* mostly contain studies by full-time P–12 teachers.

Chapter 8

1 An earlier version of this paper was presented as a lecture in July 1991 at the Institute in Teacher Education, Simon Fraser University in Burnaby, British Columbia, Canada.
2 See discussions of the deskilling and reskilling of teachers by Apple (1986) and Densmore (1987).
3 See Zeichner 1992b, Zeichner & Tabachnick, 1991, and Zeichner 1994 for the results of some of these investigations.
4 See Britzman, 1991, pp. 46–49 for a brief but insightful discussion of different views of the theory–practice relationship.
5 It should be noted that these materials are still being widely promoted throughout North America. For example, the inside front cover of the November 1991 issue of Kappan is a full page advertisement for the newly revised reflective teaching materials.
6 See Lawn (1989) for a discussion of this issue in relation to teacher research.
7 See Kozol (1991) for a vivid documentation of some of these problems in U.S. schools.
8 See Children's Defense Fund (1991) for documentation of some of these factors in the U.S. See Schorr (1989) for a discussion of the interrelatedness of educational, social and economic factors in the U.S.
9 Copies of the Madison teachers' action research reports can be obtained at no cost from the author. Contact the author at zeichner@wisc.edu.
10 This report, "Lego TC Logo: bridging the gender gap," can also be obtained from the author.

Chapter 9

1 This chapter is a revised version of Zeichner, K. (2006). Reflections of a university-based teacher educator on the future of college and university-based teacher education. *Journal of Teacher Education*, 57(3), 326–340.
2 Darling-Hammond and Berry argue that a bargain was struck in this second wave of reform that involved greater regulation of teachers through more rigorous selection, preparation, and certification rules in exchange for some deregulation of teaching and fewer rules prescribing what is to be taught, when, and how.
3 For a discussion of the relationship between these changes in education and the growth of worker participation in the U.S. economy as a whole, see Levin (1990).
4 See Elmore & McLaughlin (1988) for examples of the arguments that seek to demonstrate that teachers need to be active creators rather than passive consumers of solutions to the problems of schools.
5 For a history of community involvement in schools, see Grant (1979).
6 See Wise (1979) and Apple (1987) for discussions of these efforts to improve schools through greater prescription and standardization. Apple's discussion links these occurrences in schools to efforts to standardize and rationalize other kinds of work and to a crisis in the structure of the U.S. economy.

7   Madeline Hunter's teaching strategy is sometimes referred to as the "Essential Elements of Instruction." See Gentile (1988).

8   See Apple (1986) for a discussion of the intensification of teachers' work. One interesting example of this intensification that has arisen in Madison is a result of recent rules implemented by the state with regard to teacher education programs. As a result of new policies that require student teachers to be in the schools for the public school semester of 20 weeks (rather than the university calendar of 15 weeks), many local cooperating teachers are now saying that they only want to work with University of Wisconsin students for one rather than two semesters so that they can have some time alone with their classes without the additional responsibilities of being a teacher educator. Before this new requirement, teachers had about a month between semesters without a student teacher in their classrooms. Madison teachers are also feeling the effects of increased committee work associated with the recent involvement of teachers in curriculum development and evaluation and other special projects. See Liston & Zeichner (1991, Chapter 7) for a discussion of recent efforts by Madison elementary teachers to persuade their school board to provide them with more time during the school day to engage in a variety of noninstructional activities. See Carnoy & MacDonnell (1990) for a specific example of how the decentralization of school decision making both upgrades the status of teachers and professionals and places severe demands on their time and energy.

9   One reason for the cultural distance between schools and communities in urban areas is related to the demographics of the student and professional staff in these schools. For example, in New York City, about 75 percent of public school students are people of color, while about 75 percent of the administrative and teaching staff are not. This same phenomenon exists in practically every large urban school district in the U.S. See Bastian et al. (1986).

10 This phenomenon of involvement but lack of influence for communities in their schools is not new. For an analysis of this trend in relation to community involvement mandates of the National Teacher Corps, see Popkewitz (1975).

11 The lack of meaningful parental influence also exists with regard to the parental involvement components of the recent federal mainstreaming legislation, PL 94–142, and related state laws. While parents' rights are specifically stated in both federal and state mainstreaming statutes, parental involvement in program development and student assessment is very limited. For a summary of the literature on parental involvement in the area of mainstreaming, see Gartner et al. (1987).

12 Teachers and principals are not generally enthusiastic about parent participation in curriculum development, instruction, and school governance, oftentimes perceiving community empowerment to be a threat to teacher empowerment. See Moles (1982, November) and Olson, L. (1990, April 4).

13 These connections are also important in rural schools where poverty has also contributed to school failure for many students. See Rosewater (1989).

14 Gutmann argues that teachers should be given enough autonomy to prevent the ossification of their office, but not so much power as to lead to the insolence of their office.

15 This situation of polarization is evidenced by the separate literatures that have evolved stressing a particular form of empowerment. On the one hand, as was pointed out earlier, the mainstream educational literature advocating teacher empowerment (e.g. Bolin, "Empowering Leadership," and Lieberman, *Building a Professional Culture in Schools*) emphasizes teacher empowerment, but gives only minimal attention to community empowerment. On the other hand, much of the literature advocating community empowerment (e.g. Williams, *Neighborhood Organizing for Urban School Reform*) asserts the rights of

communities, but largely ignores how the authority of professional educators will be preserved.

16 The Institute for Democracy in Education, coordinated by George Wood in Athens, Ohio, publishes the journal *Democratic Education*. The Rethinking Schools Group, coordinated by a group of Milwaukee public school teachers, publishes a newspaper by the same name.

17 Not all school choice plans would violate the democratic restraint of nondiscrimination. For a discussion of this issue, see Zerchykov (1987).

18 The gap between the wealthy and the poor in the U.S. is the largest it has been in many years and it continues to grow wider as we continue to experience the inadequate allocation of our nation's resources to social services of almost every kind. For example, in 1987, according to the Washington, D.C.-based Center on Budget and Family Priorities, the poorest fifth of American families received only 4.6 percent of the national family income, while the top fifth's share was 43.7 percent. This gap was the largest in 40 years, as was the number of Americans who are ill-housed, poorly educated, and without health care.

19 While I will not focus here on the kinds of specific changes in the economic, political, and social structures of the society that I would personally support, one example of the kind of programs I have in mind can be found in Raskin's proposals for promoting the common good in society. While I do not agree with everything that Raskin proposes, I find the general direction of his proposals to be very close to my own sympathies. See Raskin (1986).

20 In an earlier paper that was sent to the Holmes Group, a group of us referred to reforms that lead beyond themselves to contribute to a more just and equitable society as "nonreformist reforms" (Apple, 1989).

21 For a discussion of government research priorities, see Biddle (1989).

Chapter 10

1 This chapter is a revised version of Zeichner, K. (1991). Contradictions and tensions in the professionalization of teaching and democratization of schools. *Teachers College Record*, 92(3), 363–379.

2 Although there have been other conceptualizations of different agendas for teacher education reform, including some of my own (e.g. Cochran-Smith & Frieds, 2001; Liston & Zeichner, 1991), this framework captures the major distinctions that have been made in the literature among different approaches.

3 There have been many instances, for example, where teacher educators have attempted to pursue social justice goals within a performance-based program using teaching standards (e.g. Vavrus, 2002).

4 By 2004, 49 states had reported to the U.S. Department of Education that they had developed standards that prospective teachers must meet to qualify for initial teacher certification (Spellings, 2005).

5 The American Association of Colleges for Teacher Education sponsored another widely publicized effort to articulate the knowledge base for beginning teachers (Reynolds, 1989).

6 To date, the U.S. Department of Education has given more than 40 million dollars on a noncompetitive basis to the nonprofit American Board for the Certification of Teacher Excellence. Currently, five states accept Passport to Teaching (Paige, 2005).

7 Some would argue that university-based teacher education never had a lot of credibility outside its own inner circle or even in the institutions in which programs are housed (e.g. Labaree, 2004). In some parts of the country, nearly as many teachers enter teaching through alternative routes as through traditional routes (Humphrey & Wechsler, 2005).

8 It should be noted that some of these school district-based programs employ university teacher educators, but they choose whom they want to employ and determine the conditions of the programs.

9 No college or university teacher educator that I have met in the past 30 years has advocated that we should prepare teachers to teach in a manner in which pupils totally construct knowledge or in which providing knowledge to pupils is seen as undesirable. What college- and university-based teacher education has done, however, is to integrate new research about the process of learning into its preparation programs (Bransford, Brown, & Cocking, 1999).

10 The main professional organizations for university-based teacher education in the U.S. are the American Association of Colleges for Teacher Education and the Association of Teacher Educators.

11 The meeting was held at the Carnegie Foundation for the Advancement of Teaching in June 2002.

12 It should be pointed out that not everyone in the current U.S. Department of Education has expressed such an extreme view on limiting teacher preparation to a training model. For example, the most recent report of the secretary of education on teacher quality states that "it is practically impossible to develop menu-like prescribes for every situation. Today's teacher preparation programs must train their graduates to assess student learning styles and to make sound decisions, choosing from various instructional approaches and methods" (Spellings, 2005, p. 13). With regard to the importance of teachers' cultural competence, the report states that "teachers in high-need schools must have an understanding of the needs of diverse populations and have the skills to develop a set of culturally relevant teaching strategies" (Spellings, 2005, p. 14).

13 It is rare that full-time student teaching is the first clinical teaching experience in any program, as was the norm in the past.

14 Information about the Madison Professional Development School Partnership can be found at http://labweb.education.wisc.edu/pds/.

15 This idea has been around for a long time (e.g. see Smith, 1980).

16 For example, as of July 2005, the U.S. Congress had allocated more than US$192 billion dollars to support the invasion and subsequent occupation of Iraq, whereas most of our public school systems are going deeper into debt, in some cases in the hundreds of millions of dollars. In the United States, which has the largest prison population in the world (more than 2.1 million inmates), state spending on prisons and jails grew in the 1980s and 1990s at six times the rate of state spending on tertiary education (Justice Policy Institute, 2002).

References

Abbate-Vaughn, J. (2008). Highly qualified teachers for our schools: Developing knowledge, skills and dispositions to teach culturally and linguistically diverse students. In M.E. Brisk (Ed.), *Language, culture and community in teacher education.* (pp. 175–202). New York: Erlbaum/Routledge.

Abdal-Haqq, I. (1997). *Professional development schools: Weighing the evidence.* Thousand Oaks, CA: Corwin Press.

Achinstein, B., Ogawa, R., & Speiglman, A. (2004). Are we creating separate and unequal tracks of teachers? The effects of state policy, local conditions, and teacher characteristics on new teacher socialization. *American Educational Research Journal, 41*(3), 557–603.

Ahlquist, R. (1991). Position and imposition: Power relations in a multicultural foundations class. *Journal of Negro Education, 60*(2), 158–169.

Altrichter, H., & Gstettner, P. (1993). Action research: A closed chapter in the history of German social science? *Educational Action Research, 1*(3), 329–360.

Altrichter, H., Pasch, P., & Somekh, B. (1993). *Teachers investigate their work: An introduction to the methods of action research.* London: Routledge.

American Association of Colleges for Teacher Education. (1980). *Multicultural teacher education: Guidelines for implementation.* Washington, DC: Author.

American Association of Universities. (1999). *Resolution on teacher education.* Washington, DC: Author.

American Council on Education. (1999). *To touch the future: Transforming the way teachers are taught.* Washington, DC: Author.

Anderson, G., Herr, K. & Nihlen, A. (2007). *Studying your own school: An educator's guide to practitioner action research* (2nd ed.). Thousand Oaks, CA: Corwin Press.

Angelotti, M., Capella, D., Kelly, P., Pope, C., Beal, C., & Milner, J. (2001). Preservice teacher research: How viable is it? *English Education, 34*(1), 79–85.

Annie E. Casey Foundation (2008). *2008 Kids count data book.* Baltimore, MD: Author.

Apple, M. (1986). *Teachers and texts: A political economy of class and gender relations in education.* New York: Routledge.

Apple, M. (1987a). The de-skilling of teachers. In A. Lieberman (Ed.), *Teacher renewal* (pp. 59–75). New York: Teachers College Press.

Apple, M. (1987b). Will the social context allow a tomorrow for tomorrow's teachers? In J. F. Soltis (Ed.), *Reforming teacher education: The impact of the Homes Group report.* New York: Teachers College Press.

Apple, M. (1989). *Toward tomorrow's schools.* Unpublished manuscript. Buffalo: State University at Buffalo, School of Education.

Apple, M. (2001). *Educating the "right" way: Markets, standards, God, and inequality.* New York: Routledge-Falmer.

Apple, M. (2006). *Educating the right way: Markets, standards, God, and inequality* (2nd ed.). New York: Routledge.

Artiles. A., Harry, B., Reschly, D.J., & Chinn, P.C. (2002). Over-identification of students of color in special education: A critical overview. *Multicultural Perspectives, 4*(1), 3–10.

Atkin, M. (1994). Teacher research to change policy: An illustration. In S. Hollingsworth & H. Sockett (Eds.), *Teacher Research and Educational Reform* (pp. 103–120). Chicago: University of Chicago Press.

Atwell, N. (1987). *In the middle: Writing, reading and learning with adolescents.* Portsmouth, NH: Heinemann, Boynton/Cook.

Ayala, J. (2006). Electronic portfolios for whom? *Educause Quarterly,1,*12–13.

Ayers, W. (1989). Reforming schools and rethinking classrooms: A Chicago chronicle. *Rethinking Schools, 40*(1), 6–10.

Baines, L. (2006). Deconstructing teacher certification. *Phi Delta Kappan, 88*(4), 326–329.

Ball, D. & Cohen, D. (1999). Developing practice, developing practitioners: Toward a theory of professional education. In L. Darling-Hammond & G. Sykes (Eds.), *Teaching as a learning profession: Handbook of policy and practice.* (pp. 3–32). San Francisco: Jossey-Bass.

Ball, D. (2000). Bridging practices: Intertwining content and pedagogy in teaching and learning to teach. *Journal of Teacher Education, 51*(3), 241–247.

Ball, D. (April, 2007). *The case for ed schools and the challenge.* Dewitt Wallace-Reader's Digest Distinguished lecture. Presented at the annual meeting of the American Educational Research Association, Chicago.

Ballou, D., & Podgursky, M. (2000). Reforming teacher preparation and licensing: What is the evidence? *Teachers College Record, 102*(1), 5–27.

Banks, J., Cochran-Smith, M., Moll, L., Richert, A., Zeichner, K., Darling-Hammond, L. & Duffy, H. (2005). Teaching diverse learners. In L. Darling-Hammond & J. Bransford (Eds.), *Preparing teachers for a changing world* (pp. 232–274). San Francisco: Jossey-Bass.

Baptiste, H. P., Baptiste, M. L., & Gollnick, D. (Eds.). (1980). *Multicultural teacher education: Preparing educators to provide educational equity* (Vol. 1). Washington, DC: American Association of Colleges for Teacher Education.

Barber, B. (1997). Public schooling: Education for democracy. In J. Goodlad & T. McMannon (Eds.), *The public purpose of education and schooling* (pp. 21–32). San Francisco: Jossey Bass.

Barth, R. (1989). School: A community of leaders. In A. Lieberman (Ed.), *Building a professional culture in schools* (pp. 129–147). New York: Teachers College Press.

Barth, R. (1990). *Improving schools from within.* San Francisco, CA: Jossey-Bass.

Bartlett, L., Knight, J., & Lingard, B. (1992). Restructuring teacher education in Australia. *British Journal of Sociology of Education, 13,* 19–36.

Bastian, A., Fruchter, N., Gittell, M., Greer, C., Haskins, K. (1986). *Choosing equality: The case for democratic schooling.* Philadelphia, PA: Temple University Press.

Beckman, D. R. (1957). Student teachers learn by action research. *Journal of Teacher Education, 8*(4), 369–375.

Berliner, D. (2006). Our impoverished view of educational reform. *Teachers College Record*. Retrieved September 10, 2006, from www.tcrecord.org

Bestor, A. (1953). *Educational wastelands: The retreat from learning in our public schools*. Urbana: University of Illinois Press.

Beynon, J., Grout, J., & Wideen, M. (2004). *From teacher to teacher educator: Collaboration within a community of practice*. Vancouver: Pacific Education Press.

Biddle, B. (1989). Implications of government funding policies for research on teaching and teacher education. *Teaching and Teacher Education, 5*(4), 275–282.

Bigelow, B., Christenson, L., Karp, S., Miner, B., & Peterson, B. (1994). *Rethinking our classrooms: Teaching for equity and justice*. Milwaukee, WI: Rethinking Schools.

Bigelow, B., Miner, B., & Petrison, B. (1991). *Rethinking Columbus*. Milwaukee, WI: Rethinking Schools.

Bissex, S. (1987). Why case studies? In G. Bissex & R. Bullock (Eds.), *Seeing ourselves: Case-study research by teachers of writing* (pp. 7–20). Portsmouth, NH: Heinemann.

Blair, J. (2002, January, 23). City schools feel the pain of fiscal bites. *Education Week, 21*(1), 1–10.

Bold Approach (2008). *A broader, bolder approach to education*. Statement published by a Taskforce sponsored by the Economic Policy Institute. Retrieved June 17, 2008, from www.boldapproach.org

Bolin, F. (1989, Fall). Empowering leadership. *Teachers College Record, 91*(1), 81–96.

Book, C. (1996). Professional development schools. In J. Sikula (Ed.), *Handbook of research on teacher education* (2nd ed., pp. 194–210). New York: Macmillan.

Boyle-Baise, L. (2002). *Multicultural service learning: Educating teachers in diverse communities*. New York: Teachers College Press.

Boyle-Baise, L., & McIntyre, D. J. (2008). What kind of experience? Preparing teachers in PDS or community settings. In M. Cochran-Smith, S. Feiman-Nemser & D.J. McIntyre (Eds.), *Handbook of research on teacher education* (3rd ed., pp. 307–330). New York: Erlbaum/Routledge.

Bransford, J., Brown, A., & Cocking, R. (Eds.). (1999). *How people learn: Brain, mind, experience, and school*. Washington, DC: National Academy Press.

Bransford, J. D., Brown, A. L., & Cocking, R. R. (Eds.). (2000). *How people learn: Brain, mind, experience, and school* (Expanded ed.). Washington, DC: National Academy Press.

Brisk, M. E. (Ed.). (2008). *Language, culture and community in teacher education*. New York: Erlbaum/Routledge.

British Columbia Teachers' Federation (n.d) *The story of the 2005 BC teachers' strike*. Retrieved June 2, 2007, from bctf.ca.

Britzman, D. (1991). *Practice makes practice: A critical study of learning to teach*. Albany, NY: SUNY Press.

Brodhagen, B. (1992). *Assessing and reporting student progress in an integrative curriculum*. Madison, WI: Madison Metropolitan School District.

Brown, H. (1938). A challenge to teachers' colleges. *Social Frontier, 4*(37), 327–329.

Buck, P. & Sylvester, P. (2005). Preservice teachers enter urban communities: Coupling funds of knowledge research with critical pedagogy in teachers' education. In N. Gonzalez; L. Moll & C. Amanti (Eds.), *Funds of knowledge: Theorizing practices in household, communities and classrooms* (pp. 213–232). New York: Erlbaum/Routledge.

Bullough, R. (2008). Rethinking portfolios: Case records as personal teaching texts for study in preservice teacher education. In R. Bullough *Counter narratives: Studies of teacher education and becoming and being a teacher* (pp. 177–192). Albany, NY: SUNY Press.

Burbules, N., & Torres, C.A. (Eds.). (2000). *Globalization and education: Critical perspectives*. New York: Routledge-Falmer.

Calderhead, J. (1989). Reflective teaching and teacher education. *Teaching and Teacher Education 5(1)*, 43–51.

Calderhead, J., & Gates, P. (Eds.). (1993). Introduction. In *Conceptualizing reflection in teacher development* (pp. 1–10). London: Falmer Press.

Campbell, S. S. (March, 2008). *Mediated field experiences in learning progressive teaching: A design experiment in teacher education.* Paper presented at the annual meeting of the American Educational Research Association, New York City.

Carey, K. (2004). *The funding gap: Many states shortchange low income and minority students.* Washington, DC: The Education Trust.

Carlson Learning Company. (1996). *Discovering Diversity Profile.* Mount Prospect, IL: Author.

Carnegie Task Force on Teaching as a Profession. (1986). *A nation prepared: Teachers for the 21st century.* New York: Carnegie Corporation.

Carnoy, M. (1995). Structural adjustment and the changing face of education. *International Labor Review, 134(6)*, 653–674.

Carnoy, M., & MacDonnell, J. (1990). School district restructuring in Santa Fe, Mexico. *Educational Policy, 4(1)*, 49–64.

Carpenter, T., & Fennema, E. (1992). Cognitively guided instruction: Building on the knowledge of students and teachers. In W. Secada (Ed.), Curriculum reform: The case of mathematics in the U.S. Special issue of the *International Journal of Educational Research* (pp. 457–470).

Carr, W., & Kemmis, S. (1986). *Becoming critical: Education, knowledge and action research.* London: Falmer Press.

Carroll, D.; H. Featherstone; J. Featherstone; S. Feiman-Nemser; & D. Roosevelt (Eds). (2007). *Transforming teacher education: Reflections from the field.* Cambridge, MA: Harvard Education Press.

Carter, K. (1993). The place of story in the study of teaching and teacher education. *Educational Researcher, 22*, 5–12.

Center for the Future of Teaching and Learning. (2001). *Teaching and California's future: The status of the teaching profession 2001.* Santa Cruz: Author.

Center X Community of Educators. (under review). Supporting urban educators: Lessons from Center X's first decade. *Democracy and Education.*

Charters, W. W., & Waples, D. (1929). *The commonwealth teacher training study.* Chicago: University of Chicago Press.

Children's Defense Fund. (1991). *Child poverty in America.* Washington, DC: Children's Defense Fund.

Children's Defense Fund. (2001). *The state of America's children.* Washington, DC: Author.

Children's Defense Fund. (2007). *America's cradle to prison pipeline.* Washington, DC: Author.

Chubb, J. (1988). Why the current wave of educational reform will fail. *The Public Interest, 94*, 28–49.

Clark, K. (July, 2007). *Declines in spending on public higher education in Wisconsin: An analysis of the University of Wisconsin system budget.* Madison: WISCAPE Policy Brief, University of Wisconsin-Madison.

Clark, R. (1999). *Effective professional development schools.* San Francisco: Jossey Bass.

Clarke, S. C. T. (1969). The story of the elementary teacher education models. *Journal of Teacher Education, 20*(3), 283–293.

Clewell, B. & Villegas, A. M. (2001a). *Ahead of the class: A handbook for preparing new teachers from new sources.* Washington, DC: The Urban Institute.

Clewell, B. C., & Villegas, A. M. (2001b). *Absence unexcused: Ending teacher shortages in high-need areas.* Washington, DC: The Urban Institute.

Clifford, G. J. (1973). A history of the impact of research on teaching. In R. Travers (Ed.), *Second handbook of research on teaching* (pp. 1–46). Chicago: Rand McNally.

Clifford, G. J., & Guthrie, J. W. (1988). *Ed school.* Chicago: University of Chicago Press.

Clift, R., & Brady, P. (2005). Research on methods courses and field experiences. In M. Cochran-Smith & K. Zeichner (Eds.), *Studying teacher education: The report of the AERA panel on research and teacher education* (pp. 309–424). Mahwah, NJ: Lawrence Erlbaum.

Clift, R., Veal, M. L., Johnson, M., & Holland, P. (1990). Restructuring teacher education through collaborative action research. *Journal of Teacher Education, 41*(2), 52–62.

Clinchy, E. (1989). Chicago's great experiment begins: Will radical decentralization bring school reform? *Equity and Choice, 5*(3), 40–44.

Cochran-Smith, M. (1994). The power of teacher research in teacher education. In S. Hollingsworth & H. Sockett (Eds.), *Teacher research and educational reform* (pp. 142–165). Chicago: University of Chicago Press.

Cochran-Smith, M. (1999). Learning to teach for social justice. In G. Griffin (Ed.), *The education of teachers. Ninety-eight yearbook of the National Society for the Study of Education* (pp. 114–144). Chicago: University of Chicago Press.

Cochran-Smith, M. (2001). The outcomes question in teacher education. *Teaching and Teacher Education, 17*, 527–546.

Cochran-Smith, M. (2004). *Walking the road: Race, diversity and social justice in teacher education.* New York: Teachers College Press.

Cochran-Smith, M., Davis, D., & Fries, M. K. (2003). Multicultural teacher education: Research, practice, and policy. In J. Banks & C.A.M. Banks (Eds.), *Handbook of research on multicultural education* (2nd ed., pp. 931–975). San Francisco: Jossey Bass.

Cochran-Smith, M., & Donnell, K. (2006). Practitioner inquiry: Blurring the boundaries of research and practice. In J. L. Green, G. Camilli, and P. B. Elmore (Eds.), *Complementary Methods for Research in Education* (2nd edition, pp. 503–518). Mahwah, N.J.: Lawrence Erlbaum Associates.

Cochran-Smith, M., & Fries, M. K. (2001). Sticks, stones and ideology: The discourse of reform in teacher education. *Educational Researcher, 30*(8), 3–15.

Cochran-Smith, M., & Lytle, S. (1992). Communities for teacher research: Fringe or forefront. *American Journal of Education*, 298–324.

Cochran-Smith, M., & Lytle, S. (1993). *Inside/outside: Teacher research and knowledge.* New York: Teachers College Press.

Cochran-Smith, M., & Lytle, S. (1999). The teacher research movement: A decade later. *Educational Researcher, 28*(7), 15–25.

Cochran-Smith, M., & Zeichner, K. (Eds.). (2005). *Studying teacher education: The report of the AERA Panel on Research and Teacher Education.* Mahwah, NJ: Lawrence Erlbaum.

Coley, R., & Thorpe, M. (1986). *A look at the M.A.T. model of teacher education and its graduates.* Princeton, NJ: Educational Testing Service.

Comer, J. (1980). *School power: Implications of an intervention project.* New York: Free Press.

Comer, J. (1988). Educating poor and minority children. *Scientific American, 259*(5), 42–48.

Committee on Policy for Racial Justice. (1989). *Visions of a better way: A black appraisal of public schooling* (p. 27). Washington, DC: Joint Center for Political Studies Press.

Compton, M., & Weiner, L. (Eds.). (2008). *The global assault on teaching, teachers and their unions.* New York: Palgrave Macmillan.

Conant, J. (1963). *The education of American teachers.* New York: McGraw-Hill.

Conklin, H. G. (2008, March). *Modeling compassion in critical, justice-oriented teacher education.* Paper presented at the annual meeting of the American Educational Research Association, New York City.

Cookson, P. W. (1987). Closing the rift between scholarship and practice: The need to revitalize educational research. *Educational Policy, 1*, 321–331.

Cooper, M. (1989). Whose culture is it anyway? In A. Lieberman (Ed.), *Building a professional culture in schools* (pp. 45–54). New York: Teachers College Press.

CREDE. (2002). *Five standards for effective pedagogy.* Santa Cruz, CA: Center for Research on Education, Diversity, and Excellence.

Crittenden, B. (1973). Some prior questions in the reform of teacher education. *Interchange, 4*(2-3), 1–11.

Cruickshank, D. (1987). *Reflective teaching.* Resort, VA: Association of Teacher Educators.

Cutler-Landsman, D. (1991). *Lego TC Logo: Bridging the gender gap.* Middleton, WI: Elm Lawn Elementary School.

Dahlstrom, L. (2006). Critical practitioner inquiry: Creating voices among subaltern professionals. In L. Dahlstrom & J. Mannberg (Eds.), *Critical educational visions and practices in neoliberal times* (pp. 57–70). Umea, Sweden: Umea University, Department of Education and Teacher Education in Swedish and Social Sciences.

Dana, N. F., & Silva, D. Y. (2001). Student teachers as researchers: Developing an inquiry stance toward teaching. In J. Rainer & E. Guyton (Eds.), *Research on the effects of teacher education on teacher performance* (pp. 91–104). Dubuque, IA: Kendall Hunt.

Darling-Hammond, L. (1989). Policy and professionalism. In A. Lieberman (Ed.), *Building a professional culture in schools* (pp. 55–77). New York: Teachers College Press.

Darling-Hammond, L. (Ed.). (1994). *Professional development schools: Schools for developing a profession.* New York: Teachers College Press.

Darling-Hammond, L. (2000a). Reforming teacher education and licensing: Debating the evidence. *Teachers College Record, 102*(1), 28–56.

Darling-Hammond, L. (2000b). *Studies of excellence in teacher education*. Washington, DC: American Associates of Colleges for Teacher Education.

Darling-Hammond, L. (2001). *The research and rhetoric on teacher certification: A response to teacher education reconsidered.* Stanford, CA: Stanford University School of Education.

Darling-Hammond, L. (2004). Inequality and the right to learn: Access to qualified teachers in California's public schools. *Teachers College Record, 106*(10), 1936–1966.

Darling-Hammond, L. (2006). *Powerful teacher education*. San Francisco: Jossey-Bass.

Darling-Hammond, L., & Berry, B. (1988). *The evolution of teacher policy.* Washington, DC: Rand Corporation.

Darling-Hammond, L., Berry, B., & Thoreson, A. (2001). Does teacher certification matter? Evaluating the evidence. *Educational Evaluation and Policy Analysis, 23*(1), 57–77.

Darling-Hammond, L., & Bransford, J. (Eds.). (2005). *Preparing teachers for a changing world*. San Francisco: Jossey Bass.

Darling-Hammond, L., & Chung Wei, R. (in press). Teacher preparation and teacher learning: A changing policy landscape. In D. Plank, B. Schneider & G. Sykes (Eds.), *AERA handbook of education policy research*. Washington, DC: American Educational Research Association.

Darling-Hammond, L., French, J., & Garcia-Lopez, S. P. (Eds.). (2002). *Learning to teach for social justice*. New York: Teachers College Press.

Darling-Hammond, L., Hammerness, K., Grossman, P., Rust, F., & Shulman, L. (2005). The design of teacher education programs. In L. Darling-Hammond & J. Bransford (Eds.), *Preparing teachers for a changing world.* (pp. 390–441). San Francisco: Jossey-Bass.

Davies, D. (1989). *The benefits and barriers to parental involvement*. Boston: Institute for Responsive Education.

Day, C. (1984). Teachers' thinking, intentions and practice: An action research perspective. In R. Halkes & J. Olson (Eds.), *Teacher thinking* (pp. 73–84). Lisse: Swets & Zeitlinger.

Delpit, L. (1986). Skills and other dilemmas of a progressive black educator. *Harvard Educational Review, 56*(4), 379–386.

Delpit, L. (1988). The silenced dialogue: Power and pedagogy in educating other people's children. *Harvard Educational Review, 58*, 280–298.

Delpit, L. (1995). *Other people's children: Cultural conflict in the classroom*. New York: New Press.

Densmore, K. (1987) Professionalism, proletarianization, and teacher work. In T. Popkewitz (Ed.), *Critical studies in teacher education* (pp. 130–160). London: Falmer Press.

Dillon, S. (2006). Schools cut back subjects to push reading and math. *The New York Times*, March 28. Retrieved August 28, 2006, from http://www.nytimes.com

Diniz-Pereira, J. (2002). Globalizations: Is the teacher research movement a critical and emancipatory response? *Educational Action Research 10*(3), 373–398.

Diniz-Pereira, J. E. (2005, October). Teacher education for social transformation and its links to progressive social movements: The case of the Landless Workers Movement in Brazil. *Journal for Critical Education Policy Studies, 3*(2). Retrieved June 8, 2007, from http://www.jceps.com/print.php?articleID=51

Doig, S. (1994). *Pinning the tale on the donkey: The placement of teacher voice in educational research*. Paper presented at the annual meeting of the Australian Association of Research in Education, New Castle.

Duffy, G. (1994). Professional development schools and the disempowerment of teachers and professors. *Kappan, 75*, 596–601.

Edelman, M. W. (1989). Children at risk. In F. Macchiarola & A. Gartner (Eds.), *Caring for America's children* (pp. 20–30). New York: Academy of Political Science.

Education Commission of the States. (1986). *What's next? More leverage for teachers*. Denver, CO: Author.

Education Trust. (2000). *Honoring the boxcar: Equalizing teacher quality*. Washington, DC: Author.

Education Trust. (2001). *The other gap: Poor students receive fewer dollars*. Washington, DC: Author.

Elliott, J. (1990). Teachers as researchers: Implications for supervision and for teacher education. *Teaching & Teacher Education, 6*(1), 1–26.

Elliott, J. (1991). *Action research for educational change*. Milton Keynes, UK: Open University Press.

Elliott, J., & Adelman, C. (1973). Reflecting where the action is: The design of the Ford Teaching Project. *Education for Teaching, 92*, 8–20.

Ellwood, C. (1992). *Teacher research: For whom?* Paper presented at the annual meeting of the American Educational Research Association, San Francisco.

Elmore, R., & McLaughlin, M. W. (1988). *Steady work: Policy, practice, and the reform of American education*. Santa Monica, CA: Rand Corporation.

Evans, C., Stubbs, M., Frechotte, P., Neely, C., & Warner, J. (1987). *Educational practitioners: Absent voices in the building of educational theory* (Working Paper No. 170). Wellesley, MA: Wellesley College Center for Research on Women.

Fallon, D. (2006). The buffalo upon the chimneypiece: The value of evidence. *Journal of Teacher Education, 57*(2), 139–154.

Fals-Borda, B. (1992). *Convergences in theory and action for research, learning and management*. Paper presented at the Second World Congress on Action Learning, University of Queensland, Australia.

Fecho, B. (1992). *Language inquiry and critical pedagogy: Co-investigating power in the classroom*. Paper presented at the annual meeting of the American Educational Research Association, San Francisco.

Feiman-Nemser, S. (2001). From preparation to practice: Designing a continuum to strengthen and sustain teaching. *Teachers College Record, 103*(6), 1013–1055.

Feiman-Nemser, S., & Beasley, K. (2007). Discovering and sharing knowledge: Inventing a new role for cooperating teachers. In D. Carroll, H. Featherstone, J. Featherstone, S. Feiman-Nemser & D. Roosevelt (Eds.), *Transforming teacher education: Reflections from the field* (pp. 139–160). Cambridge, MA: Harvard Education Press.

Feiman-Nemser, S., & Buchmann, M. (1985). Pitfalls of experience in teacher education. *Teachers College Record, 87*, 47–65.

Feistritzer, E., & Haar, C. (2008). *Alternative routes to teaching*. Upper Saddle River, NJ: Pearson Education Inc.

Feldman, A. (1993). Promoting equitable collaboration between university researchers and school teachers. *Qualitative Studies in Education, 6*, 341–357.

Feldman, A., Rearick, M., & Weiss, T. (2001). Teacher development and action research: Findings from six years of action research in schools. In J. Rainer & E. Guyton (Eds.), *Research on the effects of teacher education on teacher performance* (pp. 105–118). Dubuque, IA: Kendall Hunt.

Fennema, E., Carpenter, T., & Franke, M. (1995). Knowledge, action research, and cognitively guided instruction in mathematics. Unpublished paper, Wisconsin Center for Education Research, University of Wisconsin-Madison.

Fine, M. (1987). De-institutionalizing educational inquiry. In Council of Chief State School Offices (Eds.), *School success for students at risk* (pp. 89–119). Orlando, FL: Harcourt Brace Jovanovich.

Finn, C., & Kanstoroom, M. (2000). Improving, empowering, dismantling. *The Public Interest, 140*, 64–73.

Finn, P. J. & Finn, M. E. (Eds.). (2007). *Teacher education with an attitude: Preparing teachers to educate working-class students in their collective self-interest.* Albany, NY: SUNY Press.

Fiske, E. (1990, February 14). Finding a way to define the new buzzword of American education: How about Perestroika? *New York Times* (p. B8).

Flexner, A. (1930). *Universities: American, English, and German.* Oxford, UK: Oxford University Press.

Floden, R. (2005, November). *Teacher preparation accreditation and program approval.* Paper presented at the Advanced Training Program in Teacher Education Design in Colleges and Universities, Beijing Normal University, China.

Florio-Ruane, S. (2001). *Teacher education and the cultural imagination.* New York: Erlbaum/Routledge.

Florio-Ruane, S., & Burak-Dohanich, J. (1984). Research currents: Communicating findings by teacher/researcher deliberations. *Language Arts, 61*, 724–730.

Fordham Foundation. (1999).The teachers we need and how to get more of them. In M. Kanstoroom & C. Finn (Eds.), *Better teachers, better schools* (pp. 1–18). Washington, DC: Author.

Foster, M. (1997). *Black teachers on teaching.* New York: Free Press.

Fraser, N. (1997). *Justice interruptus: Critical reflections on the "post-socialist" condition.* New York: Routledge.

Freedman, S., Jackson, J. & Bilks, K. (1983). Teaching: An imperiled profession. In L. Shulman & G. Sykes (Eds.), *Handbook of teaching and policy* (pp. 261–299). New York: Longman.

Freisen, D. (1995). Action research in the teaching internship. *Educational Action Research, 3*(2), 153–168.

Fueo, V., & Neves, A. (1995). Preservice teacher as researcher: A research context for change in the heterogeneous classroom. *Action in Teacher Education, 16*, 39–49.

Furlong, J. (2005). New labour and teacher education: The end of an era. *Oxford Review of Education, 31*(1), 119–134.

Gage, N., & Winne, P. (1975). Performance-based teacher education. In K. Ryan (Ed.), *Teacher education* (pp. 146–172). Chicago: University of Chicago Press.

Gandara, P., & Maxwell-Jolley, J. (2000). *Preparing teachers for diversity: A dilemma of quality and quantity.* Santa Cruz, CA: Center for the Future of Teaching and Learning.

Garmon, M.A. (1998). Using dialogue journals to promote student learning in a multicultural teacher education course. *Remedial and Special Education,19*(1), 32–45.

Gartner, A., & Lipsky, D. K. (1987). Beyond special education: Toward a quality system for all students. *Harvard Educational Review, 57*(4), 367–395.

Gay, G. (2000). *Culturally responsive teaching: Theory, research and practice.* New York: Teachers College Press.

Gentile, J. R. (1988). *Instructional improvement: A summary and analysis of Madeline Hunter's Essential Elements of Instruction.* Oxford, OH: National Staff Development Council.

Genzuk, M., & Baca, R. (1998). The paraeducator-to-teacher pipeline: A five-year retrospective look at an innovative teacher education program for Latina(os). *Education and Urban Society, 31*(1), 73–88.

Gerwitz, S. (1998). Conceptualizing social justice in education. Mapping the territory. *Journal of Educational Policy, 13*(4), 469–484.

Gibson, R. (1985). Critical times for action research. *Cambridge Journal of Education, 15*, 59–64.

Gillette, M. (1990). *Making them multicultural: A case study of the clinical teacher-supervisor in preservice teacher education.* Unpublished doctoral dissertation. University of Wisconsin-Madison School of Education.

Gilroy, D. P. (1992). The political rape of initial teacher education in England and Wales: A JET rebuttal. *Journal of Education for Teaching, 18*(1), 5–22.

Ginsburg, M. (1988). *Contradictions in teacher education and society.* Philadelphia: Falmer Press.

Gipps, C. (1993). The profession of educational research. *British Educational Research Journal, 19*, 3–15.

Girod, G. (2002). *Connecting teaching and learning: A handbook for teacher educators on teacher work sample methodology.* Washington, DC: American Association of Colleges for Teacher Education.

Giroux, H., & McLaren, P. (1987). Teacher education and the politics of engagement: The case for democratic schooling. In M. Okazawa-Ray, J. Anderson, & R. Traver (Eds.), *Teaching, teachers, and teacher education* (pp. 157–182). Cambridge, MA: Harvard Educational Review Press.

Gitlin, A. (Ed.). (1994). *Power and method: Political activism and educational research.* New York: Routledge.

Gitlin, A., Bringhurst, K., Burns, M., Cooley, V., Myers, B., Price, K., Russell, R., & Tiess, P. (1992). *Teachers' voices for school change: An introduction to educative research.* New York: Teachers College Press.

Goldberger, P. (1990, April 6). Taj Mahal: Part Vegas, part Disney, all Trump. *New York Times,* (p. B1).

Goldhaber, D.D., & Brewer, D.J. (2000). Does teacher certification matter? High school certification status and student achievement. *Educational Evaluation and Policy Analysis, 22*, 129–145.

Gollnick. D. (1991). Multicultural education: Policies and practices in teacher education. In C. Grant (Ed.), *Research and multicultural education: From the margins to the mainstream* (pp. 218–239). London: Falmer.

Goodlad, J. (1970). The reconstruction of teacher education. *Teachers College Record, 72*(1), 61–72.

Goodlad, J. (1990). *Teachers for our nation's schools.* San Francisco: Jossey Bass.

Goodlad, J. (2004). *A place called school* (25th anniversary ed). San Francisco: Jossey Bass.

Goodlad, J., & Klein, M. F. (1974). *Looking behind the classroom door.* Worthington, OH: Charles A. Jones.

Goodnough, A. (2001). Strain of fourth-grade tests drives off veteran teachers. *The New York Times,* June 14. P.A-1. Retrieved June 24, 2003, from www.nytimes.com

Gore, J. (1991). Practicing what we preach: Action research and the supervision of student teachers. In B. R. Tabachnick & K. Zeichner (Eds.), *Issues and practices in inquiry-oriented teacher education* (pp. 253–272). London: Falmer Press.

Gore, J., & Zeichner, K. (1991). Action research and reflective teaching in preservice teacher education: A case study from the U.S. *Teaching and Teacher Education,* 7(2), 119–136.

Gore, J., & Zeichner, K. (1993). Connecting action research to genuine teacher development. In J. Smyth (Ed.), *Critical perspectives on teacher development* (pp. 203–214). London: Falmer Press.

Grant, C. (Ed.). (1979). *Community participation in education.* Boston, MA: Allyn & Bacon.

Grant, C., McCarty, D., & Volpiansky, P. (1989). *Report of a school-based management study during the second pilot year: Milwaukee.* Madison: University of Wisconsin School of Education.

Grant, C., & Secada, W. (1990). Preparing teachers for diversity. In W.R. Houston (Ed.), *Handbook of research on teacher education* (pp. 403–422). New York: Macmillan.

Green, J. L., Camilli, G., & Elmore, P. B. (2006). *Handbook of complementary methods in education research.* New York: Erlbaum/Routledge.

Greene, M. (1978). The matter of mystification: Teacher education in unquiet times. In M. Greene, *Landscapes of learning* (pp. 53–73). New York: Teachers College Press.

Gregorian, V. (2001, July, 6). How to train and retain teachers. *The New York Times,* p. A17.

Grierson, A., & Pampling, T. (1989). Feminists at Cambridge. In B. Somekh, J. Powney & C. Burge (Eds.), *Collaborative enquiry and school improvement.* Norwich, UK: Classroom Action Research Network, University of East Anglia.

Griffiths, M. (1990). Action research: Grassroots practice or management tool? In P. Lomax (Ed.), *Managing staff development in schools: An action research approach* (pp. 37–51). Clevedon, UK: Multilingual Matters.

Griffiths, M., Bass, L., Johnston, M., & Perselli, V. (2004). Knowledge, social justice and self-study. In J. Loughran, M. L. Hamilton, V. LaBoskey & T. Russell (Eds.), *International handbook of self-study of teaching and teacher education practices* (pp. 651–708). Dordrecht: Kluwer Publishers.

Grimmett, P. & Mackinnon, A. (1992). Craft knowledge and the education of teachers. In G. Grant (Ed.), *Review of Research in Education* (pp. 385–456). Washington, DC: American Educational Research Association.

Grimmett, P., Mackinnon, A., Erickson, G. & Riecken, T. (1990). Reflective practice in teacher education. In R. Clift, W. R. Houston & M. C. Pugach (Eds.), *Encouraging reflective practice in education* (pp. 20–38). New York: Teachers College Press.

Grinberg, J., & Paz-Goldfarb, K. (1998). Moving teacher education into the community. *Theory into Practice,* 37(2), 131–139.

Grossman, P. (1990). *The making of a teacher: Teacher knowledge and teacher education.* New York: Teachers College Press.

Grossman, P. (2005). Pedagogical approaches in teacher education. In M. Cochran-Smith & K. Zeichner (Eds.), *Studying teacher education* (pp. 425–476). New York: Erlbaum/Routledge.

Grossman, P., & McDonald, M. (2008). Back to the future: Directions for research in teaching and teacher education. *American Educational Research Journal, 45*(1), 184–205.

Grundy, S. (1982). Three modes of action research. *Curriculum Perspectives, 2*(3), 23–34.

Grundy, S., & Kemmis, S. (1988). Educational action research in Australia: The state of the art (an overview). In S. Kemmis & R. McTaggart (Eds.), *The action research reader* (3rd ed., pp. 321–335). Geelong, Australia: Deakin University Press.

Grunwald, M. (2006, October). Billions for an inside game on reading. *The Washington Post*. Retrieved October 10, 2006, from www.washingtonpost.com.

Gurney, M. (1989). Implementor or innovator? A teacher's challenge to the restrictive paradigm of traditional research. In P. Lomax (Ed.), *The management of change* (pp. 13–28). Clevedon, UK: Multilingual Matters.

Gutmann, A. (1987). *Democratic education*. Princeton: Princeton University Press.

Guyton, E., & McIntyre, J. (1990). Student teaching and school experiences. In W.R. Houston (Ed.), *Handbook of research on teacher education* (pp. 514–534). New York: Macmillan.

Haberman, M. (1993). Predicting the success of urban teachers: The Milwaukee trials. *Action in Teacher Education, 15*(3), 1–5.

Haberman, M. (1995). *Star teachers of children in poverty*. West Lafayette, IN: Kappa Delta Pi.

Haberman, M. (1999). Increasing the number of high quality African-American teachers in urban schools. *Journal of Instructional Psychology, 26*(4), 208–212.

Haberman, M., & Post, L. (2008). Teachers for multicultural schools: The power of selection. Reprinted in M. Cochran-Smith; S. Feiman-Nemser; & D. J. McIntyre (Eds.), *Handbook of research on teacher education* (3rd edition, pp. 360–370). New York: Erlbaum/Routledge.

Hamel, F., & Merz, C. (2005). Reforming accountability: A preservice program wrestles with mandated reform. *Journal of Teacher Education, 56*(2), 157–167.

Hamerness, K., Darling-Hammond, L., Bransford, J., Cochran-Smith, M., McDonald, M., & Zeichner, K. (2005). How teachers learn and develop. In L. Darling-Hammond & J. Bransford (Eds.), *Preparing teachers for a changing world* (pp. 358–389). San Francisco: Jossey Bass.

Handal, G., & Lauvas, P. (1987). The practical theories of teachers. *Promoting reflective teaching*. Milton Keynes, UK: Open University Press.

Hansen, D. T. (2008). Values and purpose in teacher education. In M. Cochran-Smith, S. Feiman Nemser, & D.J. McIntyre (Eds.), *Handbook of research on teacher education* (3rd edition, pp. 10–26). New York: Routledge.

Hartocollis, A. (2005, July 31). Who needs education schools? *New York Education Life*, pp. 24–28.

Haycock, K. (2000). *No more settling for less*. Washington, DC: Education Trust.

Heath, R. W., & Nielson, M. (1974). The research base for performance-based teacher education. *Review of Educational Research, 44*(4), 463–484.

Heath, S. B. (1983). *Ways with words: Language, life and work in communities and classrooms*. New York: Cambridge University Press.

Helms, J. E. (1995). An update of Helms' white and people of color racial identity models. In J. G. Ponterotto, J. M. Casas, L. A. Suzuki, and C. M. Alexander (Eds.), *Handbook of Multicultural Counseling* (pp. 181–198). Thousand Oaks, CA: Sage.

Henderson, A. T. (1987). *The evidence continues to grow: Parent involvement improves student achievement.* Columbus, MD: National Committee for Citizens in Education.

Herrnstein, R., & Murray, C. (1994). *The bell curve.* New York: Free Press.

Hess, F. (2001). *Tear down the wall: The case for a radical overhaul of teacher certification.* Washington, DC: Progressive Policy Institute.

Hewitson, M., McWilliam, E., & Burke, C. (1991). Responding to teacher education imperatives for the nineties. *Australian Journal of Education, 35,* 246–260.

Hewson, P., Tabachnick, B. R., Zeichner, K., & Lemberger, J. (1999). Educating prospective teachers of biology: Findings, limitations, and recommendations. *Science Education, 83*(3), 373–384.

Hinchey, P. & Cadiero-Kaplan, K. (2005). The future of teacher education and teaching: Another piece of the privatization puzzle. *Journal of Critical Educational Policy Studies, 3*(2). Retrieved September 17, 2007, from http://www.jceps.com.

Hite, H. (1973). The cost of performance-based teacher education. *Journal of Teacher Education, 24,* 224.

Holland, R. G. (2004). *To build a better teacher: The emergence of a competitive education industry.* Westport, CT: Prager.

Hollins, E., & Guzman, M. T. (2005). Research on preparing teachers for diverse populations. In M. Cochran-Smith & K. Zeichner (Eds.), *Studying teacher education* (pp. 477–548). New York: Erlbaum/Routledge.

Holly, P. (1987). Action research cul-de-sac or turnpike. *Peabody Journal of Education, 64*(3), 71–99.

Holmes Group. (1986). *Tomorrow's teachers.* East Lansing, MI: Author.

Holmes Group. (1995). *Tomorrow's schools of education.* East Lansing, MI: College of Education, Michigan State University.

Holmes Group. (1996). *Tomorrow's schools: Principles for the design of professional development schools.* East Lansing, MI: College of Education, Michigan State University.

Honawar, V. (2007, October). Gains seen in retooled teacher education. *Education Week.* Retrieved October 27, 2007 from www.edweek.org.

Hood, S., & Parker, L. (1994). Minority students informing the faculty: Implications for racial diversity and the future of teacher education. *Journal of Teacher Education, 45*(3), 164–171.

hooks, b. (2003). *Teaching community: A pedagogy of hope.* New York: Routledge.

Houston, W. R., & Howsam, R. (1972). *Competency-based teacher education.* Chicago: Science Research Associates.

Howey, K., & Zimpher, N. (1989). *Profiles of preservice teacher education: Inquiry into the nature of programs.* Albany, NY: State University of New York Press.

Humphrey, D., & Wechsler, M. (2005). Insights into alternative certification: Initial findings from a national study. *Teachers College Record.* Retrieved April 25, 2006, from http://www.tcrecord.org.

Humphrey, D., Wechsler, M., & Hough, H. (2005, July). *Characteristics of effective alternative teacher certification programs.* Menlo Park, CA: SRI.

Hursh, D. (2005). The growth of high-stakes testing in the USA: Accountability, markets, and the decline in educational quality. *British Educational Research Journal, 31*(5), 605–622.

Hypolito, A. M. (2004). Teachers' work and professionalization: The promised land or dream denied? *Journal for Critical Education Policy Studies, 2*(2). Retrieved August 19, 2007, from www.jceps.com.

Ingersoll, R. (2001). Teacher turnover and teacher shortages: An organizational analysis. *American Educational Research Journal, 38*(3), 499–534.

Ingersoll, R. (2003). *Who controls teachers' work? Power and accountability in America's schools.* Cambridge MA: Harvard University Press.

Interstate New Teacher Assessment and Support Consortium. (1992). *Model standards for beginning teacher licensing and development: A resource for state dialogue.* Washington, DC: Author.

Irvine, J. J. (2003). *Educating teachers for diversity: Seeing with a cultural eye.* New York: Teachers College Press.

Irvine, J. J., & Armento, B. J. (2001). *Culturally responsive teaching: Lesson planning for elementary and middle grades.* Boston: McGraw-Hill.

Izumi, L., & Coburn, K. G. (2001). *Facing the classroom challenge: Teacher quality and teacher training in California's schools of education.* San Francisco: Pacific Research Institute.

Jerald, C. D. (2002). *All talk, no action: Putting an end to out-of-field teaching.* Washington, DC: Education Trust.

Johnson, C., Miranda, L., Sherman, A., & Weill, J. (1991). *Child poverty in America.* Washington, DC: Children's Defense Fund.

Johnson, D., Johnson, B., Farenga, S. & Ness, D. (2005). *Trivializing teacher education: The accreditation squeeze.* Lanham, MD: Roman & Littlefield.

Johnston, S., & Proudford, C. (1994). Action research: Who owns the process? *Educational Review, 46,* 3–4.

Jordan-Irvine, J. (1992). Making teacher education culturally responsive. In M. Dilworth (Ed.), *Diversity in teacher education: New expectations* (pp. 79–92). San Francisco: Jossey Bass.

Jordan-Irvine, J., & Armento, B. J. (2001). *Culturally responsive lesson planning for the elementary and middle grades.* Boston: McGraw-Hill.

Jordan-Irvine, J., & Fraser, J. (1998, May 18). Warm demanders. *Education Week,* p. 17.

Joyce, B., Yarger, S., & Howey, K. (1977). *Preservice teacher education.* Palo Alto, CA: Booksend Laboratory.

Justice Policy Institute. (2002, August). *Cellblocks or classrooms? The funding of higher education and corrections and its impact on African American men.* Washington, DC: Author.

Kailin, J. (2002). *Anti-racist education.* Lanham, MD: Roman & Littlefield.

Kanstoroom, M., & Finn, C. (Eds.). (1999). *Better teachers, better schools.* Washington, DC: The Fordham Foundation.

Karp, S. (1990). Parent power: Chicago's parents struggle to institute radical new school reforms. *Rethinking Schools, 4*(3), 12.

Katznelson, I., & Weir, M. (1985). *Schooling for all: Class, race, and the decline of the democratic ideal.* Berkeley: University of California Press.

Keller, B. (2002, January 30). Illinois teacher shortage grows. *Education Week, 21*(20), 20.

Kelly, A. (1985). Action research: What is it and what can it do? In R. Burgess (Ed.), *Issues in educational research: Qualitative methods*. Lewes: Falmer Press.

Kemmis, S. (1985a). Action research and the politics of reflection. In D. Boud, R. Keogh & D. Walker (Eds.), *Reflection: Turning experience into learning* (pp. 139–164). London: Croom Helm.

Kemmis, S. (1985b). Action research. In T. Husen & T. Postlethwaite (Eds.), *International encyclopedia of education: Research and studies* (pp. 35–41). Oxford, UK: Pergamon.

Kemmis, S. (1986). Of tambourines and tumbrils: A response to Rex Gibson's 'critical times for action research.' *Cambridge Journal of Education, 16*, 50–52.

Kemmis, S. (1992). *The nature of action research: Some general principles*. Paper as the basis for a series of lectures at the Instituto Ciencias de la Educacion, Universidad del Pais Vasco, Campus, Leioa (V12 Cayo), Spain.

Kemmis, S. (2007). Critical theory and participatory action research. In P. Reason & H. Bradbury (Eds), *Handbook of action research*. (2nd edition). London: Sage.

Kemmis, S., & McTaggart, R. (1988). *The action research planner*. Geelong, Australia: Deakin University Press.

Kincheloe, J. (1991). *Teachers as researchers: Qualitative inquiry as a path to empowerment*. London: Falmer Press.

Kirby, S., McCombs, J. S., Naftel, S., Burney, H., Darilck, H., Doolittle, F., et al. (2004). *Reforming teacher education: A first-year progress report on Teachers for a New Era*. Santa Monica, CA: RAND.

Koerner, J. (1963). *The miseducation of American teachers*. Baltimore: Penguin Books.

Kornfeld, J.; Grady, K. Marker, P. & Ruddell, M. (2007). Caught in the current: A self-study of state-mandated compliance in a teacher education program. *Teachers College Record, 109*(8), 1902–1930.

Kosnick, C. (1999, March). The transformative power of the action research process: Effects of an inquiry approach to preservice teacher education. *Networks, 2*(1). Retrieved June 20, 1999, from www.oise.utoronto.ca/~ctd/networks.

Kosnick, C. (2000). Looking back: Six student teachers reflect on the action research experience in their teacher education programs. *Action in Teacher Education, 22*(2), 133–142.

Kozol, J. (1991). *Savage inequalities*. New York: Crown.

Kozol, J. (2005). *The shame of the nation: The restoration of apartheid schooling in America*. New York: Crown.

Kramer, R. (2000). *Ed school follies*. Lincoln, NE: iUniverse.

Labaree, D. (1997). *How to succeed in school without really learning: The credentials race in American education*. New Haven, CT: Yale University Press.

Labaree, D. (2004). *The trouble with ed schools*. New Haven, CT: Yale University Press.

Labaree, D. (2008). An uneasy relationship: The history of teacher education in the university. In M. Cochran-Smith, S. Feiman-Nemser, & D. J. McIntyre (Eds.), *Handbook of research on teacher education* (3rd ed., pp. 290–306). New York: Erlbaum/ Routledge.

Ladson-Billings, G. (1990). Culturally relevant teaching. *The College Board Review, 155*, 20–25.

Ladson-Billings, G. (1991). *Who will teach our children? Preparing teachers to successfully teach African-American students.* Paper presented at the California State University, Hayward Teleconference on Cultural Diversity.

Ladson-Billings, G. (1994). *The dreamkeepers: Successful teachers of African-American children.* San Francisco: Jossey Bass.

Ladson-Billings, G. (1995a). Multicultural teacher education: Research, practice and policy. In J. Banks & C. A. M. Banks (Eds.), *Handbook of research on multicultural education* (pp. 747–759). New York: Macmillan.

Ladson-Billings, G. (1995b) Toward a theory of culturally relevant pedagogy. *American Educational Research Journal, 32*(3), 465–491.

Ladson-Billings, G. (1999a). Preparing teachers for diversity: Historical perspectives, current trends, and future directions. In L. Darling-Hammond & G. Sykes (Eds.), *Teaching as the learning profession: Handbook of policy and practice* (pp. 86–124). San Francisco: Jossey Bass.

Ladson-Billings, G. (1999b). *The validity of National Board for Professional Teaching Standards assessment for effective urban teachers.* Washington, DC: U.S. Department of Education.

Ladson-Billings, G. (2001). *Crossing over to Canaan: The journey of new teachers in diverse classrooms.* San Francisco: Jossey Bass.

Ladwig, J. (1991). Is collaborative research exploitative? *Educational Theory, 41,* 111–120.

Ladwig, J., & Gore, J. (1994). Extending power and specifying method within the discourse of activist research. In A. Gitlin (Ed.), *Power and method* (pp. 227–238). New York: Routledge.

Lagemann, E. (2000). *An elusive science: The troubling history of educational research.* Chicago: University of Chicago Press.

Lampert, M., & Ball, D. L. (1998). *Teaching, multimedia and mathematics: Investigations of real practice.* New York: Teachers College Press.

Langston Hughes Intermediate School (1988). *Teacher research on student learning.* Fairfax, VA: Fairfax County Public Schools.

Lawn, M. (1989). Being caught in school work: The possibilities of research in teacher-work. In W. Carr (Ed.), *Quality in Teaching: Arguments for a reflective profession* (pp. 147–162). London: Falmer Press.

Lawson, H. (1990). Constraints on the professional service of education faculty. *Journal of Teacher Education, 41,* 57–70.

Lee, J. (2002). Racial and ethnic achievement gap trends: Reversing the progress toward equity? *Educational Researcher, 31*(1), 3–12.

Levin, H. M. (1990). Economic trends shaping the future of teacher education. *Educational Policy, 4*(2), 1–15.

Levine, M. (1998). *Designing standards that work for professional development schools.* Washington, DC: National Council for Accreditation of Teacher Education.

Lieberman, A. (Ed.). (1988). *Building a professional culture in schools.* New York: Teachers College Press.

Lieberman, A. (1990). *Schools as collaborative cultures: Creating the future now.* London: Falmer Press.

Lightfoot, S. L. (1978). *Worlds apart: Relationships between families and schools.* New York: Basic Books.

Lightfoot, S. L. (1983). *The good high school: Portraits of character and culture.* New York: Basic Books.

Limbert, P. (1934). Political education at New College. *Progressive Education, 11*(2), 118–124.

Lindbloom, C., & Cohen, D. (1979). *Usable knowledge: Social science and social problem solving.* New Haven, CT: Yale University Press.

Liston, D. (1995). Work in teacher education: A current assessment of U.S. teacher education. In N. Shimahara & I. Holowinsky (Eds.), *Teacher education in industrialized nations* (pp. 87–124). New York: Garland.

Liston, D., & Zeichner, K. (1991). *Teacher education and the social conditions of schooling.* New York: Routledge.

Liswani, V. (1999). Improving the participation of girls in my grade nine agricultural lessons. In K. Zeichner & L. Dahlstrom (Eds), *Democratic teacher education reform in Africa: The case of Namibia* (pp. 94–99). Boulder, CO: Westview Press.

Little, J. W. (1993). Teachers' professional development in a climate of educational reform. *Educational Evaluation and Policy Analysis, 15*, 129–152.

Livingston, C., & Castle, S. (1989). *Teachers and research in action.* Washington, DC: National Education Association.

Loughran, J. & Russell, T. (Eds). (2002). *Improving teacher education practices through self-study.* London: Routledge.

Loughran, J.; Hamilton, M. L.; LaBoskey, V. K. and Russell T. (Eds.). (2004). *International handbook of self-study of teaching and teacher education practices.* Dordrecht: Kluwer.

Lucas, C. (1999). *Teacher education in America.* New York: St. Martin's.

Lucas, T. & Grinberg, J. (2008). Responding to the linguistic reality of mainstream classrooms. In M. Cochran-Smith; S. Feiman-Nemser, & D.J. McIntyre (Eds.), *Handbook of teacher education* (3rd ed., pp. 606–636). New York: Erlbaum/ Routledge.

Luke, C. (1992). Feminist politics in radical pedagogy. In C. Luke & J. Gore (Eds.), *Feminums and critical pedagogy* (pp. 25–53). New York: Routledge.

Lyall, K. & Sell, K. (2006). *The true genius of America at risk: Are we losing our public universities to de facto privatization?* Westport CT: Prager.

Lynd, A. (1953). *Quackery in the public schools.* Boston: Little, Brown.

Lytle, S., & Cochran-Smith, M. (1990). Learning from teacher research: A working typology. *Teachers College Record, 92(1),* 83–103.

Lytle, S., & Cochran-Smith, M. (1994). Inquiry, knowledge, and practice. In S. Hollingsworth & H. Sockett (Eds.), *Teacher research and educational reform* (pp. 22–51). Chicago: University of Chicago Press.

Macchiarola, F. (1989). Schools that serve children. In F. Macchiarola & A. Gartner (Eds.), *Caring for America's children* (pp. 170–181). New York: Academy of Political Science.

Macgillivray, L. (1997). Do what I say, not what I do: An instructor rethinks her own teaching and research. *Curriculum Inquiry, 27(4),* 469–488.

Machelli, N., & Kaiser, D. L. (Eds.), (2005). *Teacher education for democracy and social justice.* New York: Routledge.

Madigan, K., & Poliakoff, M. (2001, November). To certify or not to certify: That is not the question: A response to the Abell and NCTAF reports. *Teacher Quality Bulletin.* Washington, DC: National Council on Teacher Quality.

Maeroff, G. (1988). *The empowerment of teachers.* New York: Teachers College Press.

Mahan, J. (1982). Native Americans as teacher trainers: Anatomy and outcomes of a cultural immersion project. *Journal of Educational Equity and Leadership, 2*(2), 100–109.

Mahan, J. (1993). Teacher education in American Indian communities: Learnings from reservation sources. *Journal of Navajo Education, 11*(1), 13–21.

Mahan, J., Fortney, M., & Garcia, J. (1983). Linking the community to teacher education: Toward a more analytical approach. *Action in Teacher Education, 5*(1–2), 1–10.

Malen, B., Ogawa, R., & Kranz, J. (1990). Site-based management: Unfulfilled promises. *The School Administrator, 30*(32), 53–59.

Markow, D., Fauth, S., & Gravitch, D. (2001). *The American teacher: 2001.* New York: Metlife.

Marx, S. (2006). *Revealing the invisible: Confronting passive racism in teacher education.* New York: Routledge.

Mayumbelo, C. & Nyambe, J. (1999). Critical inquiry in preservice teacher education: Initial steps toward critical, inquiring, and reflective professionals in Namibian teacher education. In K. Zeichner & L. Dahlstrom (Eds.), *Democratic teacher education reform in Africa: The case of Namibia* (pp. 64–81). Boulder: Westview Press.

McCaffrey, D. F., Lockwood, J. R., Koretz, D. M., & Hamilton, L. S. (2004). *Evaluating value-added models for teacher accountability.* Santa Monica, CA: RAND.

McCaleb, J., Borko, H. & Arends, R. (1992). Reflection, research and repertoire in the masters certification program at the University of Maryland. In L. Valli (Ed.), *Reflective teacher education: Cases and critiques* (pp. 40–64). Albany, NY: SUNY Press.

McCann, A. (1990). Cultural and behavior: A study of Mirpuri Pakistani infant pupils. In R. Webb (Ed.), *Practitioner research in the primary school* (pp. 183–201). Lewes: Falmer Press.

McCowan, T. (2003, March). Participation and education in the Landless People's Movement of Brazil. *Journal for Critical Education Policy Studies, 1*(1). Retrieved July 3, 2007, from http://www.jceps.com/print.php?articleID=6.

McDiarmid, G.W. (1994). The arts and sciences as preparation for teaching. In K. Howey & N. Zimpher (Eds.), *Informing faculty development for teacher educators* (pp. 99–137). Norwood, NJ: Ablex.

McDonald, F. (1973). Behavior modification and teacher education. In C. Thoresen (Ed.), *Behavior modification in teacher education* (pp. 41–76). Chicago: University of Chicago Press.

McDonald, M. (2005). The integration of social justice in teacher education. *Journal of Teacher Education, 56*(5), 418–435.

McDonald, M. (2007). The joint enterprise of social justice teacher education. *Teachers College Record, 109*(8), 2047–2081.

McDonald, M., & Zeichner, K. (2009). Social; justice teacher education. In T. C. Quinn, W. C. Ayers, & D. O. Stovall (Eds.), *Handbook on social justice in education* (pp. 595–610). Oxford, UK: Taylor & Francis.

McIntyre, A. (2002). Exploring whiteness and multicultural education with prospective teachers. *Curriculum Inquiry, 32*(1), 31–49.

McIntyre, A. (2003). Participatory action research and urban education: Reshaping the teacher preparation process. *Equity and Excellence in Education, 36*(1), 28–39.

McIntyre, D. (1993). Theory, theorizing, and reflection in initial teacher education. In J. Calderhead & P. Gates (Eds.), *Conceptualizing reflection in teacher development* (pp. 39–52). London: Falmer Press.

McIntyre, D. J., Byrd, D., & Foxx, S. (1996). Field and laboratory experiences. In J. Sikula (Ed.), *Handbook of research on teacher education* (2nd ed., pp. 171–193). New York: Macmillan.

McKernan, J. (1991). *Curriculum action research.* London: Kogan Press.

McLaughlin, M. W., & Yee, S. M. (1989). School as a place to have a career. In A. Lieberman (Ed.), *Building a professional culture in schools* (pp. 23–44). New York: Teachers College Press.

McNiff, J. (1988). *Action research: Principles and practice.* London: Macmillan.

Melnick, S. & Zeichner, K. (1997). Teacher education for cultural diversity: Enhancing the capacity of teacher education institutions to address diversity issues. In J. King; E. Hollins, & W. Hayman (Eds.), *Meeting the challenge of diversity in teacher preparation* (pp. 23–39). New York: Teachers College Press.

Merino, B. (1999). Preparing secondary teachers to teach a second language: The case of the United States with a focus on California. In C.J. Faltis & P.M. Wolfe (Eds.), *So much to say: Bilingualism and ESL in the secondary school* (pp. 225–253). New York: Teachers College Press.

Meyer-Reimer, K., & Bruce, B. (1994). Teacher-researcher collaboration: Dilemmas and strategies. *Educational Action Research, 2,* 211–222.

Meyers, M. (1986). When research does not help teachers. *American Educator, 10,* 18–23, 46.

Michelli, N. & Keiser, D. (2005). *Teacher education for democracy and social justice.* New York: Routledge.

Miller, J. (1990). *Creating spaces and finding voices: Teachers collaborating for empowerment.* Albany, NY: Suny Press.

Millman, V., & Weiner, G. (1985). *Sex differentiation in schools: Is there really a problem?* New York: Longman.

Milwaukee Public Schools. (2002, January). Personal communication with the Human Resources Department, Milwaukee, Wisconsin.

Mitchell, P. (1985). A teacher's view of educational research. In M. Shipman (Ed.), *Educational research: Principles, policies and practices* (pp. 81–96). London: Falmer Press.

Moles, O. (1982, November). Synthesis of recent research on parent participation in children's education. *Educational Leadership, 40(2),* 44–47.

Moll, K., & Arnot-Hopffer, W. (2005). Sociocultural competence in teacher education. *Journal of Teacher Education, 56(3),* 242–247.

Moll, L. (1992). Literacy researching community and classrooms: A socio-cultural approach. In R. Beach, J. Green, M. Camild, & T. Smanaman (Eds.), *Multidisciplinary perspectives on literacy research* (pp. 211–244). Urbana, IL: National Council of Teachers of English.

Moll, L., Amanti, C., Neff, D., & Gonzalez, N. (1992). Funds of knowledge for teaching: Using a qualitative approach to connect homes and classrooms. *Theory into Practice, 31,* 132–141.

Moll, L., & Greenberg, J. (1990). Creating zones of possibilities: Combining social context for instruction. In L. Moll (Ed.), *Vygotsky and education* (pp. 319–348). Cambridge, UK: Cambridge University Press.

Moll, L., & Vellez-Ibanez, C. (1992). Funds of knowledge for teaching: Using a qualitative approach to connect homes and classrooms. *Theory into Practice, 31,* 132–141.

Montecinos, C. (1995). Multicultural teacher education for a culturally diverse teaching force. In R. Martin (Ed.), *Practicing what we teach: Confronting diversity in teacher education* (pp. 97–116). Albany: State University of New York Press.

Montecinos, C. (2004). Paradoxes in multicultural teacher education research: Students of color positioned as objects while ignored as subjects. *International Journal of Qualitative Studies in Education, 17*(2), 167–181.

Moore, R. (1999). Preservice teachers engaged in reflective classroom research. *The Teacher Educator, 34*(4), 259–275.

Moule, J. (2005). Implementing a social justice perspective: Invisible burden for faculty of color. *Teacher Education Quarterly, 32*(4), 23–42.

Murrell, P. (1998). *Like stone soup: The role of professional development schools in the renewal of urban schools.* Washington, DC: American Association of Colleges for Teacher Education.

Murrell, P. (2001). *The community teacher: A new framework for effective urban teaching.* New York: Teachers College Press.

National Commission on Excellence in Education. (1983). *A nation at risk: The imperative for educational reform.* Washington, DC: U.S. Government Printing Office.

National Commission on Teaching and America's Future. (1996). *What matters most, teaching for America's future.* New York: Author.

National Commission on Teaching and America's Future. (1997). *Doing what matters most: Investing in teaching.* New York: Author.

National Commission on Teaching and America's Future. (2003, January). *No dream denied.* Washington, DC: Author.

National Council for the Accreditation of Teacher Education. (2001). *Standards for professional development schools.* Retrieved August 19, 2002, from www.ncate.org.

National Governors Association. (1986). *Time for results.* Washington, DC: Author.

National Research Council. (1997). Preparation and development of teachers serving English language learners. In D. August & K. Hakuta (Eds.), *Improving schooling for language minority children* (pp. 251–273). Washington, DC: National Academy Press.

National School Boards Association (2008). *Issue brief: Federal funding for education.* Alexandria VA. Retrieved June 20, 2008, from www.nsba.org.

New York Times (2006). *Why the achievement gap persists.* Editorial printed on December 8, p.A30.

Nieto, S. (2000). *Affirming diversity: The sociopolitical context of multicultural education.* New York: Teachers College Press.

Nieto, S., & Rolon, C. (1997). Preparation and professional development of teachers: A perspective from two Latinas. In J. Jordan-Irvine (Ed.), *Critical knowledge for diverse teachers and learners* (pp. 89–124). Washington, DC: American Association of Colleges for Teacher Education.

Nixon, J. (Ed.). (1981). *A teacher's guide to action research.* London: Grant McIntyre.

Nixon, J. (1987). The teacher as researcher: Contradictions and continuities. *Peabody Journal of Education, 62*(2), 20–32.

No Child Left Behind Act of 2001, Pub. L. No. 107–110, 115 Stat. 1425 (2002).

Noddings, N. (1986). Fidelity in teaching, teacher education, and research for teaching. *Harvard Educational Review, 56*, 496–510.

Noddings, N. (1987). Fidelity in teaching, teacher education and research for teaching. In M. Okazawa-Rey, J. Anderson & R. Traver (Eds.), *Teachers, teaching and teacher education* (pp. 384–400). Cambridge, MA: Harvard Educational Review Reprint Series No. 19.

Noffke, S. (1989). *Action research: A multidimensional analysis.* Unpublished doctoral dissertation, University of Wisconsin-Madison.

Noffke, S. (1994). Action research: Toward the next generation. *Educational Action Research, 2*, 9–22.

Noffke, S., & Brennan, M. (1991). Action research and reflective student teaching at the University of Wisconsin-Madison. In B.R. Tabachnick & K. Zeichner (Eds.), *Issues and practices in inquiry-oriented teacher education* (pp. 186–201). Philadelphia: Falmer Press.

Noffke, S., & Zeichner, K. (1987). *Action research and teacher development.* Paper presented at the annual meeting of the American Educational Research Association, Washington, DC.

Noordhoff, K., & Kleinfeld, J. (1993). Preparing teachers for multicultural schools. *Teaching and Teacher Education, 9*(1), 27–39.

North, C. (2006). More than words? Delving into the substantive meaning(s) of social justice in education. *Review of Educational Research, 76*(4), 507–535.

North, C. (2008). What is all this talk about "social justice?" Mapping the terrain of education's latest catchphrase. *Teachers College Record, 110*(6), 1182–1206.

Oakes, J. (1985). *Keeping track: How schools structure inequality.* New Haven, CT: Yale University Press.

Oakes, J., Hare, S., & Sirotnik, K. (1986). Collaborative inquiry: A congenial paradigm in a cantankerous world. *Teachers College Record, 87*, 545–561.

Oakes, J., & Lipton, M. (1999). *Teaching to change the world.* Boston, MA: McGraw Hill.

Olsen, B., Lane, S., Metcalfe, E. L., Priselac, J., Suzuki, G., & Williams, R. J. (2005). Center X: Where research and practice intersect for urban school professionals: A portrait of the teacher education program at the University of California, Los Angeles. In P. M. Jenlink & K. E. Jenlink (Eds.), *Portraits of teacher preparation: Learning to teach in a changing America* (pp. 33–51). Lanham, MD: Rowman & Littlefield.

Olson, L. (1987, 3 June). Study groups giving committed teachers the chance to reflect, share, and learn. *Education Week*, pp. 23–26.

Olson, L. (1990, April 4). Parents as partners: Redefining the social contract between families and schools. *Education Week*, p. 24.

Orfield, G. & Lee, C. (January, 2005). *Why segregation matters: Poverty and educational inequality.* Los Angeles: The Civil Rights Project, UCLA. Retrieved June 20, 2008, from www.civilrightsproject.ucla.edu.

Paige, M. (2005). *Alternative teacher certification post-NCLB: The Passport to Teaching from the American Board for Certification of Teacher Excellence.* Unpublished manuscript, University of Wisconsin-Madison.

Paige, R. (June,2002). *Meeting the highly qualified teacher challenge: The second annual report on teacher quality.* Washington, DC: U.S. Department of Education.

Parks, P., Brydon-Miller, M., Hall, B., & Jackson, T. (1993). *Voices of change: Participatory research in the U.S. and Canada.* Westport, CT: Bergin & Garvey.

Patterson, R. S., Machelli, N., & Pacheco. A. (1999). *Centers of pedagogy: New structures for educational renewal.* San Francisco: Jossey Bass.

Payzant, T. (2004, February). *Should teacher preparation take place at colleges and universities?* Invited address at the annual meeting of the American Association of Colleges for Teacher Education, Chicago.

Perrodin, A. (1959). Student teachers try action research. *Journal of Teacher Education,* 10(4), 471–474.

Persell, C. H. (1977). *Education and equality.* New York: The Free Press.

Peske, H.G. & Haycock, K. (June, 2006). *Teaching inequality: How poor and minority students are shortchanged on teacher quality.* Washington, DC: The Education Trust.

Peterman, F. (2008). Defining standards that respond to the urban context. In F. Peterman (Ed.). *Partnering to prepare urban teachers: A call to activism.* (pp. 21–40). New York: Peter Lang.

Peterman, F. (Ed). (2008). *Partnering to prepare urban teachers: A call to activism.* New York: Peter Lang.

Peterson, B. (1990). The struggle with decent schools. *Democratic Education,* 4(3), 3–6.

Poetter, T. (1997). *Voices of inquiry in teacher education.* Mahwah, NJ: Erlbaum.

Pollard, A. & Tann, S. (1987). Reflective teaching in the primary school. London, Cassell.

Popkewitz, T. (1975). Reform as a political discourse: A case study. *School Review,* 84, 311–336.

Post, L., Pugach, M., Harris, S., & Hedges, M. (2006). The Teachers-in-Residence Program: Veteran urban teachers as teacher leaders in boundary spanning roles. In K. Howey & N. Zimpher (Eds.), *Boundary spanners: A key to success in urban P-16 university-school partnerships* (pp. 213–236). Washington, DC: American Association of State Colleges and Universities, National Association of State Universities and Land Grant Colleges.

Price, J. (2001). Action research, pedagogy and change: The transformative potential of action research in preservice teacher education. *Journal of Curriculum Studies,* 33(1), 43–74.

Public Information Network. (1985). *Equity and excellence: Toward an agenda for school reform.* St. Louis: Author.

Pucci, S. L., Ulanoff, S. H., & Orellana, M. F. (2000). Se hace camino al andar: Reflections on the process of preservice inquiry. *Educators for Urban Minorities,* 1(2), 17–26.

Randi, J., & Zeichner, K. (2004). New visions of teacher professional development. In M. Smylie & D. Miretszky (Eds.), *Addressing teacher workforce issues effectively: International, political, and philosophical barriers: Yearbook of the National Society for the Study of Education* (pp. 180–227). Chicago: University of Chicago Press.

Raphael, J., & Tobias, S. (1997). Profit-making or profiteering? Proprietaries target teacher education. *Change,* 29(6), 44–49.

Raskin, M. (1986). *The common good: Its politics, policies, and philosophy.* New York: Routledge & Kegan Paul.

Rawls, J. (1999). *A theory of justice* (2nd edition). Cambridge MA: Harvard University Press.

Rawls, J. (2001). *Justice as fairness: A restatement*. Cambridge MA: Harvard University Press.

Reagan, T. (1997). The case for applied linguistics in teacher education. *Journal of Teacher Education, 48*(3), 185–196.

Regenspan, B. (2002). *Parallel practices: Social justice-focused teacher education and the elementary classroom*. New York: Peter Lang.

Rennert-Ariev, P. (2008). The hidden curriculum of performance-based teachereducation. *Teachers College Record, 110*(1), 105–138.

Reynolds, M. (Ed.). (1989). *Knowledge base for the beginning teacher*. New York: Pergamon Press.

Richardson, V. (1994). Conducting research on practice. *Educational Researcher, 23*(5), 5–10.

Ridley, D. S., Hurwitz, S., Hackett, M.R., & Miller, K. (2005). Comparing PDS and campus-based preparation: Is PDS-based preparation really better? *Journal of Teacher Education, 56*(1), 46–56.

Robertson, S. (2000). *A class act: Changing teachers' work, the state, and globalization*. New York: Falmer Press.

Robertson, S. (2008). Remaking the world: Neoliberalism and the transformation of education and teachers' labor. In M. Compton & L. Weiner (Eds.), *The global assault on teaching, teachers and their unions* (pp. 11–36). New York: Palgrave Macmillan.

Robottom, I. (1988). A research-based course in science education. In J. Nias & S. Groundwater-Smith (Eds.), *The enquiring teacher: Supporting and sustaining teacher research* (pp. 6–20). London: Falmer Press.

Rock, T.C., & Levin, B.B. (2002). Collaborative action research projects: Enhancing preservice teacher development in professional development schools. *Teacher Education Quarterly, 29*, 7–21.

Rodgers, C. (2006). Turning of one's soul: Learning to teach for social justice: The Putney Graduate School of Teacher Education, 1950–1964. *Teachers College Record, 108*(7), 1266–1295.

Rogers, B. L. (2002). *Social policy, teaching and youth activism in the 1960s: The liberal reform vision of the National Teacher Corps*. Unpublished doctoral dissertation, New York University, The Steinhardt School of Education.

Rosen, A. (2003). For-profit teacher education. *The Chronicle of Higher Education, Colloquy Live*, Retrieved September 4, 2003, from http://chronicle.com/colloquylive on September 6.

Rosenholtz, S., Bassler, O., & Hoover-Dempsey, K. (1986). Organizational conditions of teacher learning. *Teaching and Teacher Education, 2*(2), 91–104.

Rosewater, A. (1989). Schools that serve children. In F. Macchiarola & A. Gartner (Eds.), *Caring for America's children* (pp. 4–19). New York: Academy of Political Science.

Ross, D. (1987). Action research for preservice teachers: A description of why and how. *Peabody Journal of Education, 64*(3), 131–150.

Rothstein, R. (2004). *Class and schools: Using social, economic and educational reform to close the Black-White achievement gap*. New York: Teachers College Press.

Rothstein, R. & Wilder, T. (October, 2005). *The many dimensions of educational inequality across races*. Paper presented at the 2005 symposium on the Social Costs of an Inadequate Education, Teachers College, Columbia, New York City. Retrieved July 14, 2006, from www.tcequity.org.

Ruddick, J. & Hopkins, D. (1985). *Research as the basis for teaching.* London: Heinemann.

Rudduck, J. (1985). The improvement of teaching through research. *Cambridge Journal of Education, 15,* 123–127.

Rugg, H. (1952). *The teacher of teachers.* New York: Harper & Brothers.

Sarason, S. (1971). *The culture of the school and the problem of change.* Boston: Allyn & Bacon.

Scannell, D. (1999). *Models of teacher education.* Washington, DC: American Council on Education.

Scheffler, I. (1968). University scholarship and the education of teachers. *Teachers College Record, 70(1),* 1–12.

Schildgren, K. (1995). *A closer look at student involvement with action research.* Unpublished paper, School of Education, U.W.-Madison.

Schneider, B. (1987). Tracing the provenance of teacher education. In T. Popkewitz (Ed.), *Critical studies in teacher education* (pp. 211–241). London: Falmer Press.

Schon, D. (1983). *The reflective practitioner.* New York: Basic Books.

Schon, D. (1987). *Educating the reflective practitioner.* San Francisco, CA: Jossey-Bass.

Schorr, L. (1989). *Within our reach: Breaking the cycle of disadvantage.* New York: Anchor Books.

Schulte, A. (2001). *Student teachers in transformation: A self-study of a supervisor's practice.* Unpublished doctoral dissertation, University of Wisconsin-Madison School of Education.

Schulte, A. (2004). Examples of practice: Professional knowledge and self-study in multicultural teacher education. In J. Loughran, M. L. Hamilton, V. K. LaBoskey, & T. Russell (Eds.), *International handbook of self-study of teaching and teacher education practices* (pp. 709–747). Dordrecht: Kluwer.

Sconzert, K., Iazzetto, D., & Purkey, S. (2000). Small-town college to big-city school: Preparing urban teachers from liberal arts colleges. *Teaching and Teacher Education, 16(4),* 465–490.

Seidl, B., & Friend, G. (2002). Leaving authority at the door: equal status community-based experiences and the preparation of teachers for diverse classrooms. *Teaching & Teacher Education, 18(4)* 421–433.

Shanker, A. (1990, March 12). Shared decision making: A question of power. *New York Times* (p. E7).

Shor, I. (1986). *Culture wars: School and society in the conservative restoration 1969–1984.* New York: Routledge & Kegan Paul.

Shor, I. (1987). Equality as excellence: Transforming teacher education and the labor process. In M. Okazawa Rey, J. Anderson, & R. Travers (Eds.), *Teachers, teaching and teacher education* (pp. 183–203). Cambridge, MA: Harvard Education Review Press.

Shor, L. (1988). *Within our reach: Breaking the cycle of disadvantage.* New York: Author.

Sirotnik, K. (2001). *Renewing schools and teacher education: An odyssey in educational change.* Washington, DC: American Association of Colleges for Teacher Education.

Sirotnik, K. (Ed.). (2004). *Holding accountability accountable: What ought to matter in public education.* New York: Teachers College Press.

Slavin, R. (1983). *Cooperative learning.* White Plains, NY: Longman.

Slavin, R. (1989). PET and the pendulum: Faddism in education and how to stop it. *Kappan, 70(10),* 752–758.

Sleeter, C. (2001). Preparing teachers for culturally diverse schools: Research and the overwhelming presence of whiteness. *Journal of Teacher Education, 52*(2), 94–107.

Sleeter, C. (April, 2007). *Equity, democracy and neoliberal assaults on teacher education.* Vice-presidential address presented at the annual meeting of the American Educational Research Association, Chicago.

Sleeter, C. (2008). Preparing white teachers for diverse students. In M. Cochran-Smith, S. Feiman-Nemser, & D. J. McIntyre (Eds.), *Handbook of research on teacher education* (3rd ed., pp. 559–582). Mahwah, N.J: Erlbaum.

Smith, B. O. (1969). *Teachers for the real world.* Washington, DC: American Association of Colleges for Teacher Education.

Smith, B. O. (1980). *A design for a school of pedagogy.* Washington, DC: U.S. Department of Education.

Smyth, J., Dow, A., Hattam, R., Reid, A., & Shacklock, G. (2000). *Teachers' work in a globalizing economy.* London: Routledge.

Solomon, R. P. (1994). *Multicultural & antiracism education survey.* Toronto: York University.

Solomon, R. P. (2007). *Over a decade of progressive urban teacher education.* Unpublished manuscript, Toronto: York University

Solomon, R. P., Manoukian, R. K., & Clarke, J. (2007). Preserve teachers as border crossers: Linking urban schools and communities through service learning. In R. P. Solomon, & D. N. R. Sekayi (Eds.), *Urban teacher education and teaching: Innovative practices for diversity and social justice* (pp. 67–87). Mahwah, NJ: Erlbaum/Routledge.

Solomon, R. P., & Sekayi, D.N.R. (Eds.). (2007). *Urban teacher education and teaching: Innovative practices for diversity and social justice.* Mahwah, NJ: Erlbaum/Routledge.

Somekh, B. (1989). The role of action research in collaborative enquiry. In B. Somekh, J. Powney, & C. Burge (Eds.), *Collaborative enquiry and school improvement.* Norwich, UK: Classroom Action Research Network, University of East Anglia.

Somekh, B. (1993). Quality in educational research: The contribution of classroom teachers. In J. Edge & K. Richards (Eds.), *Teachers develop teacher research: Papers on classroom research and teacher development* (pp. 26–38). Oxford, UK: Heinemann International.

Spellings, M. (2005, June). *The secretary's fourth annual report on teacher quality.* Washington, DC: U.S. Department of Education, Office of Postsecondary Education.

Spellings, M. (September, 2006). *The secretary's fifth annual report on teacher quality.* Washington, DC: U.S. Department of Education.

Stachowski, L., & Mahan, J. (1998). Cross-cultural field placements: Student teachers learning from communities and schools. *Theory into Practice, 37*(2), 155–162.

Stallings, J., & Kowalski, T. (1990). Research on professional development schools. In W.R. Houston (Ed.), *Handbook of research on teacher education* (pp. 251–266). New York: Macmillan.

Steiner, D., & Rozen, S. (2004). Preparing tomorrow's teachers: An analysis of syllabi from a sample of America's schools of education. In F. Hess & K. Walsh (Eds.), *A qualified teacher in every classroom* (pp. 119–148). Cambridge, MA: Harvard Education Press.

Stenhouse, L. (1975). *An introduction to curriculum research and development*. London: Heinemann.

Stiles, L. J. (1958). The all-institution approach to teacher education. *Phi Delta Kappan, 40*(3), 121–124.

Stoddart, T. (1993). The professional development school: Building bridges between cultures. *Educational Policy, 7,* 5–23.

Stones, E. (1984). *Supervision in teacher education*. London: Metheun.

Stover, D. (1988). Those inservice hot shots: Are they worth the charge? *The Executive Educator, 10*(1), 15–18, 29.

Stubbs, M. (1989). *Training would be teachers to do research: A practical account* (Research Report No. 197). Wellesley, MA: Center for Research on Women.

Sturman, A. (1997). *Social justice in education*. Melbourne: Australian Council for Education Research.

Sykes, G. (2004). Cultivating teacher quality: A brief for professional standards. In F. Hess, A. Rotherham, & K. Walsh (Eds.), *A qualified teacher in every classroom?* (pp. 177–200). Cambridge, MA: Harvard Education Press.

Sykes, G. (1989). Teaching and professionalism: A cautionary perspective. In L. Weiss, P. Altbach, G. Kelly, H. Petrie, & S. Slaughter (Eds.). *Crisis in teaching: Perspectives on current reforms.* (pp. 253–274). Albany NY: SUNY Press.

Tabachnick, B. R., & Zeichner, K. (1999). Ideas and action: Action research and the development of conceptual change teaching in science. *Science Education, 83*(3), 309–322.

Tatto, M. T. (2007a). International comparisons and the global reform of teaching. In M.T. Tatto (Ed), *Reforming teaching globally* (pp. 7–18). Oxford, UK: Symposium Books.

Tatto, T. (Ed.). (2007b). *Reforming teaching globally*. Oxford, UK: Symposium Books.

Teitel, L. (1997). Changing teacher education through professional development school partnerships: A five-year follow-up study. *Teachers College Record, 99*(2), 311–334.

Teitel, L. (2001a). An assessment framework for professional development schools. *Journal of Teacher Education, 52*(1), 57–69.

Teitel, L. (2001b). *How professional development schools make a difference: A review of the research*. Washington, DC: National Association for Accreditation of Teacher Education.

Teitel, L. (2004). *How professional development schools make a difference: A review of the research* (2nd ed.). Washington, DC: National Association for Accreditation of Teacher Education.

Thompson, M.W. (2007). Bush brother's firm faces inquiry over purchases. *New York Times,* (November, 7). Retrieved July 11, 2007, from www.nytimes.org.

Threatt, S., Buchanan, J., Morgan, B., Strieb, L., Sugarman, J., Swenson, J., Teel, K., & Tomlinson, J. (1994). Teachers' voices in the conversation about teacher research. In S. Hollingsworth & H. Sackett (Eds.), *Teacher research and educational reform* (pp. 222–244). Chicago: University of Chicago Press.

Tom, A. (1997). *Redesigning teacher education*. Albany, N.Y: SUNY Press.

Tomlinson, S. (1989). Ethnicity and educational achievement in Britain. In L. Eldering & J. Kloprogge (Eds.), *Ethnic minority children in Europe* (pp. 15–37). Amsterdam: Swets & Zeitlinger.

Too many teacher colleges major in mediocrity. (2002, May 18). *U.S.A. Today* (editorial), p. A14.

Trier, J. (2003). Inquiring into techniques of power with preservice teachers through the school film: The paper chase. *Teaching & Teacher Education, 19*(5), 543–557.

Tripp, D. (1990). Socially critical action research. *Theory into Practice, 24*(3), 158–166.

U.S. Department of Education. (2001). *The condition of education: 2001.* Washington, DC: Author.

U.S. Department of Education. (2002). *Meeting the highly qualified teachers challenge: The Secretary's annual report on teacher quality.* Washington, DC: Author.

Valenzuela, A. (Ed.). (2005). *Leaving children behind: How Texas style accountability fails Latino youth.* Albany, NY: SUNY Press. Sector Improvement Programme

Valli, L. (2000). Connecting teacher development and school improvement: Ironic consequences of a preservice action research course. *Teaching and Teacher Education, 16,* 715–730.

Valli, L., & Rennert-Ariev, P. (2002). New standards and assessments? Curriculum transformation in teacher education. *Journal of Curriculum Studies, 34*(2), 201–225.

Valli, L., Cooper, D., & Frankes, L. (1997). Professional development schools and equity: A critical analysis of rhetoric and research. In M. Apple (Ed.), *Review of Research in Education, 22* (pp. 251–304). Washington DC: American Educational Research Association.

Vavrus, M. (2002). *Transforming the multicultural education of teachers.* New York: Teachers College Press.

Vavrus, M. (2006). Teacher identity formation in a multicultural world: Intersections of autobiographical research and critical pedagogy. In D. Tidwell & L. Fitzgerald (Eds.), *Self-study and diversity* (pp. 89–114). Rotterdam: Sense Publishers.

Vick, M. (2006). It's a difficult matter: Historical perspectives on the enduring problems of the practicum in teacher preparation. *South Pacific Journal of Teacher Education, 34*(2), 181–198.

Villegas, A. M. (1991). *Culturally responsive pedagogy for the 1990's and beyond.* Princeton, NJ: Educational Testing Service.

Villegas, A.M. (2008). Diversity and teacher education. In M. Cochran-Smith, S. Feiman-Nemser, & D. J. McIntyre (Eds.), *Handbook of research on teacher education* (3rd ed., pp. 551–558). New York: Erlbaum/Routledge.

Villegas, A. M., & Davis, D. E. (2008). Preparing teachers of color to confront racial/ethnic disparities in educational outcomes. In M. Cochran-Smith, S. Feiman-Nemser, & D.J. McIntyre (Eds.), *Handbook of research on teacher education* (3rd ed., pp. 583–605). New York: Routledge.

Villegas, A., M., & Lucas, T. (2002a). *Educating culturally responsive teachers: A coherent approach.* Albany: State University of New York Press.

Villegas, A. M., & Lucas, T. (2002b). Preparing culturally responsive teachers: Rethinking the curriculum. *Journal of Teacher Education, 53*(1), 20–32.

Villegas, A. M., & Lucas, T. (2004). Diversifying the teacher workforce: A retrospective and prospective analysis. In M. Smylie & D. Miretzky (Eds.), *Developing the teacher workforce* (pp. 70–104). Chicago: University of Chicago Press.

Walsh, K. & Jacobs, S. (September, 2007). *Alternative certification isn't alternative.* Washington, DC: Thomas Fordham Institute.

Walsh, K. (2001). *Teacher certification reconsidered.* Baltimore: Abell Foundation.

Walsh, K. (2004). A candidate-centered model for teacher preparation and licensure. In F. Hess, A. Rotherham, & K. Walsh (Eds.), *A qualified teacher in every classroom* (pp.119–148). Cambridge, MA: Harvard Education Press.

Walsh, K., & Hale, C. (2004). *Increasing the odds: How good policies can yield better teachers*. Washington, DC: National Council on Teacher Quality.

Walton, P., & Carlson, R. (1997). Responding to social change: California's new standards for teacher credentialing. In J. King, E. Hollins, & W. Hayman (Eds.), *Preparing teachers for cultural diversity* (pp. 222–240). New York: Teachers College Press.

Wasley, P. (2006, June 16). Accreditor of education schools drops controversial "social justice" language. *The Chronicle of Higher Education*. Retrieved June 24, 2006, from http://chronicle.com.

Webb, R. (1990). *Practitioner research in the primary school*. Lewes: Falmer Press.

Weiner, G. (1989). Professional self-knowledge versus social justice: A critical analysis of the teacher researcher movement. *British Educational Research Journal, 15*, 41–51.

Weiner, L. (1993). *Preparing teachers for urban schools: Lessons from 30 years of school reform*. New York: Teachers College Press.

Weiner, L. (2007). A lethal threat to teacher education. *Journal of Teacher Education, 58*(4), 274–286.

Weiss, L. (1990, April). *Issues of disproportionality and social justice in tomorrow's schools*. Paper presented at the annual meeting of the American Educational Research Association, Boston.

Wheelock, A. (1992). *Crossing the tracks: How untracking can save America's schools*. New York: New Press.

White, P. (1989). An overview of school-based management: What does the research say? *NASSP Bulletin, 73*, 107, 1–8.

Whitehead, J., & Lomax, P. (1987). Action research and the politics of educational knowledge. *British Educational Research Journal, 13*, 175–190.

Whitford, B. L., & Metcalf-Turner, P. (1999). Of promises and unsolved puzzles: Reforming teacher education with professional development schools. In G. Griffin (Ed.), *The education of teachers* (pp. 257–278). Chicago: University of Chicago Press.

Whyte, J. (1985). *Getting the girls into science and technology*. London: Routledge.

Wiedman, C. R. (2002). Teacher preparation, social justice, equity: A review of the literature. *Equity and Excellence in Education, 35*(3), 200–211.

Will, G. (2006, January 16). Ed schools vs. education. *Newsweek*. Retrieved December 1, 2007, from http://www.nytimes.com.

Williams, M. (1989). *Neighborhood organizing for urban school reform*. New York: Teachers College Press.

Wilson, S., Floden, R., & Ferrini-Mundy, J. (2001, February). *Teacher preparation research: Current knowledge, gaps, and recommendations*. Seattle: Center for the Study of Teaching and Policy, University of Washington.

Wilson, S., & Tamir, E. (2008). The evolving field of teacher education. In M. Cochran-Smith, S. Feiman-Nemser, & D.J. McIntyre (Eds.), *Handbook of research on teacher education* (2nd ed., pp. 908–935). New York: Erlbaum/Routledge.

Wilson, S., & Youngs, P. (2005). Research on accountability processes in teacher education. In M. Cochran-Smith & K. Zeichner (Eds.), *Studying teacher education:*

The report of the AERA Panel on Research and Teacher Education (pp. 591–644). Mahwah, NJ: Lawrence Erlbaum.

Wineberg, S. (2001). *Historical thinking and other unnatural acts.* Philadelphia: Temple University Press.

Winter, R. (1987). *Action research and the nature of social inquiry.* Brookfield, VT: Gower.

Winter, R. (1989). *Learning from experience: Principles and practice in action research.* Lewes: Falmer Press.

Wise, A. (1979). *Legislated learning: The bureaucratization of the American classroom.* Berkeley: University of California Press.

Wittrock, M. (Ed.). (1986). *Handbook of research on teaching* (3rd ed.). New York: Macmillan.

Worth, R. F., & Hartocollus, A. (2002). Johnny can read, but does he know how to vote? *The New York Times,* June 30, p. 19.

Young, M. (1998). Rethinking teacher education for a global future: Lessons from the English. *Journal of Education for Teaching, 24*(1), 51–62.

Young, I. (1990). *Justice and the politics of difference.* Princeton, N.J: Princeton University Press.

Young, P. (2007). Thinking outside the box: Fostering racial and ethnic discourses in urban teacher education. In P. Solomon & D. Sekayi (Eds.), *Urban teacher education and teaching: Innovative practices for diversity and social justice* (pp. 109–128). Mahwah, NJ: Erlbaum/Routledge.

Zeichner, K. (1983). Alternative paradigms of teacher education. *Journal of Teacher Education, 34,* 3–9.

Zeichner, K. (1991a). Contradictions and tensions in the professionalization of teaching and the democratization of schools. *Teachers' College Record, 92,* 363–379.

Zeichner, K. (1991b). *Connecting genuine teacher development to the struggle for social justice.* East Lansing, MI: National Center for Research in Teacher Learning.

Zeichner, K. (1992a).Rethinking the practicum in the professional development school partnership. *Journal of Teacher Education, 43*(4), 296–307.

Zeichner, K. (1992b).Conceptions of reflective teaching in contemporary U.S. teacher education program reforms. In L. Valli (Ed.), *Reflective teacher education: cases and critiques* (pp. 161–173). Albany, NY: SUNY Press.

Zeichner, K. (1993a). Connecting genuine teacher development to the struggle for social justice. *Journal of Education for Teaching, 19*(1), 5–20.

Zeichner, K. (1993b). Traditions of practice in U.S. preservice teacher education programs. *Teaching and Teacher Education, 9*(1), 1–13.

Zeichner, K. (1993c). Action research: Personal renewal and social reconstruction. *Educational Action Research, 1* (2), 199–219.

Zeichner, K. (1994). Conceptions of reflective practice in teaching and teacher education. In G. Harvard & P. Hodkinson (Eds.), *Action and reflection in teacher education* (pp. 1–14). NY: Ablex.

Zeichner, K. (1995). Reflections of a teacher educator working for social change. In F. Korthagen & T. Russell (Eds.), *Teachers who teach: Reflections on teacher education* (pp. 11–24). London: Falmer Press.

Zeichner, K. (1996a). Educating teachers for cultural diversity. In K. Zeichner, S. Melnick & M.L. Gomez (Eds.), *Currents of reform in preservice teacher education* (pp. 133–175). New York: Teachers College Press.

Zeichner, K. (1996b). Designing educative practicum experiences for prospective teachers. In K. Zeichner, S. Melnick, & M. L. Gomez (Eds.), *Currents of reform in preservice teacher education* (pp. 215–234). New York: Teachers College Press.

Zeichner, K. (1999a). Action research and the preparation of reflective practitioners during the practicum. *Practical Experiences in Professional Education, 3*(1), 1–26.

Zeichner, K. (1999b). The new scholarship in teacher education. *Educational Researcher, 28*(9), 4–15.

Zeichner, K. (2000). *Ability-based teacher education: Elementary teacher education at Alverno College.* Washington, DC: American Association of Colleges for Teacher Education.

Zeichner, K. (2001). *Learning from experience with performance-based teacher education.* Paper presented at the annual meeting of the American Educational Research Association, Seattle, WA.

Zeichner, K. (2003a).Educating teachers to close the achievement gap: Issues of pedagogy, knowledge, and teacher preparation. In B. Williams (Ed.), *Closing the achievement gap* (2nd ed., pp. 99–115). Alexandria, VA: Association for Supervision and Curriculum Development.

Zeichner, K. (2003b). The adequacies and inadequacies of three current strategies to recruit, prepare and retain the best teachers for all students. *Teachers College Record, 105*(3), 490–515.

Zeichner, K. (2005a).Becoming a teacher educator: A personal perspective. *Teaching & Teacher Education, 21*, 117–124.

Zeichner, K. (2005b). Learning from experience with performance-based teacher education. In F. Peterman (Ed.), *Assessment in urban teacher education programs* (pp. 3–20). Mahwah, NJ: Lawrence Erlbaum.

Zeichner, K. (2005c). A research agenda for teacher education. In M. Cochran-Smith & K. Zeichner (Eds.), *Studying teacher education: The AERA Panel on Research and Teacher Education* (pp. 737–760). Mahwah, NJ: Lawrence Erlbaum.

Zeichner, K. (2006). Reflections of a university-based teacher educator on the future of college and university-based teacher education. *Journal of Teacher Education 57*(3), 326–340.

Zeichner, K. (2007). Professional development schools in a culture of evidence and accountability. *School-University Partnerships, 1*(1), 9–17.

Zeichner, K., & Conklin, H. (2005). Teacher education programs. In M. Cochran-Smith & K. Zeichner (Eds.), *Studying teacher education* (pp. 645–736). New York: Erlbaum/Routledge.

Zeichner, K., & Conklin, H. (2008). Teacher education programs as sites for teacher preparation. In M. Cochran-Smith, S. Feiman-Nemser, & D. J. McIntyre (Eds.), *Handbook of research on teacher education* (3rd edition, pp. 269–289). New York: Erlbaum/Routledge.

Zeichner, K. & Flessner (in press). Educating teachers for critical education. In M. Apple, W. Au, & L. Gandin. *International handbook of critical education.* New York: Routledge.

Zeichner, K., & Gore, J. (1990). Teacher socialization. In W. R. Houston (Ed.), *Handbook of research on teaching* (pp. 329–348). New York: Macmillan.

Zeichner, K., & Gore, J. (1995). Using action research as a vehicle for student teacher reflection: A social reconstructionist approach. In S. Noffke & B. Stevenson (Eds.), *Practically critical: An invitation to action research in education* (pp. 13–30). New York: Teachers College Press.

Zeichner, K., Grant, C., Gay, G., Gillette, M., Valli, L., & Villegas, A. M. (1998). A research informed vision of good practice in multicultural teacher education: Design principles. *Theory into Practice, 37*(2), 163–171.

Zeichner, K., & Hoeft, K. (1996). Teacher socialization for cultural diversity. In J. Sikula (Ed.), *Handbook of research on teacher education* (2nd ed., pp. 176–198). New York: Macmillan.

Zeichner, K., & Hutchinson, E. (2008). The development of alternative certification policies and programs in the U.S. In P. Grossman & S. Loeb (Eds.), *Taking stock: An examination of alternative certification* (pp. 15–29). Cambridge, MA: Harvard Education Press.

Zeichner, K.; Hutchinson, E. & Chagolla, R. (February, 2007). *Using portfolio artifacts as a source of data about learning to teach in culturally responsive ways.* Paper presented at the annual meeting of the American Association of Colleges for Teacher Education, New York City.

Zeichner, K., & Liston, D. (1987). Teaching student teachers to reflect. *Harvard Educational Review, 57*(1), 1–22.

Zeichner, K., & Liston, D. (1991). *Teacher education and the social conditions of schooling.* New York: Routledge.

Zeichner, K., & Liston, D. (1996). *Reflective teaching.* New York: Erlbaum/Routledge.

Zeichner, K., & Melnick, S. (1996). The role of community field experiences in preparing teachers for cultural diversity. In K. Zeichner, S. Melnick, & M.L. Gomez (Eds.), *Currents of reform in preservice teacher education* (pp. 176–198). New York: Teachers College Press.

Zeichner, K., & Miller, M. (1997). Learning to teach in professional development schools. In M. Levine & R. Trachtman (Eds.), *Making professional development schools work: Politics, practice, and policy* (pp. 15–32). New York: Teachers College Press.

Zeichner, K., & Noffke, S. (2001). Practitioner research. In V. Richardson (Ed.), *Handbook of research on teaching* (4th ed., pp. 298–332). Washington, DC: American Educational Research Association.

Zeichner, K., & Schulte, A. (2001). What we know and don't know from peer-reviewed research about alternative teacher certification programs. *Journal of Teacher Education, 52*(4), 266–282.

Zeichner, K., & Tabachnick, B. R. (1992). Reflections on reflective teaching. In B. R. Tabachnick & K. Zeichner (Eds.), *Issues and practices in inquiry-oriented teacher education* (pp. 1–21). London: Falmer Press.

Zeichner, K., & Teitelbaum, K. (1982). Personalized and inquiry oriented teacher education. *Journal of Education for Teaching, 8*(2), 95–117.

Zerchykov, R. (1987). *Parent choice: A digest of the research.* Boston: Institute for Responsive Education.

Zumwalt, K., & Craig, E. (2005). Teachers' characteristics: Research on the demographic profile. In M. Cochran-Smith & K. Zeichner (Eds.), *Studying teacher education.* (pp 111–156). Mahwah, NJ: Erlbaum/Routledge.

Index